Egypt Leading the Way

Egypt Leading the Way

Institution Building and Stability in the Financial System

Mark Huband

Published by Euromoney Books
in association with

CIB
Ezz Group
Fleming CIIC
Glaxo Wellcome Egypt
Helmy & Hamza (Baker & McKenzie)
KMPG Hazem Hassan

Published by
Euromoney Institutional Investor Publications PLC
Nestor House, Playhouse Yard
London EC4V 5EX
Tel: +44 (0)171 779 8860 Fax: +44 (0)171 779 8541
Email: books@euromoneyplc.com
Website: www.euromoneybooks.com

Copyright © 1999 Euromoney Publications PLC
ISBN 1 85564 669 2

This publication is not included in the CLA Licence so do not copy without the permission of the publisher.

All rights reserved. No part of this book may be reproduced or used in any form (graphic, electronic or mechanical, including photocopying, recording, taping or information storage and retrieval systems) without the permission of the publisher.

The views and opinions expressed in the book are solely those of the author(s) and need not necessarily reflect those of the institutions which have acted as co-publishers to the book. Although Euromoney has made every effort to ensure the complete accuracy of the text, neither it nor any co-publisher can accept any legal responsibility whatsoever for consequences that may arise from errors or omissions or any opinions or advice given.

The chapter on the regulatory environment (Chapter 15) is an adapted extract from *Breaking New Ground in Egypt, Legal Aspects*, copyright © Helmy & Hamza (Baker & McKenzie) 1999.

Typeset by Euromoney Institutional Investor and PW Reprorint, London
Printed in Dubai, United Arab Emirates by Emirates Printing Press, Dubai

The author

Mark Huband is the Cairo correspondent of the *Financial Times*, a post he has held since 1997. He has reported widely in the Middle East, and has written extensively on Egypt's economic reform programme. Prior to his appointment to this post, he was for eight years a correspondent in sub-Saharan Africa, covering political, social and economic issues while based initially in Abidjan, Côte d'Ivoire and subsequently Nairobi, Kenya. He worked for one year in the Maghreb, based in Rabat, Morocco, before taking up his post in Cairo.

Acknowledgements

The author would like to thank H.E. Dr Youssef Boutros-Ghali, Minister of Economy, for his valuable support. Special thanks to Dr Mahmoud Mohieldin, senior adviser to the Minister of Economy, Dr Ziad Baha'a Eldin, legal adviser to the Minister of Economy, Mrs Manal Hussein, executive director of the Minister's office, Mrs Amina Ghanem, economist and senior assistant to the Minister of Economy, and Mrs Nermine Abulata, economist and assistant to the Minister of Economy, for their assistance in the preparation and research for this book. Thanks are also due to senior assistants to the Minister: Mr Hany Kadry Dimian, Mr Maged S. Sourial, Mrs Mona Zobaa, and Mr Sherif Ahmed Sherif; also to economic researchers and analysts in the Ministry: Heba El-Deken, Maha Kamel, Marwa Mahgoub, Nayef Moukhtar, and Waleid Gamal Eldien.

He would also like to thank H.E. Mrs Mervat Tellawi, Minister of Insurance and Social Affairs, Mr Ashraf Shams Eldin, deputy chairman of the Capital Market Authority, Dr Sameh El-Torgoman, chairman of the Cairo and Alexandria Stock Exchanges, Mr Sherif Raafat of Concord International Investments and former chairman of the ESE, and Mr Mauro Mecagni, IMF resident representative in Cairo. Many leading businesspeople, financiers, bankers and economists also gave generously of their time, and their assistance was greatly appreciated. In particular, the author would like to thank Mr Mohamed Younes of Concord International Investments, Mr Hassan Heikal of EFG Hermes, Mr Yasser El-Mallawany of CIIC, Mr Samir Metwally and Mr Ezzat Hammoudah of Mohandes Insurance Company, Mr Christopher Vaughan of HSBC Investment Banking, Mr Hazim Al-Dalli of Nile Rating, Mr Osama Nassar of Flemings, and Ms Dina Khayat of Lazard Asset Management Egypt.

Euromoney Books would like to thank KPMG Hazem Hassan and Helmy & Hamza (Baker & McKenzie) for the preparation of Chapters 14 and 15 respectively.

The photographs in this book were supplied by Capstone Design. The co-publishers provided their own photographs.

Mural, Cairo

Contents

Foreword xii

Map xiv

1 Introduction 1
Brief history of the economic reform process 1 • A macroeconomic overview 3 • Egypt and the Asia crisis: is there a risk? 5 • The government's economic policies, 1997–98 8 • The Republic's plans to borrow: benchmarking and monitoring private sector debt 14

2 The financial system and foreign investment 19
Solid and independent institutions: the 'equity' necessary for economic growth 19 • Supervision of the financial system 21 • Incentives and regulation for proper governance 22 • Comparison of financial monitoring with MENA and other emerging markets 25 • Statistical summary of foreign portfolio and direct investment, 1990–98 26 • The role of international capital in financing Egypt's growth 27 • Foreign competition and investment in the financial sector 30 • Egypt as a regional financial centre: the importance of attracting new institutions 31

3 Regulation of the financial sector 35
The legal framework for banking, insurance and pension reform 35 • The Ministry of Economy, the Central Bank, and the Capital Market Authority 36 • The new Capital Markets Law 38 • The Foreign Investment Law and the Law on Concessions 38

4 Ratings and the information market 41
Standard and Poor's, Moody's Investors Service and Fitch IBCA sovereign ratings 41 • How the agencies rated, and why 41 • Rating agencies in emerging markets: their role and credibility 43 • Ratings of private sector companies; specialist ratings 44 • The availability of brokers' and independent research 46 • Information from the public and private sector: how open is Egypt 47

5 Domestic savings and the capital markets 49
The importance of domestic savings in increasing investment 49 • The spur of privatisation 53 • New products to enhance savings 55 • Insurance and pension reform 56 • Private pensions and social security: the Latin American model? 59

6 The stock exchange 60
Statistical summary 60 • Modernisation of the ESE 62 • Electronic trading and the new settlement system 63 • Foreigners on the ESE: consolidation among local brokers 64 • Broker regulation and codes of conduct 66 • Market indices and their constituents 67 • Progress of the new Capital Markets Law and its effects 68

7 Fund management 70
A new business for Egypt 70 • The funds established so far 73 • Cairo as a regional investment centre 77

8 The insurance sector 80
History of the Egyptian insurance and reinsurance industry 80 • The performance of the state and private companies 81 • Legal reform in the insurance sector: prospects for international control or ownership 84 • Valuing the state sector for privatisation 85 • Domestic savings and the capital markets: the role of insurance funds 86

9 The banking sector 89
Banking sector reform: ensuring institutional stability 89 • New competitive practices 92 • Foreign banks 94 • Investment banking in Egypt: a new business 95 • The prospects for privatisation and mergers 98 • Competition to bank lending: the capital markets' impact on the sector 99 • The development of micro-credits: the small and micro-enterprise unit 102 • Retail financial products: personal credit, loans and mortgages 103

10 Privatisation 106
A summary of six years of privatisation 106 • Privatisation in the financial sector 108 • The next big challenges: infrastructure and telecommunications 109 • How have privatised companies benefited from privatisation? 110 • The impact of privatisation on the private sector 111

11 Infrastructure and project finance 112
The implementation of build-operate-transfer projects, 1995–99 112 • Mega-projects of the future: Toshka and the South Valley; East Port Said 114 • Power generation and distribution 117 • Ports, airports and other transport; concessions and foreign involvement 119 • Communications: the future of Egypt Telecom and the boom in mobile telephony 121

12 Other forms of fixed foreign investment 124
Joint ventures 124 • Mergers and acquisitions 126 • Setting-up a manufacturing operation in Egypt 126

13 Egyptian industry in figures 129
Statistical summary of Egypt's GDP by sector 129 • Trade flows 130 • The growth of tertiary industries: pharmaceuticals and electronics 133 • The future for agriculture and the prospects of land reform 135

14 Taxation and incentives for foreign investors 138
Taxation 138 • Salary tax 138 • Withholding taxes on certain categories of income 139 • Unified personal income tax 141 • Corporate profit tax 144 • Real estate taxes 148 • Customs taxes 149 • Sales tax 150 • Stamp tax 150 • Social insurance contributions 150 • Important tax exemptions and other investment incentives 151 • The Investment Law 152 • Tax incentives provided by other laws 154 • Accounting and auditing 155

15 Legal environment 157
Establishing a presence 157 • Representative offices 157 • Branch offices 159 • Egyptian companies 160 • Incentives for foreign investors 166 • Banking Law 170 • Capital Markets Law 171 • Privatisation and the Public Enterprise Law 174 • Labour Law 175 • Commercial aspects of business activities 177 • Ownership of real estate 185 • Environmental Law 186 • Disputes 188 • Conclusion 190

16 Egypt leading the way 192
Fulfilling the promise of the mid-1990s 192 • Egypt in the region: economic leadership to complement political clout 194 • Conclusion 195

The co-publishers 199

Foreword

At the threshold of the 21st century, Egypt stands ready to enter a new era and to live up to the glories of its past. The structural and financial changes introduced in the country since 1991 have set it irreversibly on a path towards reform. The aim of the changes has been to forge Egypt into a market-based, liberal economy driven by the private sector, such that it can fulfil its rightful role in the global economy and rival the most developed countries in the standard of living it provides for its people.

Markets have been liberalised, prices freed and the public sector transferred through privatisation to an increasingly vibrant private sector. Meanwhile, an openness to the outside world has been instituted gradually, systematically and irreversibly. Underlining all these changes have been deep institutional reforms that have changed the laws and regulations governing economic activity in Egypt at the corporate and the public level. The driving force behind the whole process has been the need to expand, both domestically and globally.

Today, with the national budget virtually balanced, low inflation, high growth, low external debt and an increasing presence on the world stage, Egypt stands ready to enter the last phase of its reform process. In the coming years we will see a broader regeneration of the institutions in the financial sector, the regulatory environment in which they operate and, most importantly, the basic infrastructure that will guarantee the transparency and sustainability of Egypt's financial rebirth.

It is this rebirth, this continuous focus on progress, that means that Egypt will enter the first century of its eighth millennium having shed, once and for all, the shackles of its underdevelopment. The 21st century will herald a new era, in terms of both Egypt's view of the world and the world's view of Egypt.

Youssef Boutros-Ghali

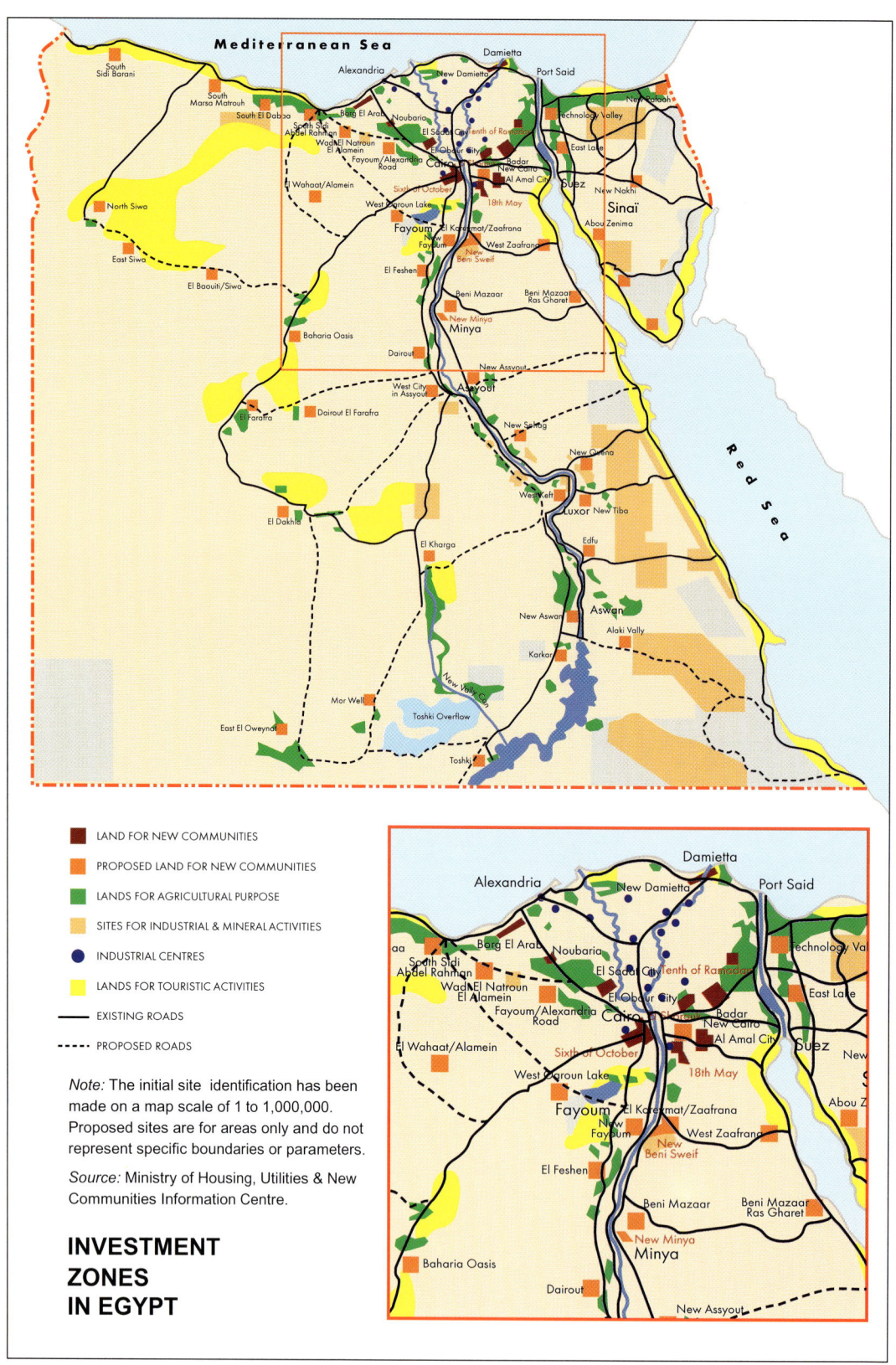

INVESTMENT ZONES IN EGYPT

Note: The initial site identification has been made on a map scale of 1 to 1,000,000. Proposed sites are for areas only and do not represent specific boundaries or parameters.

Source: Ministry of Housing, Utilities & New Communities Information Centre.

1 Introduction

Brief history of the economic reform process

The macroeconomic conditions that have allowed Egypt to weather the succession of global and domestic crises reveal the extent to which real reform has taken place and allowed the country to genuinely emerge onto the global stage. The realisation in Egypt that change was vital triggered in earnest the reform process at the start of the 1990s. As reform has accelerated throughout the decade, it has been introduced with calm and painstaking planning, with the result that the only semblance of instability has been the experience of waking the country from a long period of economic slumber.

The multinational army which drove Iraq out of Kuwait in 1991, marked the emergence of a new sense of purpose among Arab states. As important, it also provided Egypt with extensive debt relief, in recognition of its military support. This combination of circumstances was the launch pad for an unprecedented phase of economic reform which had long been necessary, but which had previously lacked the conditions for take-off.

At the heart of the reform programme launched in 1991 was the need to reduce Egypt's fiscal deficit, which by then stood at the equivalent of 20 per cent of GDP. Equally pressing was a need to reduce the 20 per cent level of inflation, and to narrow the 8 per cent current account deficit. With the signing of a stabilisation agreement with the IMF, there followed five years of cuts in the capital investment budget and subsidies. Spending cuts and major efforts to increase government revenue were rapidly introduced (see Exhibit 1.1). Simultaneously, the exchange rate was adjusted, bringing an increase in Suez Canal revenue and profits from oil. Furthermore, a general sales tax was introduced, though wages were left unchanged.

By 1996 the currency had seen a 23.7 per cent devaluation against the US dollar, the current account deficit had been reduced from −3.7 per cent of GDP to 0.9 per cent, and the fiscal balance reduced from −15.6 per cent to −1.2 per cent. With foreign currency reserves having risen from US$6.9 billion to US$20.3 billion by early 1997, the conditions were ripe for change. Currency adjustments were accompanied by reform of the financial sector, aimed at strengthening the banking system and controlling liquidity. A variety of foreign exchange rates were unified in 1991, while interest rate caps and direct credit controls to the private and public sectors were removed. The effective pegging of the currency to the US dollar was matched concurrently with the introduction of Treasury bill auctions. The auctions allowed the Central Bank of Egypt (CBE) to accumulate rapidly growing reserves, which in turn allowed for support of the exchange rate peg. As important, the auctions soaked up capital

INTRODUCTION

Exhibit 1.1
Summary of national budget operations, 1990–99, (E£ million)

	1990–91	1991–92	1992–93	1993–94	1994–95	1995–96	1996–97	1997–98	1998–99
Total revenues	**30,710**	**43,385**	**46,703**	**52,567**	**55,719**	**60,893**	**64,498**	**67,963**	**71,449**
Tax revenues	15,504	24,285	27,334	31,373	34,279	38,249	40,518	43,962	46,400
Transferred profit	6,979	8,863	9,364	9,070	10,542	11,113	11,423	10,780	10,642
Other non-tax revenue	1,393	2,694	5,004	6,619	5,724	5,715	5,867	5,293	5,446
Non-central government revenue	6,834	7,543	5,001	5,505	5,174	5,796	6,690	7,293	8,161
Total government expenditure	**50,398**	**50,963**	**52,223**	**56,264**	**58,256**	**63,889**	**66,826**	**70,783**	**74,449**
Current expenditure	27,400	33,431	40,954	45,912	46,933	51,196	53,030	55,289	58,432
Of which:									
Domestic interest payments	4,176	6,359	9,315	11,816	11,177	12,231	12,337	12,219	12,772
Foreign interest payments	2,870	3,151	3,994	4,682	3,613	3,796	3,114	2,724	2,624
Investment expenditure	15,067	15,746	11,097	10,659	11,299	12,581	14,070	15,635	16,210
Overall balance	(19,688)	(7,578)	(5,520)	(3,697)	(2,537)	(2,996)	(2,328)	(2,820)	(3,000)
Total financing	19,688	7,578	5,520	3,697	2,537	2,996	2,328	2,820	3,000
Foreign financing	14,416	2,981	298	524	(278)	(1,340)	(1,575)	(1,328)	(597)
Domestic financing	5,272	4,597	5,222	3,173	2,815	4,336	2,903	4,148	3,597
Memorandum items									
Balance as % of GDP	(17.7)	(5.4)	(3.5)	(2.1)	(1.2)	(1.3)	(0.9)	(1.0)	(1.0)
Gross domestic product	111,200	139,100	157,300	175,000	204,000	229,400	256,300	280,200	305,242

Source: Ministry of Finance

inflows, which rose to 6 per cent of GDP in 1992, creating pressure on the currency, which would have undermined the reform programme had the T-bill option not been so actively pursued.

Nine years into the reform process, what has been most remarkable is that, by adopting a cautious if steady approach, Egyptian governments have successfully weaned the public away from any nostalgia for the benefits and burdens of central planning. In doing so, they have created conditions for an economic take-off which are unique in the Arab world. The absence of credible arguments against the reform programme has been vital to its success. Change has been introduced at a pace judged prudent by the government, thereby allowing a quiet revolution to take shape. A strong commitment to stabilisation and tight monetary control have equipped Egypt with the macroeconomic foundation necessary to continue the introduction of structural reform vital to accelerating annual economic growth to the 7–8 per cent necessary to soakup the 450,000 annual arrivals to the job market.

INTRODUCTION

A macroeconomic overview

Debt forgiveness by Arab states after the Iraq war in 1991 to the value of US$7 billion, and the repatriation of around US$6 billion by Egyptians fleeing the Gulf states, led to the growth in reserves to around US$20 billion or, 14.2 months of exports as at early 1999. The war was followed by an agreement with the Paris Club of government donors for the rescheduling of US$27 billion worth of foreign debt, easing Egypt's debt service ratio 7.5 per cent by early 1999. The debt stock by this period stood at 90.6 per cent of GDP or 175.7 per cent of total annual exports, a 38 per cent drop since the launch of the stabilisation programme.

Building on this foundation, Egypt's macroeconomic position is now passing into a second stage of post-stabilisation maturity. Having brought the fiscal deficit down to 1.0 per cent and inflation down to 3.6 per cent, the government is under pressure to use the instruments at its disposal more flexibly. With the continued goal of energizing private sector activity and accelerating economic growth from its 5.7 per cent level in 1998–99, to an anticipated 6.2 per cent in 1999–2000, the issue of exchange rate flexibility is increasingly under debate. In inflation-adjusted terms, the Egyptian pound has seen a 50 per cent appreciation since 1991. The peg to the US dollar of E£3.39 has played a key role in establishing balance-sheet strength in the eyes of foreign investors. The government is now faced with the choice of either raising interest rates from their average 11.52 per cent, to contain the current account deficit and therefore risking lower growth, or of allowing interest rates to fall in order to finance a wider current account deficit, which would test creditworthiness.

Egypt's resilience in the face of a series of economic shocks in the past two years has tested the government's commitment to reform. It has also offered a true picture of how much has been achieved, while exposing the degree to which the economy remains vulnerable to shocks in a handful of industries. Significant legislative strides had clearly been made before 58 foreign tourists and six Egyptians were killed by Islamic militants in the southern city of Luxor in November 1997. But then came the time for action. The government responded by requesting that banks ease the pressure on tourist-related industries, on the assumption that within one year the industry would have recovered. This time frame proved realistic. During the first quarter of 1998–99, tourism receipts increased by 46 per cent on the previous quarter. By December 1998, both tourist arrivals and the number of nights spent had reached 87.2 per cent and 71.5 per cent respectively of their levels in December 1997, while tourism receipts for 1997–98 have reached 81 per cent of the level of a year earlier. Even so, the cost to Egypt's biggest foreign exchange earner was 1 per cent of GDP, with a 19 per cent fall in income, from US$3.64 billion in 1996–97 to US$2.94 billion a year later.

A second shock has been the oil price slump. The fall to around US$12 a barrel has added considerably to the current account deficit, owing to earnings from oil exports accounting for 6.4 per cent of GDP. Government earnings from petroleum were US$1.72 billion in 1997–98, a 32 per cent drop on the previous year. Non-tax revenue from the third main foreign exchange earner, receipts from maritime traffic using the Suez Canal, has peaked at around US$1.8 billion, and it is recognised that while this source of foreign exchange will remain

INTRODUCTION

Exhibit 1.2
National budget revenues, 1991–99, (E£ million)

	1991–92	1992–93	1993–94	1994–95	1995–96	1996–97	1997–98	1998–99
Total government revenues	**43,385**	**46,703**	**52,567**	**55,719**	**60,893**	**64,498**	**67,963**	**71,449**
Total central government revenues	**35,676**	**41,020**	**46,384**	**49,889**	**54,486**	**57,179**	**60,035**	**62,488**
Tax on income and profit:	9,996	11,114	12,003	12,134	13,707	14,589	15,306	15,800
EGPC	2,512	3,336	3,309	3,071	3,111	3,195	3,033	2,500
Suez Canal Authority	2,238	2,161	2,504	2,311	2,413	2,294	2,095	2,100
Central Bank of Egypt	1,503	847	867	945	1,578	1,784	2,019	2,000
Other	2,833	3,733	3,981	4,446	5,047	5,561	6,130	7,000
Personal income	910	1,037	1,342	1,361	1,558	1,755	2,029	2,200
Tax on business profits	9,086	10,077	10,661	10,773	12,149	12,834	13,277	13,600
Tax on property	4	8	12	21	24	3	–	–
Taxes on goods and services	6,324	7,191	8,080	9,333	10,450	11,325	12,925	14,200
Taxes on international trade	4,588	5,009	6,120	7,017	7,911	8,125	8,886	9,200
Other taxes	3,373	4,012	5,158	5,774	6,157	6,476	6,845	7,200
Stamp tax	1,839	2,067	2,657	2,874	3,074	3,168	3,215	3,300
Central government non-tax revenues	**11,391**	**13,686**	**15,011**	**15,610**	**16,237**	**16,661**	**16,073**	**16,088**
Transferred profits:	8,863	9,364	9,070	10,542	11,133	11,423	10,780	10,642
EGPC	3,715	4,626	4,610	4,443	4,717	4,788	3,870	3,300
Suez Canal Authority	3,015	3,013	2,610	3,132	3,015	2,828	2,940	2,950
Central Bank of Egypt	1,556	968	1,200	2,072	2,318	2,587	2,617	2,900
Other	577	757	650	895	1,083	1,220	1,353	1,492
Fees	475	459	963	1,220	1,359	1,427	1,483	1,553
Miscellaneous	2,053	3,863	4,978	3,848	3,745	3,811	3,810	3,893
Sale of capital assets	166	682	678	656	611	629	635	800
Local government	1,408	1,782	1,984	1,951	2,125	2,354	2,426	2,704
Public service authorities	749	881	1,050	1,085	1,097	1,220	1,428	1,657
Investment self-financing	749	881	1,050	1,085	1,097	1,220	1,428	3,800

Source: Ministry of Finance

steady, it will not increase. The same is assumed of the US$3.5 billion earned in remittances from Egyptians working abroad.

Underlying the economic reform process has been the need to diversify Egypt's sources of income. While the government has proved itself capable of weathering the serious storms of the past two years, the real lesson from these crises has been salutary rather than laudatory. The public sector banks, for example, which account for 60 per cent of total bank assets, were used by the government as a weapon with which to cushion the blow of the Luxor killings. In the longer term the resilience of the Egyptian economy has benefited from the implementation of that reform.

INTRODUCTION

The Tower of Cairo is one of the city's most famous landmarks

Egypt and the Asia crisis: is there a risk?

The macroeconomic reforms which have created the framework and institutions which have equipped Egypt to weather a succession of global and domestic crises, reveal the extent to which real reform has taken place and the groundwork done to equip it to succeed in a global market. Key factors reveal the extent to which Egypt's links with the global market are still in their infancy. Its current account deficit has not – and probably will not – reach the 4 per cent level above which it would require financing beyond the resources available through gross

Exhibit 1.3
National budget outlays, 1990–99, (E£ million)

	1990–91	1991–92	1992–93	1993–94	1994–95	1995–96	1996–97	1997–98	1998–99
Total current expenditure	27,400	33,431	40,954	45,912	46,933	51,196	53,030	55,289	58,432
Wages and salaries	7,118	8,029	9,803	11,096	12,519	14,045	15,368	17,025	18,700
Pension payments	2,138	2,763	3,526	3,914	4,146	4,256	4,300	4,647	4,809
Material and supplies	1,446	1,766	2,423	2,857	2,986	3,214	3,520	3,734	3,951
Interest payments	7,046	9,510	13,309	16,498	14,790	16,027	15,451	14,943	15,396
Of which:									
Domestic debt	4,176	6,359	9,315	11,816	11,177	12,231	12,337	12,219	12,772
Foreign debt	2,870	3,151	3,994	4,682	3,613	3,796	3,114	2,724	2,624
Subsidies and GASC debt	3,921	4,850	5,572	5,873	6,410	6,954	7,373	7,772	8,200
Defence	4,205	4,850	5,572	5,873	6,410	6,954	7,373	7,772	8,200
Social fund	0	0	150	333	520	515	645	650	700
Other	1,526	1,663	2,122	2,256	2,443	2,625	2,639	2,758	2,876

Source: Ministry of Finance

domestic product. The depreciation of the currency and the broader economic contraction to have hit the south-east Asian countries, have not and will not be experienced in Egypt, owing to its still relatively strong current account position and the reserves to support the currency (see Exhibits 1.4 and 1.5).

Equally, Egypt is a net creditor with no Asian-style debts in need of regular servicing. Nor does it have a large commodity component to its foreign trade, largely freeing it from global commodity price deflation, beyond the impact of the oil price slump.

Loss of confidence is clearly a major factor behind the crisis in Asia, and in particular the loss of confidence in the banking sector which brought with it grave doubts as to the standards of corporate governance and regulatory control in those markets. The role of the state is undoubtedly being redefined in Egypt, rather than being rapidly stripped away. While the nature of the government role in the economy is still in a state of transition, its role as a regulator is very much in evidence. Public and private sector banks, in particular, are subject to the careful oversight of the CBE. Such a role has been of major benefit in allowing the government to identify the fundamental soundness of the banking sector as a reason not to regard Egypt as sharing the unstable characteristics exposed in Asia.

Rightly or wrongly, the Asian crisis lies behind a 37 per cent drop in the value of Egyptian shares in 1998. This fall, however, must be seen against the background of an 111 per cent rise in the price of shares between March 1996 and March 1997. Egypt represents a mere 8 per cent of total emerging market capitalisation of US$1,500 billion, at around US$20 billion. Of the top 200 companies in the emerging markets, none are in Egypt. The impact on Egypt of the global crisis facing emerging markets can be seen in several specific areas. In particular, the

Exhibit 1.4
Emerging market indicators, March 1999

Country	Inflation*	Industrial production*	GDP growth*	Trade balance**	Current account**
Egypt	3.6	8	5.2	-12.3	-3.1
India	15.3	3.1	5	-9.2	-7
Indonesia	70.7	-3	-13.9	21.6	0.1
Malaysia	5.2	-9.4	-8.6	13.9	-4.8
Thailand	3.5	-3.2	-6.5	12.1	13.3
Brazil	2.3	-3.3	-0.1	-6.5	-34.9
Mexico	19	3.9	5	-7.7	-15.2
China	-1.2	8	9.6	42.4	29.7
Greece	3.7	10.9	3.5	-17.7	-4.4
Turkey	65.9	-9.1	1.6	-21	-2.6

* Annual percentage changes
** In US dollars billion

Source: IDSC

Exhibit 1.5
Selected economic indicators for Egypt, 1991–98

Year	GDP growth (%)	Inflation (%)	Fiscal deficit % of GDP	Foreign debt % of GDP	Reserves/imports (months)
1991-92	1.9	21.1	5.4	79.7	12.9
1992-93	2.5	11.1	3.5	69.2	14.4
1993-94	3.9	9.1	2.1	58.0	19.2
1994-95	4.7	9.3	1.3	58.7	18.6
1995-96	4.9	7.3	1.3	49.2	16.0
1996-97	5.0	6.2	0.93	41.2	16.2
1997-98	5.0	4.0	0.95	35.2	14.6

Source: Ministry of Economy

stock market, which has picked up steadily since December 1998, has become good value for more discerning foreign and domestic buyers. A factor which in itself has led to a significant slow-down in the pace of privatisation.

Egypt's position relative to other emerging markets is the necessary gauge by which to assess the impact of the global crisis. In 1998 the IFC composite index of emerging markets declined by 19 per cent, dragged down much further by the averages recorded in Asian and Latin American markets than by Egypt's contribution to the composite decline. On the other hand, Egypt's standing in the IFC index of emerging market prices showed a 29.55 per cent decline in December 1997 to December 1998, making it the thirteenth worst performer of the 33 markets listed. Even so, the pattern of foreign investment in Egypt has revealed the extent of its relative immunity to the global crisis. The bulk of the US$1.1 billion foreign portfolio investments made in Egyptian stocks in 1997–98 were from country and emerging market funds. It was the withdrawal of these funds which heralded the steady decline. Meanwhile, trade in the five London-listed global depository receipts (GDRs) issued by Egyptian companies reached a value of US$800 million in mid-1997 to mid-1998. Between October 1997 and September 1998, the GDRs saw a 22 per cent fall, 10 per cent less than the fall on the Egyptian Stock Exchange. The ongoing GDR trade suggested that Egyptian stocks were not themselves the object of investor doubts, and that the retrenchment by emerging market fund managers affecting Egypt was the result of the global trend. Even at the height of the crisis in 1998, international investors controlled 44 per cent of the total shares traded, 21 per cent of them on the buy side.

While not emerging unscathed from the global crisis, the risk to Egypt of Asian contagion appears slim. Even before the Asian crisis, Egyptian shares were overvalued, and a correction in February 1998 was regarded as an early stage on the road to market maturity. At the same time, the boom of 1996–97 had served to expose the institutional and regulatory shortcomings of the Egyptian capital market. Depression on the trade side in 1997 was partly compensated for by exhilaration on the infrastructural side. The stock exchange embarked on the most extensive modernisation programme in its history, the regulatory environment saw the beginnings of a legislative revolution, and the human resources of the capital markets began a steady transformation towards new levels of sophistication. The importance of all these measures was heightened by comparison to the Asian markets where the paucity of regulation, inappropriate corporate governance and a lack of confidence in capital markets institutions brought on the crisis there. By checking these shortcomings before the contagion could spread, Egypt appears to have learned some vital lessons from the experience of markets elsewhere, without in the process having to suffer the consequences of their mistakes.

The government's economic policies, 1997–98

As Egypt has moved further along a course of economic liberalisation, so it has increasingly been required to 'sell its story' to the domestic and foreign private sector investor communities, upon whose resources the government is steadily coming to rely. The challenges are clearly enormous, and the figures tend to show how much further the process of liberalisation must go before a private sector-led take-off allows the government to achieve the 7–8 per cent annual economic growth rate it requires. According to the IMF, in 1992–93, the private sector accounted for 62 per cent of GDP. By 1996–97 it had grown to around 66 per cent, where it has remained. Privatisation has reduced the size of the public sector by around 40 per cent, with the market value of the privatised companies representing around 7 per cent of GDP.

Having stabilised the macroeconomic condition of the country in the first few years of the decade, government policy in the late 1990s has been dominated by a major broadening of reform, intended to put in place the elements vital to the creation of a market economy and fostering a favourable investment climate. Coupled with this has been the need to reduce the state's economic role. The pace of privatisation has been determined by several factors, which

INTRODUCTION

arose consecutively during 1997–98. Rising foreign portfolio investor interest in Egypt and other emerging markets had allowed the government to win the domestic political argument in favour of privatisation on the basis that it could get a good price for the privatisation stocks on offer. This period, which lasted from March 1996 to March 1997, saw the Egyptian market rise 111 per cent. A period of correction, followed in early 1998 with the global reaction to the worsening crisis in Asia, during which the Egyptian market fell by 33 per cent, led to an effective suspension of the privatisation programme from August 1998, until Spring 1999.

The Suez Canal and tourism are both key earners of foreign exchange receipts

The first phase of privatisation, launched in 1996 with the successful sale of Nasr City Housing, was followed with a steady progression towards state divestment. By February 1997, the government had either part-sold, majority-sold or liquidated its stake in 81 companies, and by September this had been raised to 84 companies. In 29 of the companies in which the state had sold more than 50 per cent of its stake, it remained the largest single shareholder. In a further five companies in which less than 50 per cent was sold, it continued to hold the largest single stake, as was the case in five companies in which less than 40 per cent was sold. Meanwhile, 95 per cent of shares in 11

INTRODUCTION

Exhibit 1.6
The progress of privatisation as at December 1998

Method of privatisation	Number of companies	Sale value in E£ million
Majority sale through IPO	46	6,494
Sale to employees	25	613
Sale of assets or liquidation	27	3,041
Minority sale through IPO	20	2,207
Total	118	12,355

Source: Financial Securities

companies were sold to employees, nine companies were sold to anchor investors and two were majority-sold on the stock exchange.

The Ministry of Public Enterprise announced that it intended to sell 80 companies in 1998, but this figure was later revised to 43. By December 1998 it had sold 16, bringing to 118 the total number of companies in which shares had been sold. Of those in which the government had sold a majority stake, 14 had been sold to anchor investors, while 27 had been liquidated and 25 sold to employees (see Exhibit 1.6). Plans were made for the preparation of a further 83 public companies, of the total 314 non-financial public sector companies earmarked for sale, to undergo extensive financial restructuring intended to settle outstanding debt of E£8 billion, owed in large part to the public sector banks. In February 1999 the ministry announced plans to find foreign partners to manage the restructuring of these companies over a one-year period beginning in September 1999.

Despite privatisation and a reduction in the size of the public sector's workforce since 1991, the public sector's share of GDP remains substantial. Overall, where there has been increased growth in private sector activity, it has been in areas of the economy which remain dominated by the public sector. Meanwhile, the weight of the bureaucracy on the public purse has remained. Prior to the past three years of privatisation, 34 per cent of the workforce was employed by the government. While the state economic authorities accounted for 3 per cent of this workforce and contributed 18 per cent of GDP, the civil service remained a major drain on resources, accounting for 24 per cent of the total workforce while accounting for only 7 per cent of total economic activity. The affect, while showing a greater private sector participation, has been to limit private sector gains and expansion possibilities, despite privatisation. Meanwhile, the government estimates it needs E£375 billion in investment over the next four years to meet its 7 per cent growth target, 20 per cent of which it will provide, but the rest of which must come from the private sector.

Most controversial in the programme of economic legislation was a decision to close a tax loophole allowing banks and other companies to claim tax relief on the purchase of government bonds and T-bills. Prior to the legislation, operational income had been taxable while 90 per cent of revenue from government bonds and Treasury bills was non-taxable. This allowed banks or companies with an income from tax-exempt securities equal to or higher than their net profit before tax, to avoid paying tax altogether. Corporate bonds and stocks were not

Exhibit 1.7
Public investments, 1990–99, (E£ million)

	1990–91	1991–92	1992–93	1993–94	1994–95	1995–96	1996–97	1997–98	1998–99
Total public investments	**15,067**	**15,746**	**11,097**	**10,659**	**11,299**	**12,581**	**14.070**	**15635**	**16,210**
Social sector	*2,072*	*2,060*	*2,263*	*2,565*	*3,035*	*3,455*	*4,127*	*5,127*	*5,012*
Education	653	536	540	1,148	1,351	1,449	1,982	2,009	2,067
Health	182	161	106	86	270	289	361	770	893
Public services	1,211	1,332	1,564	1,263	1,364	1,657	1,694	2,271	1,972
Other	26	31	53	68	50	60	90	77	80
Infrastructure/construction	*4,777*	*6,408*	*6,437*	*5,976*	*5,864*	*6,702*	*7,446*	*7,457*	*7,688*
Construction	1,855	2,067	2,220	2,450	2,628	2,681	3,124	3,308	3,555
Electricity	1,509	2,544	2,412	1,915	1,804	1,891	1,999	1,790	1,795
Transport/telecoms	1,413	1,797	1,805	1,611	1,432	2,130	2,323	2,359	2,338
Economic services	*1,659*	*1,697*	*1,532*	*1,935*	*2,250*	*2,312*	*2,399*	*2,882*	*3,146*
Agriculture/irrigation	731	968	1,183	1,175	1,590	1,715	1,781	2,191	2,416
Industry/mining	928	729	349	760	660	597	617	691	730
Other investments	*1,669*	*1,683*	*865*	*183*	*150*	*112*	*99*	*169*	*364*
Public enterprise investment	4,890	3,898	*	*	*	*	*	*	*

* Public enterprise investments were removed from the national budget in 1992

Source: Ministry of Finance

subject to the amendment, nor were corporate bond and stock dividends. However, confusion about the law stemmed from uncertainty over the formula to be used to establish the cost of funding to the banks of T-bill purchases. The purpose of the legislation was to encourage greater investment on the stock exchange, which it was thought would take place if T-bill investments became less attractive to banks. It took a full six months for the calculation formula to be announced, during which time banks had heavily provisioned in expectation of a soaring tax burden. The final regulations allowed tax exemption up to the level of a bank's net worth, which was not expected when the law was first discussed.

The impact on T-bill purchases was eventually set against the background of the broader pattern of redemption and market contraction which was experienced in the wake of the Asian crisis and foreign portfolio withdrawal from emerging markets. At the beginning of 1998, E£3 billion was held by foreigners in Egyptian T-bills. This holding had dropped to E£500 million a year later, the CBE consequently having to pay out US$700 million for redemptions, which tested the policy of pegging the currency (see Exhibit 1.8).

T-bill redemption was one of several factors which placed a strain on Egypt's US$20 billion foreign exchange reserves, and raised the issue of Egypt's policy of pegging the currency to the US dollar (see Exhibit 1.9). Differences of opinion over how to explain a dollar shortage, which became apparent in October 1998 and continued to remain an issue

INTRODUCTION

Abu Simbel

during the first quarter of 1999, helped to further clarify the relationship between the government and the financial sector. Dollar holdings by the four state-owned commercial banks had slipped from US$2 billion in December 1996, to –US$2.3 billion by March 1998. The purpose had been to ensure that the CBE reserves remained at the US$20 billion mark, perceived as a key indicator of Egypt's economic strength and the vital component in the dollar peg.

The dollar shortage also emerged in the wake of a 30 per cent increase in imports in 1998, largely explained by a major growth in the import of cheap consumer goods from Asia. The fall in earnings from oil and tourism, coupled with a growing trade deficit, which had reached

Exhibit 1.8
Foreign exchange reserves, 1990–98

	1990–91	*1991–92*	*1992–93*	*1993–94*	*1994–95*	*1995–96*	*1996–97*	*1997–98*
Net international reserves (US$ billion)	5.6	12.9	14.4	19.2	18.6	19.3	20.2	20.1
CBE reserves/E£ in circulation (%)	–	–	297	296	276	260	262	227
Reserves/imports % (months of G&S)	–	–	–	19.7	18.6	16	16.2	13.9
CBE reserves/foreign exchange deposits	–	–	149	177	155	160	140	176

Source: Central Bank of Egypt

Exhibit 1.9
Egypt's balance of payments, 1990–98, (US$ million)

	1990–91	*1991–92*	*1992–93*	*1993–94*	*1994–95*	*1995–96*	*1996–97*	*1997–98*
Trade balance	**(7,175)**	**(6,174)**	**(7,003)**	**(7,306.8)**	**(7,853.5)**	**(9,498.1)**	**(10,219.4)**	**(11,770.6)**
Exports	4,250	3,880.1	3,725.1	3,337.3	4,957	4,608.5	5,345.4	5,128.4
Petroleum	2,333.9	1,897.7	2,111.3	1,772.1	2,176	2,225.6	2,577.8	1,728.4
Other	1,196.1	1,982.4	1,613.8	1,565.2	2,781.0	2,382.9	2,767.6	3,400
Imports	(11,425)	(10,054.1)	(10,728.2)	(10,647.1)	(12,810.5)	(14,106.6)	(15,564.8)	(16,899)
Services (net)	*3,575.9*	*4,463.6*	*3,561*	*3,673.7*	*4,041.8*	*5,791.5*	*6,192.8*	*4,594.5*
Receipts	*7,153*	*8,189.1*	*8,332.2*	*8,677.3*	*9,555.6*	*10,636*	*11,240.9*	*10,443.8*
Suez Canal	1,662	1,950.2	1,941.1	1,990.3	2,058.4	1,884.5	1,848.9	1,776.5
Tourism	1,646	2,529	2,375	1,779.3	2,298.9	3,009.1	3,646.3	2,940.5
Investment income	1,167	994.8	882.9	1,197	1,625.5	1,829.4	2,052.3	2,080.4
Other	2,678	2,715.1	3.133.2	3,710.7	3,572.8	3,912.8	3,693	3,646.4
Payments	*3,577.1*	*3,725.5*	*4,771.2*	*5,003.6*	*5,513.8*	*4,844.5*	*5,048.1*	*5,849.3*
Investment income	1,529.7	1,320.1	1,455	1,319	1,484.7	1,290.8	1,085.3	940.8
Private transfers	*2,568*	*3,028.5*	*3,835.1*	*3,232.4*	*3,279*	*2,797.6*	*3,255.6*	*3,518.5*
Current account excluding official transfers	**1,031.1**	**1,318.1**	**393**	**(403.7)**	**(532.7)**	**(909.0)**	**(771)**	**(3,657.6)**
Official transfers	4,851	1,351.8	1,902.1	813.6	918.6	723.6	889.6	885.3
Current account balance	**3,819.9**	**2,669.9**	**2,295.1**	**409.9**	**385.9**	**(185.4)**	**118.6**	**(2,772.3)**
Capital/financial account	457.3	(1.6)	1.821.4	2,510.9	429.7	1,017.3	2,040.7	3,765.4
Direct investment abroad	(30.9)	(120)	(118.7)	(35.9)	47.6	(15.3)	(47.2)	(110.2)
Direct investment in Egypt	1,124.7	1,152	1,139.6	1,320.8	782.7	626.9	769.7	1,107.6
Portfolio investment	4.3	9.2	4.8	2.5	4.1	257.6	1,462.9	(248)
Other investment	(1,555.4)	1,042.8	795.7	1,223.5	309.5	148.1	(144.7)	3,006

Exhibit 1.9 continued

Net borrowing	531.6	(267.8)	80.8	228.2	1,084.2	88.5	224.7	919.7
M/L-term loans	496.9	321	295.2	364.5	302.5	(75)	(112.5)	(54.3)
Drawings	1,037.3	954	818.4	644.5	729.4	472.4	415.9	525
Repayments	(540.4)	(632.2)	532.2	(280)	426.9	(547.4)	(528.4)	(579.4)
MT credit	134.7	(589.6)	214.4	(136.3)	171.3	(283)	(250.5)	322
Drawings	911.9	498.4	271.9	214	162.7	56.2	77.4	546.5
Repayments	777.2	(1,088)	486.3	(350.3)	334	(339.2)	(327.9)	(224.5)
ST credit	n/a	n/a	n/a	n/a	953	446.5	587.07	652
Other assets	1,093.6	1,189.5	1,143.7	1,399	1,406.4	237	(1,589.9)	317.2
Other liabilities	993.4	414.5	428.8	403.7	12.7	(177.4)	1,220.5	1,769.1
Net errors/omissions	480.7	1,330.4	195	814.6	61.4	(261.3)	(247)	(1,128.1)
Overall balance	**3,843.3**	**3,998.7**	**4,311.5**	**2,106.2**	**754.2**	**570.6**	**1,912.3**	**(135)**
Change in CBE's reserve assets	(3,846.3)	(3,998.7)	(4,311.5)	(2,106.2)	(754.2)	(570.6)	(1,912.3)	135

Source: Central Bank of Egypt

US$11.7 billion by the time the dollar shortage became apparent, brought calls for the reserves to be allowed to fall to finance the current account deficit, which had grown in response to the burgeoning investment climate.

The government's response centred on regarding the issue as essentially a structural one, stemming primarily from the mechanics of interbank currency trading. The government insisted that there was no need to allow a devaluation of the currency on the basis of the pressure on the reserves, and maintained that the current account deficit, which had reached 3.2 per cent by March 1999, was not unbridgeable and would only become a cause for concern if it reached 3.5–4.0 per cent. Meanwhile, the need for liquidity was addressed, and action was taken to prevent Egypt's 111 licensed foreign exchange bureaux from introducing their own devaluations in light of the squeeze.

The Republic's plans to borrow: benchmarking and monitoring private sector debt

Egypt's net credit position in the international market place has inspired lengthy discussion of the need to fully exploit the sound economic fundamentals established since 1991. Egypt's debt service ratio of 7.7 per cent on its total US$29.8 billion debt is clearly manageable. Moreover, the relation between the debt and reserves has heightened the potential advantage to be gained from pursuing the development of a debt market. The actual current value of the debt is placed at around US$18 billion, or 33 per cent of GDP, below the US$20 billion level of the reserves, implying a net credit position. Egypt's strong debt position is regarded as a vital component in

Exhibit 1.10
Value of exports by commodity groups, 1990–98, (US$ million)

	1990–91	1991–92	1992–93	1993–94	1994–95	1995–96	1996–97	1997–98
Total exports	**4,250**	**3,880**	**3,725**	**3,337**	**4,955**	**4,608**	**5,345**	**5,128**
Agricultural commodities	*226*	*257*	*199*	*238*	*614*	*339*	*270*	*243*
Cotton	83	35	37	45	306	109	107	103
Vegetables	23	42	27	25	33	21	20	11
Citrus fruits	38	58	42	35	17	23	20	12
Potatoes	28	40	19	21	104	28	17	27
Rice	5	33	26	45	64	71	38	28
Fresh onions	7	7	3	6	22	1	1	2
Other	42	42	45	61	68	86	67	60
Industrial commodities	*3,467*	*3,359*	*3,276*	*2,899*	*4,150*	*3,540*	*3,880*	*3,413*
Petroleum sector	*2,334*	*1,898*	*2,111*	*1,772*	*1,948*	*2,226*	*2,578*	*1,728*
Crude oil	1,463	1,172	1,279	932	837	1,192	1,293	676
Petroleum products	508	479	524	567	792	657	814	714
Jet & vessel fuel	363	247	308	273	319	377	471	338
Spinning and weaving	*529*	*575*	*451*	*496*	*1,078*	*574*	*605*	*759*
Cotton yarn	318	283	204	212	480	199	204	288
Cotton textiles	75	87	65	66	161	42	30	20
Clothes	115	170	152	163	285	161	195	258
Other	21	35	30	55	152	172	176	193
Engineering industry	*80*	*119*	*91*	*93*	*51*	*126*	*146*	*286*
Wood furniture	26	38	23	14	16	4	9	12
Transport/parts	10	13	11	34	2	25	19	57
White goods	n/a	11	9	7	2	11	14	6
Other	44	57	48	38	31	86	104	211

Source: Central Bank of Egypt

the financing of economic growth, particularly in the funding of private sector infrastructure projects which the government is keen to see expand (see Exhibit 1.11). Consequently, the private sector has sought finance through bond issues. By January 1999 there were 23 Egyptian corporate bond issues, worth E£2.67 billion. Between August 1997 and a year later, trade in bonds rose from E£390.6 million to E£734.7 million. The absence of an adequately equipped electronic trading mechanism is hampering the growth of the corporate bond market, and consequently a secondary market. Of the current corporate bond issues, nine are fixed rate, while the remaining floating rate bonds base their coupon on the 91-day T-bill rate to a

INTRODUCTION

Cairo skyline

maximum of TB+1 per cent.

The benchmarking provided by the corporate bond issues has clearly led the way to establishing broad conclusions as to the cost of money. A sovereign Eurobond issue, which had been discussed in 1997 as a means of establishing a sovereign benchmark, was postponed in light of the Asian market turmoil, though is still considered a possibility. Meanwhile, the government financing has been achieved by issuing, in August, September and October 1997 seven-year government bonds, each of E£500 million. The wish to avoid the premium that an external sovereign bond issue would have implied, lay behind the government's decision to postpone a Eurobond issue. The decision was relatively straightforward, as the need for cash was not great. Further 10- and 15-year bonds were planned for early 1999, by which time the depth of the bond market is expected to have been established. In so doing, the corporate bonds are expected to become a reference point as a safe-asset device. This will give the private sector a benchmark, and also provide a future mortgage market with its key reference point. The CBE remains content to postpone the sovereign bond issue while investors are content to use Egypt's investment-grade ratings as a benchmark. Commercial banks have been ready to underwrite corporate bonds being issued by the private sector, based on their own investment criteria. Meanwhile, the CBE prevents any banks from paying dividends if funds are inadequate. It also requires of banks to lend in foreign currency to customers who can repay in foreign currency. Much of the prudential regulation introduced to govern the conduct of commercial banks and allow monitoring of private sector debt, was introduced in the wake of the Mexican currency crisis of 1994.

Central bank monitoring of private sector debt has led to several early warnings alerting bankers to the economic health of particular sectors. A 15 per cent fall in the value of luxury real estate projects in 1998 led to the leading commercial banks warning against further investment in an area that was in danger of saturation. The CBE asked the banks to link exposure to real estate to their total loans portfolio and bank equity. This has been in response to a 113 per cent growth in the amount of private sector corporate lending as a proportion of bank assets, from 15 per cent of assets in 1991 to 32 per cent in 1998. Household credit, which banks are keen to expand as they offer a widening range of retail banking products, has seen a 269 per cent increase as a proportion of total bank loans in the same period, from 2.6 per cent in 1991, to 9.6 per cent in 1998. The government's determination to force all banks to abide by International Accounting Standards (IAS) has been evident since the IAS rules were adopted in 1997. Government action to drive down inflation during the early 1990s means that the level of Egypt's total banking sector assets are large relative to the size of the economy. This has increased the need for tight monitoring, and for the IAS rules to be firmly applied. In its 1998 *Egypt Sovereign Report*, Fitch IBCA rating agency calculated that 13.4 per cent of loans in 1997 were non-performing. While 81 per cent of those loans were provisioned, three banks which accounted for 26 per cent of total bank assets were below the 8 per cent capital adequacy threshold, while eight banks had failed to abide by a 30 per cent single counterparty exposure

Exhibit 1.11
Egypt's deficit and financing sources, 1996–98, (E£ billion)

	1996–97				1997–98			
	Revised estimate	%	Actual 9 months	%	Revised estimate	%	Actual 9 months	%
Total expenditure	66.8		47.7		71.7		50.6	
Total revenues	64.9		45.6		69.1		47.8	
Overall deficit	(1.9)		(2.1)		(2.6)	100	(2.8)	100
Financing sources	1.9	100	2.1	100	2.6	50	2.8	46.4
External	(1.5)	(78.9)	(1.5)	(71.4)	(1.3)	150	(1.3)	146.4
Domestic	3.4	178.9	3.6	171.4	3.9	92.3	4.1	139.3
Non-bank	2.9	152.6	3.7	176.2	2.4		3.9	–
Savings	1.8		1.6		–		2.9	
Treasury bill	1.6		2		–		(2.3)	
Treasury bond	0.4		0.4		–		(0.1)	
Government bonds	(0.9)		(0.3)		2.4		3.4	
Bank finance	0.5	26.3	(0.1)	(4.8)	1.5	57.7	0.2	7.1

Source: Ministry of Finance

INTRODUCTION

Exhibit 1.12
Commercial banks' lending and discount balances, 1992–98, (E£ million)

	1992	*1993*	*1994*	*1995*	*1996*	*1997*	*1998*
Total	**40,424**	**49,617**	**59,674**	**81,755**	**99,491**	**116,654**	**130,348**
Local currency positions	**32,417**	**37,882**	**43,855**	**65,267**	**78,444**	**87,645**	**95,775**
Government sector	2,645	3,288	1,393	10,489	12,066	8,677	4,283
Public business sector*	14,620	16,914	20,872	21,548	23,881	26,179	23,148
Private business sector	12,828	14,743	17,370	26,113	34,610	43,373	56,579
Household sector	1,187	1,880	3,383	6,265	7,573	9,109	10,742
Foreign sector	1,137	1,057	837	852	314	307	1,023
Foreign currency positions	**8,007**	**11,735**	**15,819**	**16,488**	**21,047**	**29,009**	**34,573**
Government sector	536	813	844	916	983	2,095	2,942
Public business sector*	1,403	1,520	3,075	2,913	3,697	4,361	4,277
Private business sector	5,034	8,033	10,405	10,983	14,344	20,082	24,370
Household sector	436	692	775	935	1,101	1,585	1,654
Foreign sector	598	677	720	741	922	886	1,330

* Including public business sector companies subject to Law No. 203 and other public sector companies
Source: Central Bank of Egypt

limit. Some Cairo banks admit that the CBE rarely sees the full picture of their loan portfolios, owing largely to an inadequacy of staff to assess the details of each of the country's four state-owned commercial banks, 32 investment banks and commercial banks, 21 public specialised banks, and 18 agricultural banks, all of which are supervised by the CBE. Banks are required to maintain an aggregate credit position, but against a background of growing pressure to lend to individuals against securities.

2 The financial system and foreign investment

Solid and independent institutions: the 'equity' necessary for economic growth

The character of the financial institutions which comprise the Egyptian financial system, has evolved at a similar pace to the growth of the market those institutions serve. Outside the banking sector, there are 144 brokerage companies licensed to operate on the Egyptian Stock Exchange (ESE), as well as several major investment banks and nine fund managers.

The growth of the financial services sector has been the most vivid result of the liberalisation of the Egyptian economy. The relative youth of the personnel developing this industry is occasionally startling, when viewed against the task they are undertaking. A significant number of the leading individual players in the financial sector have emerged from one of two key areas. Many emerged well equipped to deal with Egypt's new challenges, having played a key role in the creation of joint-venture banks in the mid-1970s. Others returned to Egypt in the early 1990s, after periods of effective exile from the country following the nationalisation of all major industry after 1962. Many others are young, determined professionals who have relatively recently gained invaluable experience in the offices of leading global banks and financial institutions in the United Kingdom, the United States and elsewhere, before returning with their skills to Egypt.

The institutions which have emerged in the past five years as the powerhouse of Egypt's economic transformation are thus the product of a variety of traditions. In garnering them into an identifiable industry with a solid and independent institutional base, the regulatory authorities governing the financial sector have relied extensively upon prudential regulations which are the result of intensive coordination between the industry and the regulators, as they attempt to tailor regulations to suit the evolving economic climate.

The government estimates that it will require E£375 billion in investment over the next four years to meet its 7 per cent growth target. It is prepared to provide 20 per cent of this sum, which effectively means that the various arms of the financial sector will have to energize E£300 billion in domestic and foreign investment. Can Egyptian financiers generate this amount?

Central to any assessment of the institutions charged with the task of mobilising these funds, is the question of whether the supervisory and monitoring functions of the regulators are adequate to ensure that the industry becomes and remains equipped to handle growing

THE FINANCIAL SYSTEM AND FOREIGN INVESTMENT

The CBE's major task in the 1990s has been managing the successful expansion of the capital market

volumes of trade. A major preoccupation to have faced policy-makers since the growth in capital inflows in 1991–92, spurred by the fiscal and structural policy reforms, has been the need to supervise the financial sector effectively. The three years immediately following the Gulf War saw reserves rise by US$11 billion, which the CBE absorbed by sales of government securities, the proceeds from which were deposited in the CBE. The post-war bonanza was accompanied, however, by a decline in the terms of trade and a contraction of investment. The subsequent emergence of a financial services industry, after 1994, prepared Egypt for a second phase of capital inflows, in the form of foreign portfolio investment which required skilled management and the launch of a search for investment opportunities. Trading on the ESE has increased by 43 per cent since 1993, while the market capitalisation of the exchange has risen from 8 per cent of GDP to around 33 per cent in the same period.

Against this background of expansion, the institutions of the financial system – both the regulatory bodies and the private and public-private companies they are charged with regulating – have jointly created a cohesive financial services industry which within five years is expected by some analysts to be generating 2–3 per cent of GDP. The spread of companies, particularly those offering brokerage, is regarded as sustainable despite the three largest companies holding around 30 per cent of the brokerage market. Increasingly stringent rules governing the practice of brokers are promoting the need for adequate back-office operations to support the exchange floor brokerage, allaying concerns about quality of service. Such rules are introduced following extensive discussions involving representatives of the brokerage companies, the ESE and the regulatory Capital Market Authority (CMA), which has a paternalistic rather than dictatorial attitude towards the numerous young players in this burgeoning though increasingly sophisticated industry.

Supervision of the financial system

The process of supervision of the Egyptian financial system has witnessed profound change since the launch in 1991 of the economic reform programme. It is in the area of supervision that some of the most significant strides have in fact been taken, although the system regulators are occasionally regarded by investment bankers, brokers and fund managers as having slowed the pace of reform by failing to match the pace of the emergent financial sector with the creation of appropriate regulations. The key supervisors – the Central Bank of Egypt (CBE) as overseer of the banking sector, and the Capital Market Authority (CMA) as overseer of the financial services sector – have overseen the maintenance of systemic stability while also adapting their roles to new needs and complexities.

Despite being 101 years old, the CBE has played the traditional role of a central bank for less than half that time. After the passing of Law No. 163 of 1957, the CBE acted as a banking supervisor, conducting off-site monitoring and surveillance of bank performance, as well as on-site inspection of the financial condition of the banks. Such supervision was extended in 1988, with Law 144 (Law No. 144 of 1988) subjecting the state-owned banks to on-site monitoring by the Central Audit Organisation (CAO) in coordination with external auditors. While the CBE supervision concentrates on the degree of compliance with credit controls, tariff schedules, interest rate ceilings and bank solvency, the CAO is charged with ensuring that the state-owned banks comply with rules governing the activities of all public sector companies, and not only the financial performance of the banks.

Since the launch of reforms in 1991, the CBE has drawn heavily upon the experiences of other emerging markets, to assess the best ways in which to advance its supervisory role and regulatory structure. A key element in the development of its strategy was the Mexican currency crisis of 1995. The CBE has retained particularly close scrutiny of capital inflows since that crisis. From 1991–94 Egypt's interest differential with US interest rates resulted from a sharp tightening of credit. This led to a rise in capital inflows of around US$600 million in 1994–96, which the CBE responded to

Exhibit 2.1
Net flow of international finance into Egypt, 1996–97 and 1997–98, (US$ million)

	1996–97	*1997–98*
Total net flows	2,307.9	1,192.2
External debt	13.3	281.5
Bilateral loans	-82.7	-139.4
Utilisation	135.5	68.3
Repayments	-218.2	-207.7
International institutional loans	-94.2	167.8
Utilisation	142.3	416.7
Repayments	-236.5	-248.9
Medium/long-term credits	-253.3	-39.2
Utilisation	15.9	135.4
Repayments	-269.2	-174.6
Short-term credits	443.5	292.3
Official grants	698.7	653.8
Direct investments into Egypt	498	676
Direct investments abroad	-3.7	-95.4
Portfolio investment in Egypt	1,101.6	-323.7

Source: Central Bank of Egypt

with the sale of government securities. The inflows also led to a growth in the foreign currency reserves of the commercial banks. After a steady rise of capital inflows in 1994–96, the total grew to around US$2 billion between 1996 and 1998 (see Exhibit 2.1).

For the CBE, managing the clearly successful expansion of the capital markets – the main beneficiary of these capital inflows – has been the major task of the 1990s. High capital inflows could have created inflationary pressure which would have undermined the government's macroeconomic management of the country. Equally, rapid credit growth carried with it the danger of misallocation of funds in poorly managed projects. The CBE has continued to soak up capital inflows as the cornerstone of its strategy to counter pressure on the currency, while also retaining tight fiscal control as a way of keeping inflation down to its early 1999 level of 3.6 per cent.

The changing nature of the Egyptian business environment has created new pressures on the broad policy direction of the CBE, particularly in its resistance to devaluation. In early 1999 the CBE ordered foreign exchange bureaux to bring their rates to within the scope of the official rate it had set. Such use of its supervisory powers over the financial system have allowed it to postpone debate over the issue of the exchange rate, even while the need for an 11 per cent increase in foreign trade remains a central feature of government policy as part of its drive to increase economic growth. The maintenance of the exchange rate in the absence of major improvements in economic output and the quality of exports is regarded as unlikely to improve the competitiveness of Egyptian goods, while a steady devaluation is seen as key to improving both domestic efficiency and Egypt's global market share of trade.

The central bank's response to the growth of the capital markets has been complemented by that of the CMA, which has concentrated on promoting good governance within the institutions into which these foreign capital inflows – in tandem with much greater domestic investment – have been channelled. In the meantime, the ESE has developed its own rules for members, allowing it to evolve steadily into becoming a self-governing body equipped with the power to censure brokerage companies. The evolution of the supervisory powers of the CMA has been strongly influenced by both the learning process prevalent among the brokers, as well as the pace of technological advances at the ESE, which has allowed both the CMA and the ESE in its surveillance capacity to perform hands-on supervision of the electronic trading system installed in 1999.

Incentives and regulations for proper governance

The framework for proper governance of the Egyptian financial system has been put in place, striking a balance between incentives and regulation viable for the participation of the private sector in the system. Pressure on the regulators stems less from the passing of regulations, than from their ability to enact those regulations. Among key reformers there is the desire to see penalties for transgression rather than incentives to abide by regulations. Broadly, the direction of the regulatory environment has been determined by the view that the state should play the key role as a regulator, while the players on the financial scene create the economic vehicles for investment. The state's role is to prevent any single group securing oligarchistic rights, while allowing the market to establish the processes of investment.

The Capital Market Authority (CMA), which was established in 1980 as a relatively weak regulator of a market which was at that time moribund, now has the intention of promoting itself as a centre of excellence, with the aim of inspiring equally high standards in those subject to its authority. At the heart of successive reappraisals of the rules governing the capital markets has been the need to take into consideration the ability of the market players to develop their business, in terms of both trade and personal skills. The best example of this has been the application of prudential regulations, four sets of which have been introduced since 1994. At the heart of the CMA's message to the often newly-arrived brokers at the ESE is that they should know their clients, to whom they should offer advice and information as to the real condition of the market, with the aim of encouraging investors to move from speculation to investment. To this end, equal access to information through timely and accurate disclosure is rigorously applied.

The CMA's encouragement of the business side of capital markets activity is an essential part of the government's broad role in the reform process. The CMA's active participation in fostering a climate favourable to investment, investment vehicles, financial risk and the role of financial intermediaries, has greatly assisted in diminishing the legacy of suspicion of such intermediaries, which is a hangover from Egypt's socialist past. The children of those who nationalised Egyptian industry in the 1960s, are now actively engaged in its privatisation. Meanwhile, the CMA has used the regulatory powers invested in it by the Capital Markets Law of 1992 to cajole and persuade members of the ESE to abide by rules which they themselves have had an opportunity to assist in formulating. Where the system has detected abuses, action has been taken, though not to the severe extreme allowable under the 1992 law. The legislation allows for heavy fines and lengthy prison terms for those discovered to have manipulated the market or committed insider trading. So far these penalties have not been imposed, though occasional suspension of brokers has taken place in response to malpractice.

Equipping the banking sector with the incentives for proper governance is dependent upon regarding the regulator – the CBE – as able and willing to enact the regulatory powers with which it has been armed since Law No. 163 of 1957. By this law, banks can have their registration cancelled and their licence withdrawn if they break the law, the subsequent decrees by which the law is implemented 'or decisions taken by the Board of Directors of the Central Bank of Egypt'.

Since the launch of the economic reform programme in 1991, six specific measures have been introduced by the CBE, intended to ensure stability within the system. These measures demand: capital adequacy at a risk ratio of a minimum of 8 per cent; a liquidity ratio of 20 per cent for local currency and 25 per cent for foreign currency; standards of asset classification and provisioning as laid down by the World Bank. They prohibited banks from having claims against one client, either in the form of a credit facility or capital ownership, which exceeds 30 per cent of the bank's capital base; state that all but branches of foreign banks operating in Egypt

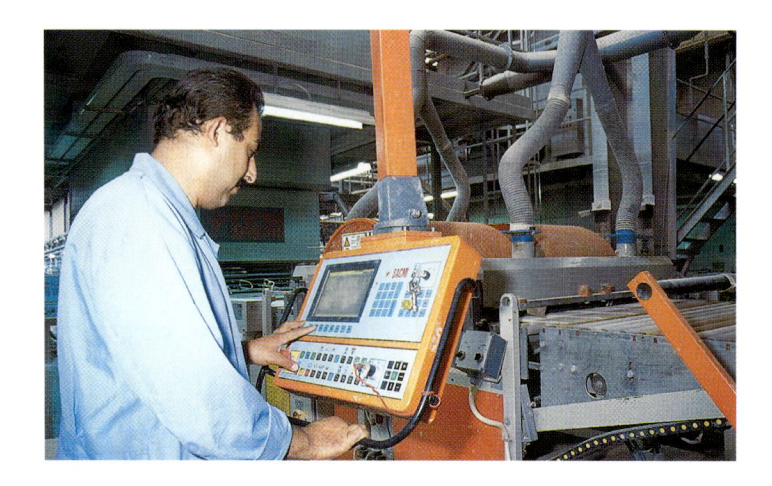

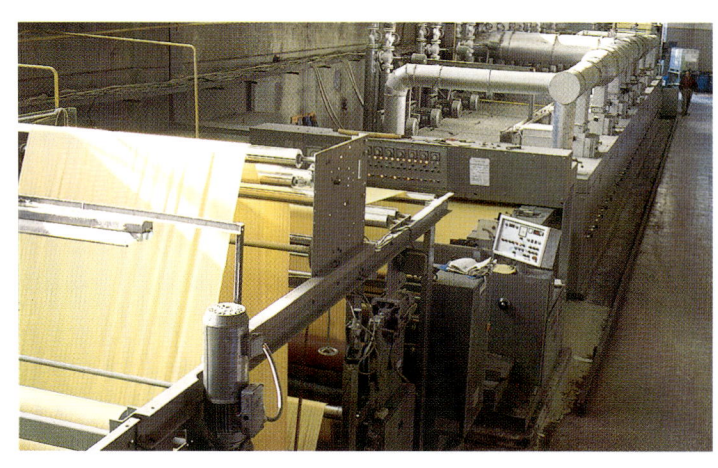

Companies operating in one of the new industrial centres outside Cairo – Tenth of Ramadan (top) and Sixth of October

are prohibited from depositing more than 40 per cent of their capital base or 10 per cent of total investments abroad with one foreign correspondent; and, prohibit banks retaining more than 10 per cent of their capital base in a single foreign currency.

The CBE's role in the formulation of monetary policy, which the bank itself regards as having been its major achievement, in particular in the fight against inflation, is well recognised. In its role as a regulator, bankers regard the CBE as being as effective as its ability to support and follow up its regulations. While the quantity of supervision is regarded as being in place, the analysis and implementation is occasionally the subject of criticism, particularly in the area of efficient monitoring of country risk exposure. Timing is clearly of crucial importance, and the CBE is widely regarded as having dealt with most potential problems as far in advance as has been possible. This has been the case particularly when it has been necessary to remind commercial banks of the importance of retaining sound asset quality. However, the variability in assessment of the asset quality and risk is an area in which there is growing pressure for improvement.

Comparison of financial monitoring with MENA and other emerging markets

Egypt's integration into the global economic system remains limited. Comparisons with other markets are consequently far from straightforward, as any such comparison would have to take into account not just the monitoring process as it currently stands, but the stage which new and future legislation has reached, in trying to address current shortcomings. The extent to which Egypt compares favourably or unfavourably with other regional and emerging markets in terms of its own systemic monitoring requires acknowledgment of the evident variety of market development within the markets with which Egypt may be compared. Within the Middle East and North Africa (MENA), there are only a handful of markets with which comparison is relevant. Morocco, Tunisia, Jordan, Lebanon, Bahrain and other Gulf states have evolved systems of monitoring which reflect a variety of attitudes towards how best the market should develop. Driving Egypt's monitoring effort are the guidelines laid down by the International Organisation of Securities Commissions (IOSCO), as well as its accordance with the Basle concordats of 1975 and 1983 for the process of banking regulation and monitoring.

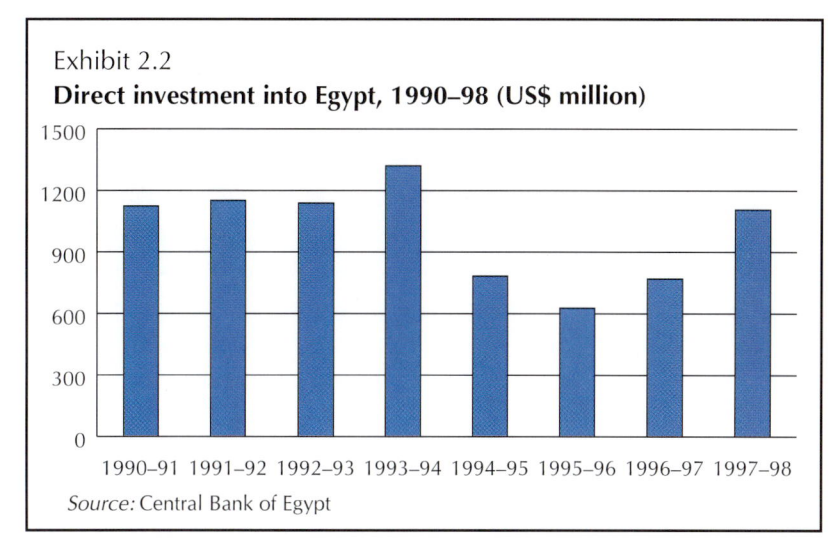

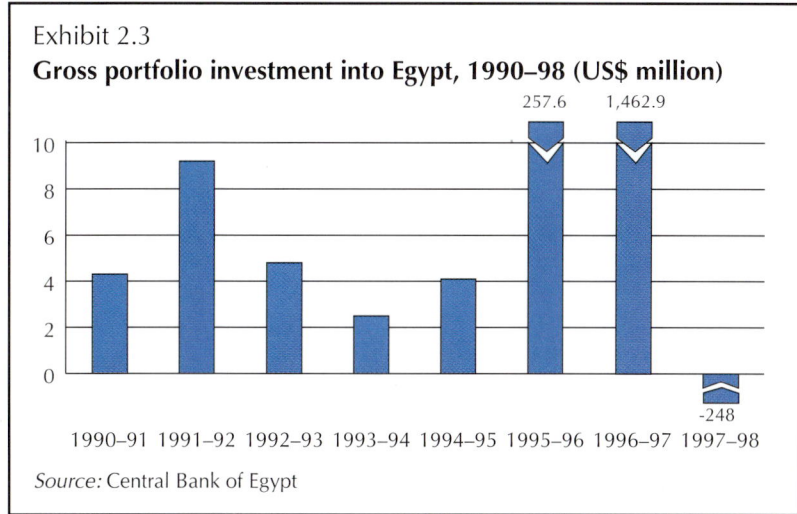

Exhibit 2.2
Direct investment into Egypt, 1990–98 (US$ million)
Source: Central Bank of Egypt

Exhibit 2.3
Gross portfolio investment into Egypt, 1990–98 (US$ million)
Source: Central Bank of Egypt

From a comparative perspective, Egypt is regarded by players in the banking sector and capital markets as exercising a sound process of monitoring compared with other regional and emerging markets, though a process which requires more resources as both sectors expand. In the banking sector, the Basle standard insists that regulators impose a minimum risk asset ratio of 8 per cent on banks. Compliance with Basle is strictly applied in Egypt, which has enhanced the banks' reputations for soundness. capital markets monitoring has become centred on enforcing observance of standards of disclosure in the documentation of offerings, and the periodic announcements of any material events, as well as measures to counter insider dealing, rules governing related-party transactions, corporate governance, shareholder minority rights, and takeover regulations. Incorporating these provisions within the monitoring system is a priority for officials currently drawing up a new Capital Markets Law. Comparisons between

Egypt and other emerging markets: Mexico, Thailand and Indonesia – where the state is withdrawing from the banking sector and creating a regulatory environment, are favourable. In Egypt the need to maintain routine and adequate monitoring in the banking sector is accepted, and stands out by comparison with emerging markets that have seen crises consequent to poor procedures. The test will come when the public sector banks, which hold more than 60 per cent of total bank assets, are no longer under the direct control of the CBE and the Ministry of Economy. Constant monitoring will then require much greater human resources at the CBE than is currently the case.

Statistical summary of foreign portfolio and direct investment, 1990–98

The changing patterns of foreign direct and portfolio investment are clearly commensurate with the changes witnessed in the legislative environment, as it has shifted in favour of the private sector. Any assessment of the liberalisation policies of the 1990s should be seen against the background of the low growth period of the 1980s. By 1989, foreign direct investment (FDI) into Egypt accounted for 2 per cent of the country's total sources of external funding. The pattern of FDI has shown it to have been particularly present in the area of technology, while also having been encouraged to provide the private sector with technical assistance, licensing agreements, the use of trademarks and local content subcontracting agreements.

Assessment of the impact of the liberalisation policies only become valid in 1993–94, by which time the combination of the evolving investment climate had been married with the impact of legal changes introduced in 1989. Law No. 230 of 1989 ruled that private capital of any nationality could participate independently or jointly with other nationalities in any investment field within the investment law, which excludes the petroleum sector and tourism. Crucially, it allowed foreigners to buy land for productive purposes, and ensure that there would be no price controls or profit ceilings on the products. By the end of 1993, 2,418 investment projects had been approved, with a value of E£43,934 million, a 20 per cent increase on the previous year and a 46 per cent increase on the 1990 level. However, only 41 per cent of the 1993 figure was accounted for by FDI. In 1994 the total value decreased by 41 per cent, to E£25,652 million. By 1995, foreign participation in the capital of approved projects rose to E£35,183 million (US$10,317 million), a 37 per cent increase which was to set the upward trend into 1996–97, which saw FDI leap to US$498 million, and in 1998 to US$676 million.

FDI levels since 1991 have been more than matched by burgeoning foreign portfolio investment (FPI) on the ESE (see Exhibits 2.2 and 2.3). It is revealing that prior to 1996, the figures showing FPI into Egypt have little of the substance of those figures available since then. The privatisation programme, which had theoretically begun five years earlier, really only raised Egypt's international profile with the sale in 1996 of Nasr City Housing. Foreign trading

Exhibit 2.4
Value of foreign direct investment into Egypt by sector and region in 1998, (E£ million)

	Arab countries	Non-Arab countries	Total
Sectors:			
Manufacturing	493	335	828
Agriculture/construction	113	1,387	1,500
Tourism	603	90	693
Financial services	25	117	142
Total	1,234	1,929	3,163
Investment in free zones	48	153	201
Grand total	1,282	2,082	3,364

Source: GAFI

Exhibit 2.5
Value of Egyptian domestic investment by sector 1995–98, (E£ million)

	1995	1996	1997	1998	Total
Sectors:					
Manufacturing	1,006	1,380	4,264	5,841	12,491
Agriculture/construction	76	88	493	2,731	3,388
Tourism	745	1,675	4,481	4,776	11,677
Financial services	1,290	1,394	3,560	1,484	7,728
Total	**3,117**	**4,537**	**12,798**	**14,832**	**19,405**
Investment in free zones	68	318	2,596	1,024	4,006
Grand total	**3,185**	**4,855**	**15,394**	**15,856**	**23,411**

Source: GAFI

on the ESE has clearly reflected the pattern of market performance. In 1996 foreign trading accounted for around 23 per cent of purchases and 16 per cent of sales. This compares sharply with 1995, when foreigners accounted for a mere 5.37 per cent of purchases and 2.31 per cent of share sales. However, this proportion should be seen against the background of the value of the shares traded. Foreign purchases in 1997 accounted for 21.27 per cent of the value of traded shares, and 11.87 per cent of shares sold. Equally, in 1998 the value of trade in foreign purchases accounted for 18.16 per cent of purchases and 22.49 per cent of shares sold. In 1998 the value of the total market in shares traded by foreigners was E£18.405 billion, a 500 per cent rise on 1996 but an 11 per cent fall on 1997.

The role of international capital in financing Egypt's growth

Necessity has played the major role in developing strategies aimed at encouraging inflows of international capital to Egypt. Assessments of the level of capital already in the country vary,

Exhibit 2.6
Sources of direct investment into Egypt, 1996–98, (US$ million)

	July 1996 to March 97		July 1997 to March 98	
	Value	% of total	Value	% of total
Total	**498**	**100**	**711.6**	**100**
United States	425.7	85.5	541.6	80.1
Germany	13.8	2.8	6.8	1.0
France	6.5	1.3	60.5	8.9
United Kingdom	9.0	1.8	7.6	1.1
Italy	0.6	0.1	3.7	0.5
Switzerland	0.5	0.1	2.1	0.3
Japan	4.1	1.8	43.1	6.4
South Korea	2.2	0.4	0.5	0.1
Saudi Arabia	2.4	0.5	16.8	2.5
Kuwait	–	–	0.8	0.1
Lebanon	12.4	2.5	–	–
Oman	5.1	1.0	5.8	0.9
UAE	–	–	15.3	2.3
Others	14.2	2.9	7.0	1.1

Source: Central Bank of Egypt

and several key events have revealed the extent to which past estimates have proved well below actual levels. Leading fund managers estimate that there are about three million people in Egypt capable of investing up to E£20,000. The sale of shares in the Mobinil mobile telephone company saw E£2 billion invested by 130,000 individual subscribers, a much higher level than anticipated by those managing the issue. Equally, the launch of mutual funds in 1994 saw a large number of subscribers, again many more than had been anticipated. In 1998, Egyptian investors accounted for 81.86 per cent of total traded value as buyers on the ESE. The necessity for greatly increasing foreign capital is clear, as a means of increasing the economic growth rate to the desired 6–7 per cent level.

According to the IMF, steady growth increasing by 0.1–0.2 per cent per year requires investment to reach 26.5 per cent of GDP in order to achieve 5.6 per cent growth. If growth were to be accelerated, in order to reach the government's target of 6.9-7 per cent, investment would have to reach 26.1 per cent of GDP, if it were accompanied by a 25 per cent improvement in productivity. To achieve 8 per cent growth, there is a need for E£75 billion of investment every year. Domestic savings and investment are reckoned to be able to achieve a maximum 65 per cent of this, accounting for E£48.75 billion, leaving the remaining E£26.25 billion to be found from foreign investors. So far the most successful year for combined FPI and FDI was 1998, which saw E£3.3 billion spent by foreigners for share purchases, and US$989 million spent in FDI, a total of E£6.6 billion.

THE FINANCIAL SYSTEM AND FOREIGN INVESTMENT

Investment banks in Egypt have assessed the most advantageous prospect for long-term investment to be in equity rather than debt. Foreign investment in joint-venture banks, power generation, mobile telephones, port projects and the cement and pharmaceutical industries have revealed both the breadth and depth of foreign interest in Egyptian equities. The same investment banks are wary, however, of attempting to lure foreign investors with partial privatisations in industries which foreign investors are historically unlikely to be interested. Commodities, and industries which require a substantial level of imported raw materials, are areas which are unlikely to attract the desired level of foreign investment and with the notable exception of the utilities, these are the industries which remain to be sold as part of the privatisation programme.

In 199, in an attempt to improve the quality of the privatisation stocks on offer, the government called on foreign companies to manage their restructuring prior to sale. Tailoring the market to international standards is therefore becoming a more prominent aspect of government strategy. This has undoubtedly helped maintain foreign investor interest, despite the worldwide withdrawal of foreign investors from emerging markets during 1998. Three key investments helped Egypt remain above the fray of the emerging markets crisis, and kept the investment drive very much alive. First was the US$1.32 billion earned by the government from the sale of two mobile telephone licence, to consortia involving both foreign and Egyptian partners. Then the sale of the private sector Amoun Pharmaceuticals to Glaxo Wellcome Egypt for US$117 million marked a major expansion in the Glaxo Wellcome presence in Egypt. These three deals accounted for 71 per cent (US$702 million) of total FDI of US$989 million between January and December 1998.

Such spectacular success in attracting this high level of FDI is testimony to Egypt's attractiveness in the most advanced industrial sectors. With the spotlight returning to new privatisations, private sector IPOs and the long-awaited sale of either one of the four state-owned commercial banks or a share in the public sector utilities, similar successes are not expected to punctuate the investment programme in 1999. Investment bankers regard the ongoing foreign interest in Egypt as sustainable and deep, with significant interest from Gulf investors matching that of European and US investors. Dominating foreign investment patterns will be increases in growth and efficiency within quoted companies, with an increasing emphasis on efficiency. For foreign investors, the liquidity of the capital markets remains a vital component in their assessment of the attractiveness of different emerging economies. The need to broaden the Egyptian market is clear. In 1998, the top 10 companies accounted for 57.7 per cent of trade on the ESE in terms of volume traded, and for 61.56 per cent of trade, in terms of value traded, of the total 876 companies listed. The expectation among investment banks is that FDI will continue to grow, while domestic investment will see a less steady rise. The foreign appetite for Egyptian stocks remains high, with foreign buyers accounting for around 20 per cent of stocks in the first three months of 1999, as portfolio investors sought to take advantage of cheap markets.

Foreign competition and investment in the financial sector

The skills acquired through partnerships between the National Bank of Egypt and Chase Manhattan, which led to the creation of Commercial International Bank (CIB), have spread from the commercial banking sector into investment banking, asset management and the development of retail banking, as well as banking involvement in insurance. The liberalisation of the economy after 1991 allowed a generation of highly-skilled bankers to thrive in the developing capital markets. This course of events prepared the Egyptian market for the dramatic increase in stock market activity after 1996, and led to the creation of financial sector companies determined to exploit the burgeoning array of opportunities.

Foreign competition within the activities of the financial sector has been limited by the array of skills on offer from Egyptian companies. Fundamentally, foreign companies are regarded as strong in their quality of service and range of products, but their ability to penetrate the Egyptian market without a local partner is hampered by the dominance of well-connected local companies. Foreign companies are reckoned by the CMA to take up to four years to establish a regular supply of business. Consequently, foreign investment banks have tended to act more as advisers on private sector company restructuring than on share issues. This has been evident in the growing number of companies which have established holding companies, as the first stage of their restructuring, on the advice of local offices of foreign investment banks. Thirty private sector holding companies were established in 1998.

Foreign companies hold 10 per cent in equity stakes in the Egyptian financial sector. The pattern of investment has shifted as the market has grown more sophisticated, and companies have sought to create a regional business based in Cairo. The most significant consolidation in the market in 1999 was the merger by Robert Fleming, the UK-based investment banking and brokerage company, of its Cairo joint-venture brokerage company Fleming Mansour, with CIIC. The new company, Fleming CIIC Securities, was created out of a merger of Fleming Mansour and Intercapital Securities – CIIC's brokerage arm – in a move which gave the new company 16 per cent share of the Egyptian brokerage market. Fleming's and CIIC have equal shares in the new company, which is capitalised at US$100 million. The merger came in the wake of the failure of CIIC's brokerage partnership with ING Barings, which had held a 29 per cent stake in CIIC's operation.

The restructuring within ING Barings, which has led to a major part of its emerging market business being effectively abandoned, is similar to that within other foreign companies which were poised to move in to the Egyptian market. UBS, the Swiss bank, had been in discussion with the major Cairo investment bank, brokerage and asset management company, EFG-Hermes, about taking an equity stake in the company. The talks were abandoned when UBS merged with SBC. Other Swiss banks operating in Cairo also have limited if lucrative niches. Credit Suisse closed down its retail and commercial banking operations in 1997, to concentrate on investment banking, bridging loans and project finance. As with Credit Suisse, UBS tends to despatch experts from Switzerland or London to advise on major deals, with a consequent impact on the size of local operations. UBS offers private banking, as well as managing US$100 million of the assets of the CBE, as one of four banks mandated to do so.

Most foreign competitors have identified local groups they can use, either on an ad hoc basis or through joint ventures. They are now awaiting the growth in the liquidity of the market itself to engender the dynamism which will require them to establish a permanent presence in Egypt, rather than merely retaining small representative offices able to bring in experts when they are needed. A disparity in standards of due diligence is often cited as a reason for foreign companies having been faced with an uphill struggle to establish themselves. And, as with the wait for market growth, the raising of standards is something which is expected to make it easier for foreign companies to find business, once the playing field has been levelled between them and the local companies. The growth of the market, to an attractive size for foreign investors and therefore foreign companies considering Egypt as a sound base, will be determined by the earnings growth of the private sector. The average price-earnings ratio for the top 20 Egyptian stocks in terms of market capitalisation in 1998 was 9.6.

The stunted growth of the Egyptian secondary market is regarded as a key area in need of development, if the primary market is itself to grow. For the first eight months of 1998, 55.9 per cent of total volume traded on the ESE was accounted for by 20 companies, 16 per cent of which were new issues. A total of 12.8 per cent of trade in the stocks of these 20 companies was in bank stocks, and 10.5 per cent in cement stocks. The narrow market and the need for increased capitalisation are now regarded as priority areas for the development of the capital markets, in order to attract greater foreign interest, and with it foreign investment in the financial sector itself.

Egypt as a regional financial centre: the importance of attracting new institutions

Between 1993 and 1998 the number of participants in the Egyptian capital markets rose from 48 to 159, including both local and foreign companies. This growth in activity has been the single biggest factor in broadening the scope of the sector to include regional aspirations, and forced the major global financial institutions to assess whether they should establish a presence in the Egyptian market. Coupled with the development of the market itself, and central to this assessment, has been the evolution of the legal environment in favour of investment. Law No. 95 of 1992 streamlined existing legislation, including the legal framework, facilitating the expansion of the securities industry. The activation of the privatisation programme led to a revitalisation of stock market turnover, from E£531 million in 1991 to a value traded in 1998 of E£18 billion. The size of the Egyptian market has played a key role in attracting institutions to Egypt who will be pivotal in establishing it as a regional financial centre. In two years, between January 1997 and January 1999, the capitalisation of the Egyptian market rose by 61 per cent, from E£56.4 billion to E£91.2 billion. Stock market growth has been accompanied by a growth in the corporate bond market from miniscule to being an active market of 23 issues worth E£2.6 billion by the end of 1998. The trading volume of corporate bonds increased by 88 per cent between 1997 and

THE FINANCIAL SYSTEM AND FOREIGN INVESTMENT

Glaxo Wellcome has expanded its presence recently in Egypt, reflecting the country's spectacular success in attracting high levels of FDI in advanced industrial sectors

the end of 1998, from E£390.6 million to E£734.7 million. Legal reform has both led and bolstered the increase in market activity, as the private sector has sought to use the capital markets while also remaining cautious about plunging into the market before its institutional and technological foundations have been firmly established. In October 1997, the Ministry of the Economy published the Egyptian Accounting Standards, requiring joint-stock companies to prepare future accounts based on IAS. A stock market compensation fund has meanwhile been designed to cover potential settlement losses arising from defaults by capital markets institutions.

The legislative measures put in place since the introduction of the Capital Markets Law of 1992, laid the foundation for a transparent environment. The ambition of creating a regional financial centre based on these advances in the Egyptian market has emerged subsequently, as the strengths of the market have become evident. Fundamentally, Egypt has been advantaged by both the timing of its reforms and the size of the domestic market it has been able to activate as a means of perpetuating those reforms. Without 65 million people, two million of whom are ready and able to invest, the reforms would have been more difficult to sustain. Meanwhile, other markets in the region have failed to match the pace, breadth and dynamism of those in Egypt. Reasons of geography and communication have also helped, with Cairo located at the mid-point of the Middle East and North Africa, although demographics and market volume are much more important.

It is the ambition of the private sector companies in the forefront of capital markets activity

Exhibit 2.6
Listed securities on the Egyptian Stock Exchange, January 1999

Common	Official	Unofficial (1)	Unofficial (2)	Total
Stocks				
Agriculture	4	17	2	23
Building and contracting	11	78	23	112
Building materials	4	37	3	44
Cement	5	2	2	9
Chemicals	7	16	1	24
Computer/information technology	–	7	1	8
Distribution	5	2	1	8
Engineering	10	50	4	64
Financial services	4	90	20	114
Food and beverages	12	54	3	69
Gas and mining	–	8	1	9
Housing	11	56	12	79
Mills	7	3	1	11
Paper and packaging	4	33	5	42
Pharmaceuticals	10	24	3	37
Support services	4	33	5	42
Textiles and clothing	14	32	2	48
Trade	5	52	12	69
Transport & telecoms	10	16	3	29
Travel and tourism	5	37	10	52
Total	**132**	**633**	**111**	**876**
Preferred				
Building and contracting	1	–	7	8
Building materials	–	1	–	1
Engineering	–	1	–	1
Financial services	–	–	1	1
Food and beverage	–	1	–	1
Support services	–	1	–	1
Trade	–	2	–	2
Travel and tourism	–	1	1	2
Total	**1**	**7**	**9**	**17**

Bonds	Government	Corporate
Housing bonds	19	
Treasury bonds	5	
National development bonds	92	
Fixed		6
Floating		13
Total	**116**	**19**

Source: Financial Securities

which is determining the extent to which the sound fundamentals of the Egyptian market can be transformed into creating a regional financial centre. Two aspects of this evolution have already become evident. The first is the regional business now being sought by EFG-Hermes, the Cairo-based brokerage, investment banking and asset management company. EFG-Hermes lead managed the sale of 20 per cent of Fastlink, Motorola's Jordanian subsidiary in a deal worth US$27 million. It also lead managed the sale of 33 per cent of Jordan Cement to the French company Lafarge, in a US$100 million deal, and is advising a Yemeni group on the purchase of 51 per cent of Ethiopian Tobacco Enterprises in a US$36 million deal. The company is now looking to the Gulf, Lebanon and Iran for expansion opportunities, having decided that the Maghreb markets of North Africa are less attractive. Such activity marks the shift from local to regional, and is certain to be followed by EFG-Hermes' main competitor in the Egyptian market, Fleming CIIC. The creation of Fleming CIIC in March 1999, brought together a well-established Egyptian partner capitalised at E£600 million which has handled business worth E£5.5 billion since its establishment in 1994, with a global company – Robert Fleming – able to offer global reach and extensive research.

The success at the regional level of EFG-Hermes, which has no foreign partner despite having discussed and then abandoned plans to create a partnership in 1997 with UBS, and the expected further growth of CIIC in partnership with Robert Fleming, reflects two sides of Egypt's capital markets development. There is a great variety of opinion as to how best to grow the sector as the market grows. Key to determining future developments is the pattern of investment being attracted to Egypt. Increasingly, portfolio and direct investment into Egypt are emanating from the Gulf states, much of it through Gulf banks which have established their own branches in Cairo. This growth was reflected in the overall leap in foreign activity in the market, which saw the market share by foreigners rise by 212 per cent between 1996 and 1998 from 13 per cent to 40.6 per cent. Total trading value by foreigners in 1998 was E£7.5 billion, while volume in terms of the value of shares traded by foreigners was 38.2 per cent. An IPO by the Gemma porcelain manufacturer in late-1998 was 50 per cent subscribed by foreign investors. Even so, net portfolio investment by foreigners was -US$248 million, compared with US$1.463 billion in 1996–97.

The overall growth in foreign activity on the exchange is not explained by foreign institutions having established a presence in Egypt. Among leading Cairo financiers, there are those who regard the permanent foreign presence as unnecessary, due to Egypt's close proximity to the foreign markets from which it is drawing funds, as well as the increasingly sophisticated technology available to the market, and the fact of local companies having established sound reputations. Reform of existing institutions is regarded by leading investment banks as a higher priority than attracting new institutions to the Egyptian market. In particular, the reform of the public sector banks and insurance companies is sought, as a means of widening the product range available to the market and increasing momentum. Vehicles for increasing domestic savings, which currently stand at around 18 per cent of GDP, are viewed as essential if Egypt's attractiveness is to be sustained and enhanced, owing to the strength of its role as a regional market drawing fundamentally on its domestic strengths. Meanwhile, the coming period of development is more likely to see consolidation among local institutions, perhaps involving joint ventures with foreign partners, rather than the establishment in Cairo of more foreign institutions.

3 Regulation of the financial sector

The legal framework for banking, insurance and pension reform

Egypt's banking and insurance sectors remain two key areas whose reform is regarded by both government and private sector alike as key determinants of the future development of the Egyptian capital market. The role of the banks as financial intermediaries is hampered by the vast disparity of assets and potential between the dominant public sector banks and the flexible though geographically limited joint venture banks. Meanwhile the commercial insurance sector is regarded as having so far failed to play its key role in economic development, either as an industry able to attract clients or as a flexible source of investment funds. Both areas have been subject to substantial legislative change, which has cleared the way for privatisation in both sectors, intended to accelerate their role in economic development.

Banking Law No. 155 of 1998 was the most far-reaching piece of legislation to have been applied to the banking sector since 1974 – when joint venture banks were established by the public sector banks in partnership with foreign banks. Until 1998, the public sector banks were subject to the same law as all public sector companies, namely Law No. 97 of 1983, which did not allow the transfer of shares from the appropriate public sector companies, except to another public sector company. Law 97 has remained in force, despite the introduction of Law No. 203 of 1991, the Privatisation or 'Public Sector Companies Law', which allowed public sector companies to be grouped into holding companies, which could in turn sell shares in the constituent companies as part of the privatisation programme. Not all public sector companies were moved under the authority of Law 203, and consequently could not be sold. One sector which remained under Law 97 was that of the public sector banks. In order to instigate the change necessary to prepare the public sector banks for privatisation, Law No. 155 of 1998 allowing the private sector to own shares in the public sector banks was passed, with some strong criticism in parliament from both opposition and government MPs.

Privatisation of the public insurance sector required similar legislative changes as had been the case with the public sector banks, although owing to the history of the insurance companies the process was less complicated, as amendments had already opened the market up to foreign involvement prior to the decision to allow full privatisation. Law No. 156 of 1998 was essentially designed to bring the public insurance sector into parity with the provisions affecting the public banks. The law amended Law No. 10 of 1981, the Law for Insurance Supervision and Regulation. The original law had been amended in 1991 to allow foreigners to own 49 per cent of the state-owned insurance companies. Law 156 increased this proportion to 100 per cent. The legal change in 1998 allowed foreigners to take all the seats on the boards of directors of the insurance companies. The law also stated that if a single individual or institution wanted to buy 5–10 per cent of the company it must notify the insurance industry regulator, and that permission must be sought if a stake were to reach 10 per cent or more.

Two decrees issued by the Ministry of Economy followed the introduction of Law 156, and were intended to improve the practical framework for the sector, which has been accused of inefficiency. Decree No. 356 of 1998 explains how investors should go about notifying the regulator of their intention to buy the 5 or 10 per cent stakes in the insurance companies. The second decree, Decree No. 45 of 1999, was intended to address the problems of claimants in receiving payments from the insurance companies. The decree was an amendment to the executive Decree No. 362 of 1996, and created a framework for policy holders' rights and claims from the companies.

Variety within the social security system already exists, but is currently being reformed with a view to enhancing the role of private pension and private insurance schemes once the existing companies widen the products to allow them a more creative role in the insurance market. The Ministry of Insurance and Social Affairs was restructured in a 1998 cabinet reshuffle as a precursor to changing the entirety of the legislation affecting pensions and insurance. The aim of new legislation will be to simplify laws introduced in 1975, which have many complicated tiers for contributions and benefits. Changes are expected in the upper and lower limits that employers and employees are obliged to pay, as well as in the levels of maximum and minimum contributions – which is likely to result in the minimum levels being raised. The proportion of contributions paid by employers and employees will also change.

The Ministry of Economy, the Central Bank, and the Capital Market Authority

The authority of all Egyptian institutions is ultimately derived from the ministry under whose auspices the institution falls. While specific legislation may define a particular institution in its own statutes as being independent, this independence is within the context of the degree of influence to which it is subject by the relevant ministry. The logic of this arrangement stems from the view that all institutions should be accountable to the Council of Ministers, and should therefore be represented by a minister who attends meetings of the council.

The Central Bank of Egypt (CBE)

Under the provisions of Law No. 120 of 1975, the CBE is defined as an 'independent legal entity'. As such it is an entity within which there are numerous departments, which has its own legal identity and against which a legal action, for example, could be taken. The appointment of the governor of the CBE falls within the remit of the state president, while the deputy governor is appointed by the prime minister. As one example of the CBE's independence, its own management is appointed internally, without reference to the Ministry of Economy, whose minister is the CBE representative on the Council of Ministers. Even so, as the watchdog of the banking sector, the CBE defers to the Ministry of Economy on several fronts. It is the Minister of Economy who is required to chair the annual general meetings of the four state-owned banks, for example. The boards of governors of the state-owned banks are appointed by the prime minister, not the CBE, which oversees them. A major change will take place with the introduction of legislation governing the Central Bank, which will eventually remove the CBE and banking in general from the control of the Ministry of Economy. The Cabinet has been reviewing the existing CBE Law No. 250 of 1960 and Presidential Decree No. 2336 of 1960, which are the foundation of CBE powers. Under the planned amendments, the CBE would report directly to the President rather than the Minister of Economy. The aim would be to create more autonomy for the CBE. The progress of this legislation has so far been slow, and the new legislation is not expected to be placed before parliament during 1999.

In the meantime, the CBE's role in formulating economic policy is varied. The Ministry of Economy has limited influence over CBE decisions affecting the exchange rate, despite the issue having a direct impact on the economic policy of the Ministry of Economy. However, the ministry is responsible for drawing up the regulations governing the CBE, the state insurance companies and the Capital Market Authority (CMA), and therefore has considerable influence over these institutions at the level of practice.

The Capital Market Authority (CMA)

The CMA is also defined as a public entity, but as one which 'follows the Ministry of Economy'. There is some ambiguity in the law as to how independent the CMA actually is. As with the CBE, its chairman is appointed by the president, and other members of its directorial board by the prime minister. However, the Ministry of Economy has specific powers over the CMA, which it does not have over the CBE. The minister can impose or cancel the ceiling on share price movements, which is currently 5 per cent in either direction, as well as having the power to issue the schedules for minimum and maximum commissions paid to brokers. The minister also has to approve the establishment of other stock exchanges, may approve the establishment of new kinds of business within the stock exchange, and is responsible for issuing the decree which establishes the committee of appeal to which brokers accused of malpractice can appeal and to which the minister can make one of the five appointees. Even so, the CMA regards itself as independent in the sense that it can make a decision, and then go through what its personnel generally regard as the routine of seeking Ministry of Economy approval.

The relative powers of the key institutions influencing the evolution of the capital markets have been forced to evolve as the level of activity has increased. From the perspective of Egypt's leading asset managers, the role of the CBE should be to assist in the development of the secondary market in government paper, rather than to buy and sell Treasury bills. The central goal of the CBE is regarded by some as that of developing an active money market for itself, by engendering repurchases to accommodate market-makers in government stock. The powers of the CMA have been forged not only by its relationship with the Ministry of Economy, but also by the ongoing contact with the brokerage community. Some brokers regard the CMA as playing too active a role in influencing business practice, by making its feeling known as to whether sales should take place during periods of market decline. Its role as a regulator is regarded by brokers as generally sound, but occasionally intrusive, and perhaps exceeding its statutory powers.

The new Capital Markets Law

As Egypt's capital markets becomes more sophisticated, so the legislation governing the activities of the growing number of active institutions will be updated. The existing Capital Markets Law, Law No. 95 of 1992, covers both joint stock companies that offer shares to the public, as well as companies that deal with securities, underwriting, company formation, venture capital, clearance and settlement, the management of securities portfolios and investment funds, mutual funds and book-keeping. Several other laws have been introduced since 1992, which have implications for the capital markets. However, a new capital markets law is expected to be written by the end of 1999. The new law will be significant for two reasons. First, it will modify and update the existing law regarding the issues of corporate governance, insider dealing, shareholder minority rights, and the structure of the Egyptian Stock Exchange (ESE). Secondly, it will clarify trading laws and penalties to be applied when companies fail to abide by the rules of the CMA.

Further to the Capital Markets Law a new and separate Central Depository, Central Registry, Clearance and Settlement and Securities Law is also to be introduced. It is expected to be put before parliament in 1999 and to be applicable even before the new Capital Markets Law itself. The introduction of new securities law will address the limited references made to these areas of capital markets activity, and clarify their function within the system as a whole. The current law only refers briefly to these elements of the capital markets, and is regarded as providing little definitive guidance as to how the increasingly sophisticated functions relate to each other.

The Foreign Investment Law and the Law on Concessions

In order to facilitate investment in Egypt and to provide more incentives and guarantees, Law No. 230 of 1989, which provides certain incentives and guarantees for foreign investors doing business in Egypt, was repealed and replaced by Law No. 8 of 1997, a unified investment guarantees and incentives law. Law 8 covers the areas of investment specified, namely, land reclamation, housing, industrial enterprises, tourism and agricultural projects, services to the oil sector, transport services including air and maritime transport, infrastructure related to drinking water, waste water, electricity, roads, communications, financial leasing, as well as projects financed by the government's Social Fund for Development (SFD). In the financial services sector, the law covers underwriting and venture capital activities. The law also covers selected hospital and medical treatment centres, and the production of computer software and computer systems.

Law 8 gave the Council of Ministers discretion to approve other investment projects in accordance with this legislation, even if the character of the project did not fall within the law's specified scope. Simultaneously, the law greatly reduced the variety of documentation required before a company could be incorporated, thereby reducing the time taken for incorporation to as little as 24 hours. However, key concessions were excluded from the specifics of the law, in particular petroleum production, for which foreign investors are required to draw-up concession agreements with the Egyptian General Petroleum Corporation (EGPC), creating production-sharing agreements under which the foreign partner will receive up to 40 per cent of the oil produced.

The attraction of Law 8 was not only that it had streamlined previous legislation, but that it offered wide-ranging guarantees to companies that were approved for incorporation in Egypt. As a fundamental break with Egypt's past, the law specifically guaranteed that no administrative body would have the power to revoke or suspend the company's licence to use the property in which it had established its operations, except in cases where the company had exceeded the conditions of its licence. This was effectively a guarantee against expropriation, of the kind which had taken place during the period of nationalisation from 1959-61. Specific guarantees against expropriation are also made in Law 8. The new law also offered extremely attractive tax holidays to new companies, in part to encourage them to establish their operations in areas of the country which had benefited least from development. The basic tax holiday from corporate income tax lasts for five years, starting in the fiscal year after production has begun. Companies established in new industrial zones, urban communities, remote areas, or those working on projects financed by the SFD, benefit from a 10-year tax holiday. As part of the government's drive to encourage people and companies to establish themselves outside the Nile Valley, 20-year tax holidays are offered. Added to these, the interest on bonds, debentures and securities earned by all these companies, are exempt from taxes if the securities are offered to the public and are listed on the ESE.

Encouraging new companies to set-up their business forms a key part of Law 8, and consequently a flat rate of 5 per cent is charged as duty on equipment and machinery imported for use by a new company. Price control and profit margin limitations on projects established under this law were scrapped upon its introduction. Profits can be repatriated as part of the exchange market liberalisation of 1991. A variety of exemptions from several tenets of existing workforce and company laws were introduced for companies operating under Law 8. Further exemptions are offered by the law to companies operating in the public and private free zones. Companies created to operate in the free zones enjoy unlimited exemption from all Egyptian income taxes, though free zone products are subject to duty of 1 per cent of the value of goods entering or leaving the free zone, or to an annual duty of 1 per cent of the annual value added to the project.

REGULATION OF THE FINANCIAL SECTOR

Vital to creating an increasingly dynamic private sector role in the economy has been the rapid move by the government towards creating build-operate-transfer projects in key infrastructure sectors. The amendment of existing legislation in Law No. 100 of 1996, allows for private local and foreign investors to build power generation plants and to sell electricity to distribution companies nationwide. Amendments to Law No. 12 of 1976, allow local and foreign investors to apply for permits to operate, manage and maintain public utilities for a period of up to 99 years. Law No. 3 of 1997 allows local or foreign private investors to build, operate and maintain roads, from which they will be allowed to collect tolls, while the same law allows them to build, operate and then transfer to the government, airports and runways. In the same area, Law No. 18 of 1998 transformed Telecom Egypt into a private joint-stock company, and allowed the private sector to operate mobile telephone networks.

For a more detailed discussion of investment incentives and taxation see Chapter 14.

4 Ratings and the information market

Standard & Poor's, Moody's Investors Service and Fitch IBCA sovereign ratings

The extent of reform and the general health of the Egyptian market were looked at against the background of growing global interest in emerging markets during the mid-1990s. International rating agencies have revealed a diversity of opinion over the lengths to which Egypt has gone to cement its market reforms and tailor the climate to the needs of foreign investors. For each of the three leading agencies, a credit rating is an opinion on the risk of default on fixed-income securities. Standard and Poor's takes into account a wide variety of positive and negative factors when assessing a country's creditworthiness. Government commitment to fiscal control, the ratio of external debt service commitments to annual exports, the pace of reform in emerging markets and the extent of government commitment to those reforms, as well as macroeconomic features such as per capita income. The debt burden and savings rates are all taken into consideration during the rating process. Moody's guidelines evaluate an issuer's ability to generate cash in a variety of economic circumstances, and its readiness to use that cash to meet its obligations to its creditors. The analysis focuses on cashflow relative to its prospective debt service obligations, and more importantly the margin an issuer's cashflow will have over its debt service under possible stress. Fitch IBCA takes a similarly broad view of the trends within an economy when making its assessment, in particular the pace of reform within emerging markets, the character of the debt burden, exchange rate policy and political stability.

How the agencies rated, and why
Moody's Investors Service
The first agency to offer a rating of the Egyptian economy came after five years of structural reform during which major strides had been taken towards fully liberalising the economy and tailoring reforms to encourage a rise in investment levels. Moody's originally awarded Egypt a non-investment grade speculative rating on its foreign currency debt of Ba2 in 1996, which it revised upwards to Ba1 in November 1997, thereby still remaining below investment grade. The rating was a disappointment to Egypt's reformers. The rationale behind the rating was

explained against a background of reforms which the agency believed required judgement over time to assess their sustainability. The agency acknowledged that Egypt had, by 1997, experienced an improvement in its credit fundamentals, as well as a deepened commitment to market-oriented structural reform. It also acknowledged that prudent macroeconomic policies had brought a sharp reduction in the fiscal deficit and inflation, and that debt relief since 1991 had brought the foreign currency debt into manageable proportions. Despite stabilisation and reform, acknowledged as setting the stage for sustainable growth, 'the reforms are still in an early phase and the strength of the private sector's response to the new policy environment remains uncertain'.

The challenge to Egypt, the agency concluded, was to sustain growth without destabilising the external accounts. The assessment stressed the fact that the domestic savings rate remains relatively low, and that the main sources of foreign exchange – oil, tourism and worker remittances – are vulnerable to shocks. The agency stressed the resilience of the economy, reflected in the fact that with its low foreign currency debt burden and high foreign currency reserves, Egypt could respond to shocks reasonably flexibly. Even so, the agency stated that the ability of the government to handle shocks was not the same as creating the conditions in which the possibility for those shocks actually receded. 'The roots for widespread social discontent do exist. The authorities will eventually have to respond to growing sentiments for greater political openness,' the agency's report stated.

Fitch IBCA

Greater encouragement was drawn from an investment-grade solicited rating awarded by Fitch IBCA in August 1997 which was then reconfirmed following further research, in October 1998. The resulting assessments awarded a BBB- (BBB minus) long-term foreign exchange rating, short-term foreign exchange rating of F3, and a long-term local currency rating of A- (A minus). The original assessment was made prior to a series of shocks to the economy, and the killing in Luxor of 58 foreign tourists, the impact of the Asian crisis on investment patterns in emerging markets, and the fall in oil prices. The later Fitch IBCA assessment recorded the impact of these shocks on the economy, and concluded that while they depressed growth by 1 per cent and widened the current account deficit by 3.5 per cent of GDP, domestic demand and the external position were deemed sufficiently robust to allow the government to maintain its reform programme.

The agency stated that it was the ability to survive the shocks which had confirmed its view that the economy had been substantively reformed. On its more detailed analysis, the agency highlighted the weaknesses in the economy which had led it to award the lowest of its investment grade ratings. In particular, savings and investment ratios were identified as remaining well below the level necessary to achieve the government's 6-7 per cent annual economic growth target. In strong contrast to Moody's report, Fitch IBCA gave little importance to political factors, deeming the government popular while Islamic fundamentalist movements had fragmented.

Standard and Poor's

The calculations made by Fitch IBCA were similar to those of Standard and Poor's, whose June 1997 solicited rating drew heavily upon the government's strong commitment to reform as a source of confidence. The agency awarded Egypt a BBB- (BBB minus) foreign currency rating, and an A- (A minus) local currency rating, both of which it concluded had a stable outlook. The agency calculated, correctly, that the current account would slip into deficit, but that this could be comfortably financed by foreign equity inflows. It also correctly predicted that the external debt service would remain light and manageable, and that shifts in the market could be financed from the substantial foreign exchange reserves. S&P's award reflected the reality of other emerging markets, particularly when taking into account the 18 per cent external debt service, which is among the lowest when compared with similar markets. At the other end of the scale, Egypt's then US$19 billion (now US$18.9 billion) of foreign exchange reserves were drawn upon as an important signal that, being among the highest among similar markets, money in circulation and the banking system's foreign currency deposits were covered. S&P explained the higher local currency rating on the basis that it was recognition of the government's sound fiscal policies and the steep drop in inflation.

The agency identified low per capita income of around US$1200 a year, and weak social infrastructure, as cause for concern in terms of the test they may impose on the government's readiness to push through its reforms. The report also cited the net government debt burden, of 51 per cent of GDP, as well as the low domestic savings rate of 18 per cent, and the concentration of foreign exchange earnings in the oil, tourism and remittances sectors, as being of concern.

Rating agencies in emerging markets: their role and credibility

Opinions vary greatly as to how appropriate are the assessments of rating agencies when operating in emerging markets, owing in part to the variety of perspectives on the impact of political risk upon the economic fundamentals. Essentially, rating agencies act as the providers of a benchmark by which companies and banks can access funds on global capital markets. In the absence of a sovereign bond issue – of the kind which Egypt, for example, has been considering but has yet to undertake – such a benchmark is a valuable asset. The restructuring of private sector business and the impact of privatisation on the competitive sectors of the Egyptian economy, has enforced a period of extensive and rapid restructuring on Egyptian industry.

Egypt's three sovereign credit ratings can be used by Egyptian companies as a benchmark for borrowing. Egyptian companies are also obliged to seek their own ratings if they intend to issue corporate bonds, thus giving the rating agencies a vastly more micro-level role in the economy. A corporate rating assesses the company using similar criteria to that of the sovereign rating. The company's ability to meet debt obligations, as well as the soundness of its finances, are the key criteria. In the case of banks, a rating involves an overall evaluation of sovereign risk, as well as an assessment of the efficacy of the regulatory, supervisory, accounting and auditing practices of a specific country's banking system. By taking these into account, a common platform for the analysis of a particular banking market can be established. For the Cyprus-based rating agency Capital Intelligence, which specializes in bank ratings in the Middle East and North Africa, the evaluation of a bank's overall performance and risk are derived from both quantitative and qualitative analyses. Risk is assessed in terms of credit, liquidity, interest rates, currency risk, and the risk of fraud. A rating will be given which reflects a bank's strengths and weaknesses relative to other rated banks in the same market.

The conclusion of the rating agency is essentially an opinion, based on numerous factors. The fact that, as in the case of Egypt, two rating agencies can give the country investment-grade ratings, while a third does not, reflects the divergence of opinion. Clearly there is nothing exact or obviously scientific about the conclusions drawn. It is not a matter of drawing together the figures and making an assessment on the basis of the economic fundamentals. As Moody's makes clear, 'We will use various financial ratios and mathematical credit risk models as helpful analytical tools, but they can quickly become irrelevant to each specific company's risk profile as any one of a multitude of new factors enters into the picture over time.' These new factors are often of the greatest significance in emerging markets, which are by their nature passing through periods of structural reform and are therefore subject to a greater variety of opinion on the part of the rating agencies.

It is noticeable from the Egyptian ratings of the past few years, that the conclusions have stemmed not from ignoring some facts and including others, but from giving a variety of weight to some facts over others. Analysis of political stability is less of an issue in the reports of agencies awarding investment grade ratings, than that of the report awarding Egypt a below investment-grade rating. The relative weight of economic and political reform is clearly open to a wide variety of opinion. Such variety makes it necessary to gather a variety of opinion, rather than relying upon one agency assessment. In this way, the value of the rating process is strengthened, and the ultimate purpose – that of providing risk assessment to would-be investors – while also opening up capital markets to borrowers based on the benchmark, enhances the credibility of the rating process.

Ratings of private sector companies; specialist ratings

The growing need among Egyptian private sector companies for investment finance has played a key role in expanding the financial services sector, as more companies have sought finance from the capital markets as an alternative to bank credit. One consequence of this development has been the growth in the corporate bond market, which had by March 1999 grown to include nine fixed-rate and 14 floating-rate bonds. Approval for the issue of corporate bonds of a value in excess of company capital has, since the issue of Decree No. 397 of 1998, been contingent upon companies seeking a rating prior to the bond issue. As a key area of the financial services sector, this requirement led to the creation of Nile Rating, currently Egypt's sole rating agency. The company is 60 per cent owned by Fitch IBCA, the UK rating agency, with 20 per cent stakes held by the Arab Monetary Fund and the International Finance Corporation. Prior to the establishment of Nile Rating, Egypt's Commercial International Bank (CIB) had sought a rating with a view to issuing bonds on foreign money markets. The purpose had been to assess creditworthiness by way of a variety of benchmarks, drawing upon both individual ratings and the three sovereign ratings Egypt currently holds.

Nile Rating currently has mandates for the rating of 19 Egyptian private sector companies. Five of these are yet to be published and eight are currently in the process of being rated. The remaining six companies have been awarded in the past year. The methodology used is that developed by Fitch IBCA. These take into account factors of industry risk, the company's market position, management ability, accounting quality, past and forecast financial results, revenue structure and earnings protection, operating efficiency, cashflow, debt structure and financial flexibility, capital structure, and matters pertaining to ownership.

The six companies for which Nile Rating has published assessments have all achieved investment-grade ratings. The company's first rating was of El-Rashidi El-Mizan, a food processing company producing sesame seed paste and biscuits. The company enjoyed high cash flows but was heavily indebted with net debts equivalent to 3.3 times earnings before interest, taxes, depreciation and amortisation (EBITDA). The company was awarded a BBB- (BBB minus) rating, essentially on the basis of its high cashflow. A second BBB- (BBB minus) rating was awarded to MEGA for Investments – a financial investment house, which refrained from publishing the report into its credit assessment. In December 1998, Nile Rating awarded Orascom Construction Industries an AA+ rating, on the basis of its EBITDA margin of 18.8 per cent, which saw the company generate revenues of E£1.3 billion in 1998. Leverage measured by total debt to EBITDA was put at 1.2x, which was deemed manageable. Pursuant to the issuing of the bond, OCI issued E£280 million of seven-year bonds to finance E£250 million of short-term borrowing. A further rating was issued to Alexandria Carbon Black. Based on assessment of the company's position as the sole carbon black producer in the Middle East and North Africa, providing improved strength and overall performance in rubber tyres, as well as a high level of technical skill in a market dominated by three global producers, the company was awarded an A- (A minus) credit rating. Nile Rating's highest rating to date was awarded to Commercial International Bank, which had already achieved a BBB- (BBB minus) long-term and A-3 short-term rating by Standard & Poor's of the United States in May 1998. Nile Rating assessed CIB on the basis of having achieved high profits during periods of high inflation in Egypt during the early 1990s, while continuing to raise profits significantly as inflation has fallen. Increased competition stemming from the low net interest margins still saw CIB retain higher margins than its competitors, leading Nile Rating to award CIB a AA+ long-term and F1+ short-term rating. The sixth rating to have been awarded to an Egyptian private sector company is the AA- (AA minus) award to the Lakah Group, owners of the Arab Steel Company, which allowed the group to secure a bond issue underwritten by Banque de Caire for the purpose of financing company debt.

Specialist ratings have become a feature of the rating process in Egypt following the government's decision to sell part of its stake in the insurance sector. Three insurance companies and the Egypt Reinsurance Company are all to be valued by investment banks by mid-1999, while A.M. Best, the US-based specialist insurance rating agency, will assess the companies' ability to meet obligations to policyholders. In 1996, the four insurance and reinsurance companies were each awarded a BBB rating by S&P, deeming them invest grade.

When the assessment is finalised, A.M. Best will assign two types of rating opinions, Best's Ratings and Best's Financial Performance Ratings (FPR). Best's Ratings range from A++ (Superior) to F (In Liquidation). FPR ratings are numerical ratings and range from nine (Very Strong) to one (Poor). FPR ratings may be assigned to small or new companies that do not qualify for a Best's Rating. The ratings are based on a comprehensive evaluation of a company's financial strength, operating performance and market profile, and compared with quantitative and qualitative standards or norms. Quantitative evaluation is based on an analysis of a company's reported financial performance for at least the past five years, while qualitative results are made by comparisons with other companies based on the performance of insurance industry segments comprising companies with a comparable business mix and size. The primary source of information is data received directly from the companies. In addition, assessment is based on meetings with company management to discuss operations, financial condition, competitive market position and future business plans. On this basis, an opinion is given as to the financial strength, operating performance and market profile of an insurer.

The availability of brokers' and independent research

Egypt's burgeoning information market has become one of the features to distinguish it from other markets in the region. This has been the direct consequence of two trends. First, the presence of foreign companies in the market has exposed local companies to the premium placed on information, leading to the realisation that information can be used to the advantage of companies. Second, as an increasing number of financial intermediaries have been licensed, so they have sought to distinguish themselves by the quality of their service. Key to this process has been the research they have carried out, initially on sectors of the economy, and more recently on particular companies.

While the prospectuses issued by corporate financiers and submitted for approval by the Capital Market Authority (CMA), are regarded as 'error-proof', owing to the strict guidelines laid down for such research, the research carried out by brokers for particular clients is a tailored, non-standard marketing tool. Just as the market has developed in sophistication since 1996, so the demands of investors for adequate information has grown. The CMA insists that brokers provide their clients with a full picture of a company's prospective fortunes, as a key aspect of their role as financial intermediaries. Moreover, the growing sophistication of investors, as well as the variety of stocks, investment instruments and opportunities, means that investors themselves have generally become a great deal more discerning. Leading finance houses reckon that without information being provided on a regular basis, there would be a drastic diminution in the number of investors. Consequently, the financiers are now pressuring companies to be more open and to allow a more in-depth and regular assessment of their finances. While the financial services sector itself has assisted in forcing transparency, encouraging companies to do so is a formidable task, owing to secrecy having become habitual. Institutional investors have, on occasion, been given false information by companies, though the practice is not thought to be widespread and has been detected reasonably quickly. Generally local brokers and fund managers believe companies have been stung by a lack of information, as the dangers inherent in rumours are regarded as much more destructive than a solid and published analysis. The problem for brokers is, often, that companies do not have all the information that is necessary. One leading broker reckoned that the six companies listed with global depository receipts on the London Stock Exchange, plus three other Egyptian companies, were capable of providing adequate information for brokers to offer as research to clients. For fund managers, the experience is similar, the conclusion being that while the larger companies are ready to open their books, smaller companies are either reluctant or do not have the information at all. This factor has become more important since early 1998. As the Egyptian market has opened to foreign investors, so its broad parameters are known. Consequently, foreign investors who are most attuned to the high standards of research available in developed markets have demanded more individual company research, and less of the sectoral research which had introduced them to the Egyptian market in 1996–97.

Independent research by investment banks which have not established a permanent presence in Egypt, has tended to be tailored to the needs of foreign investors seeking to compare the advantages of investing in Egypt over other emerging markets. Consequently, this research has offered a broad impression of the movement of the market. This type of information is in fact increasingly available, and consequently more up to date. Regular research bulletins are available from official sources, in particular the CMA and the Ministry of Economy, which both publish updated information on the markets.

Information from the public and private sector: how open is Egypt?

Transparency has become the sought-after ideal among the main architects of Egypt's reform process. The chief stumbling block to creating greater openness is the perception that information made public is likely to be used for negative rather than positive purposes. Companies reluctant to divulge their secrets generally assume that if they do allow their rivals to see factual information about their affairs, such information will allow those rivals to emulate the successes and avoid the shortcomings revealed by such information.

A key change has begun to take place, which is allowing companies both to assess the value of greater transparency, and is also leading to a greater awareness of information management. At the centre of this change has been the view that rumour is more damaging than fact. The scale of leverage of some of Egypt's leading private sector companies had long been rumoured. With the establishment of Nile Rating, analysis of the financial condition of large Egyptian companies has become less subject to rumour. A total 19 companies are now either in possession of a rating from the agency or are in the process of being rated. While the agency itself has voiced concern about the openness of companies, it is also aware that the very process of scrutiny to which it subjects the companies inviting it to provide ratings is new to the companies themselves. The key to their readiness to allow the rating agency to examine their books has been their own need to raise investment finance. Private sector companies are required to seek a rating before being permitted to issue corporate bonds. As many regard the capital markets as a more favourable source of investment finance than the banks, they are prepared to make the concession and seek a rating. Of the six ratings published so far by Nile Rating, four of the companies have permitted the rating report to be published, suggesting that they are not overly concerned about allowing their competitors to see how they were rated and why.

The government's demand for ratings, and the process of information sharing and the possible publication of results, applies to the small group of companies in need of investment finance. Clearly many companies have yet to follow this route. In the meantime, the requirements upon all companies to follow auditing and accounting standards which will provide an adequate picture of their financial situation is becoming more widely voiced. This process is hampered by a non-uniform legal environment. By law, financial and non-financial enterprises with at least 25 per cent ownership by the government must submit themselves to audit by the official Central Accounting Agency (CAA), whose practices are not consistent with International Accounting Standards (IAS) by which all Egyptian companies must abide by 2005 as required by Egypt's membership of the World Trade Organisation. Egyptian companies with less than 25 per cent state ownership, meanwhile, are not subject to the CAA system. The government in 1997 ordered companies to abide by IAS standards, but implementation of the decree has not been as effective as had been anticipated, though the Ministry of Economy has developed accounting standards for the banking and insurance sectors in accordance with IAS standards.

Within government itself, there is a growing tendency towards providing information. Regular economic publications from the Ministry of Economy, as well as monthly economic bulletins from the Central Bank of Egypt, the Cabinet Information and Decision Support Centre (IDSC), and the Egyptian Stock Exchange, have allowed for much closer tracking of economic patterns and statistical analysis than was the case even two years ago. With the acceleration of the economic reform process, the government's own need for information has greatly increased, and with this the process of collecting, collating and distributing information has become more routine. However, while this has become more streamlined in ministries which have realised the importance and value of detailing the condition of the economy, there are marked variations in both the quality of information, its reliability and accessibility.

5 Domestic savings and the capital markets

The importance of domestic savings in increasing investment

Egypt's relative strengths are rooted in the combination of having the largest domestic market in the region, comparatively rapid moves towards market liberalisation, and an economy which has sufficient diversity to allow for growth on a variety of fronts. Reform has not however led to Egypt's rapid incorporation into the global economy, largely owing to its continued small size relative to the size of the population, and to the economic growth rate.

The current transition from closed economy to global player has required profound reform at the micro level, which the macro reform programme has made possible. The development of the market will require several more years to be evident in the vital areas of increased company earnings, company efficiency, and export growth. This transitional stage requires much greater access to domestic savings than is currently being tapped. This alone will ensure that growth rates continue to rise, the secondary market develops, and foreign direct investment (FDI) is attracted by growing domestic market potential (see Exhibit 5.1).

Exhibit 5.1
Egypt's domestic savings, 1995–98, (E£ million)

	1995		1996		1997		1998	
	March	June	March	June	March	June	March	June
Total savings	136,140	140,959	151,709	157,699	173,588	183,944	196,060	203,703
Savings in banks Time/savings deposits	117,211	120,943	128,692	133,476	146,009	154,850	161,612	166,897
In local currency	79,853	82,177	89,897	94,412	108,450	116,77	124,507	128,698
In foreign currency (including demand deposits)	37,358	38,776	38,795	39,064	37,559	38,074	37,105	38,199
Net sales of investment certificates	16,968	17,714	20,285	21,031	23,879	24,714	29,202	30,694
Post office saving deposits	1,961	2,302	2,732	3,192	3,700	4,380	5,246	6,112

Source: Central Bank of Egypt

DOMESTIC SAVINGS AND THE CAPITAL MARKETS

The estimate of up to three million people in Egypt currently being capable of investing up to E£20,000, a total up to E£80 billion, reveals how limited have been moves towards accessing domestic savings, which are estimated to stand at 18 per cent of GDP, or E£54.9 billion. Domestic investment in the Egyptian Stock Exchange (ESE) in 1998 amounted to E£14.2 billion. Only seen against the background of the very recent past, the figures look impressive. In 1992 there were 25,000 local individual retail investors on the ESE. In seven years this has risen by 700 per cent, to two million, including the 300,000 individual investors in mutual funds. But for economic growth to increase by 0.1–0.2 per cent per year to reach 5.6 per cent growth requires investment to reach 26.5 per cent of GDP. If growth were to be accelerated, in order to reach the government's target of 6.9–7 per cent, investment would have to reach 26.1 per cent of GDP, if accompanied by a 25 per cent improvement in productivity. To achieve 8 per cent growth, there is a need for E£75 billion of investment every year. Domestic savings and investment are reckoned to be able to achieve a maximum of 65 per cent of this, accounting for E£48.75 billion, leaving the remaining E£26.25 billion to be found from foreign investors.

The main obstacle to the development of the capital markets is seen by fund managers as being the absence of a domestic distribution service for securities. Essential to developing this service is an increase in the commission paid to brokers, as a means of widening the net of potential investors. While the government is applauded for having revitalised the moribund stock exchange, this effort has not been matched by the creation of a well-oiled brokerage industry beyond the main cities of Cairo and Alexandria. Most brokers function essentially to process orders, without enough basic business to sustain the large number of small brokers. An increase in brokers' commissions is regarded by leading fund managers as controversial but vital, if the stock market is to play its role successfully. With this measure are needed more effective use of nationwide institutions through which securities can be sold, in particular the state-owned banks and post offices. Belief that Egypt can draw upon greater domestic savings stems not only from estimates based on test cases, but also on evidence from the Rayan Islamic investment company, which attracted investments from small depositors worth E£1.9 billion between 1982 and 1986, before it collapsed and was exposed as the biggest fraud in Egyptian history. The further development of Egypt's Islamic investment companies (ICCs) led to as many as 105 such companies being established by 1988, when many of them collapsed. As a sign of the extent to which they had managed to attract funds, the IICs officially attracted 502,826 depositors between 1985 and 1988, collecting E£3.8 billion in deposits, which at current levels was equivalent to 7.8 per cent of GDP, or 10 per cent of total banking deposits or 17 per cent of the deposits of the state-owned banks. The attraction of the market to individual investors has never been in doubt, but essential to accelerating investment rates is the need to create investor confidence in the financial sector intermediaries. Public awareness of the opportunities is regarded as limited, while brokerage companies are criticised for often failing to furnish potential investors with adequate guidance and information.

While the number of individual investors continues to prove insufficient to generate the necessary growth rate, other vehicles have been sought to tap into domestic savings. The role of

DOMESTIC SAVINGS AND THE CAPITAL MARKETS

non-bank financial intermediaries, in particular pension and social insurance funds, is a common feature in all emerging markets. The growing cost of social insurance has necessitated an overhaul of the market, to allow contributory pensions to force an increase in domestic savings. The role of these intermediaries is determined by the level of assets of the pension funds and

Exhibit 5.2
Egypt's domestic liquidity, 1995–98, (E£ million)

	1995		1996		1997		1998	
	March	June	March	June	March	June	March	June
Total domestic liquidity	147,388	152,577	162,331	168,532	183,044	193,902	202,840	210,487
Money supply	30,177	31,634	33,639	35,056	37,035	39,052	41,228	43,590
Currency outside banks	21,033	21,519	23,010	23,643	24,846	25,839	28,645	29,517
Demand deposits in local currency	9,144	10,115	10,629	11,413	12,189	13,223	12,583	14,073
Quasi money	117,211	120,943	128,692	133,476	146,009	154,850	161,612	172,798
Time/savings deposits local currency	79,853	82,177	89,897	94,412	108,450	116,776	124,507	128,698
Counterpart assets								
Net foreign assets	49,132	48,017	47,648	48,164	54,394	56,110	44,061	45,138
Domestic credit	129,363	133,215	150,673	155,777	174,137	183,506	206,521	211,525
Other items (net)	-31,107	-28,655	-35,990	-35,409	-45,487	-45,714	-47,742	-46,176

Source: Central Bank of Egypt

Exhibit 5.3
Egypt's domestic credit, 1995–98, (E£ million)

	1995		1996		1997		1998	
	March	June	March	June	March	June	March	June
Total domestic credit	129,363	133,215	150,673	155,777	174,137	183,506	206,521	211,525
Net claims on government*	42,099	41,762	41,247	42,714	40,279	43,650	48,372	46,900
Treasury bills	25,290	22,827	20,432	24,504	21,299	28,955	34,808	35,295
Securities	36,988	39,399	39,666	38,525	42,268	42,248	43,122	42,966
Credit facilities	36,916	37,742	38,033	38,435	37,151	34,305	30,218	32,965
Government deposits	57,095	58,206	56,884	58,750	60,339	61,858	59,776	64,336
Claims on:								
Public business sector	26,159	25,019	29,512	28,560	32,438	32,110	30,724	29,394
Private business sector	48,509	52,965	64,397	68,440	82,306	87,969	105,132	112,396
Household sector	12,596	13,469	15,517	16,063	19,114	19,777	22,293	22,835

* T-bills + securities + credit facilities less government deposits

Source: Central Bank of Egypt

DOMESTIC SAVINGS AND THE CAPITAL MARKETS

Private sector activity now accounts for around 62 per cent of total economic activity

insurance companies relative to GDP, which in Egypt stands at around 40 per cent. The large relative size of Egyptian assets, which are double those of Jordan, Morocco and Tunisia, has been offset by low returns earned from these assets in the 1980s and 1990s, when balances of the social insurance system fell from 38 per cent of GDP in 1986 to 29 per cent in 1992. More efficient use of social insurance fund assets is now being achieved, with the establishment in 1998 of an investment unit within the ministry responsible. As a key source of domestic savings, the fund is now an active player in the market with the launch in 1998 of the E£1 billion Egypt International Fund. The Ministry of Insurance and Social Affairs has a direct computer link with the ESE, and is planning to have a permanent staff at the exchange to track stock prices and is also seeking to have representatives on the boards of the companies in which it is an investor. But the fund has yet to invest what amounts to the shortfall between investment generated from abroad and that generated domestically, to a level adequate for the total level to meet total investment requirements.

The spur of privatisation

The twin vehicles of privatisation and an increased role for the private sector have driven Egypt's economic fortunes since liberalisation of the economy started in 1991. Private sector activity now accounts for around 62 per cent of total economic activity. The government intends that privatisation will reduce the public sector's industrial sector role by 25 per cent, to around 13 per cent. Public sector output is projected to fall from 9.6 per cent of GDP to 3.2 per cent. The rate of change depends upon the pace of privatisation, which has slowed markedly since 1996–97, when several of the most attractive companies were sold. The four methods employed by the government to carry out its privatisation programme – majority initial public offerings, sales to employees, liquidations and minority IPOs – have raised a total E£12.36 billion since 1994. Taking an average of 20 per cent as being the level of stock market activity conducted by foreigners, and leaving aside the Egyptian global depository receipts traded on the London Stock Exchange, it appears that around E£9.8 billion of the proceeds from privatisation have been provided by Egyptian domestic investors. Seen against the amount of total savings believed available in the country, this amount is small, suggesting that a great deal more is awaiting investment if the right investment and the right investment vehicles can be found.

Investment bankers and fund managers remain keen to see the privatisation programme accelerated as a means of utilizing domestic savings more effectively. However, they also remain convinced that it is the Egyptian private sector companies which have retained their shares within their founding families and not the remaining privatisation stocks, which are the real potential drivers of the economy. A comparative analysis of the change in profitability of 56 privatised public enterprises, shows that by the end of 1998, 22 had experienced an average 48 per cent fall in profits after privatisation, compared with an average 51 per cent rise in net profits in the first year since privatisation of the remaining 34 companies. On average, 65 per cent of privatised companies had seen their share price fall below their initial flotation price by December 1998 (see Exhibits 5.4 and 5.5). Of the 17 private sector companies which had previously not been listed but which carried out IPOs between January 1997 and December 1998, seven saw the value of their shares increase by an average 44 per cent, while those which fell did so by an average 20 per cent. The overall downward trend of the Egyptian market in common with other emerging markets in the wake of the Asian crisis accounted for much of the decline in share values. But the broad conclusion drawn from the Egyptian market, which saw a 32 per cent decline in share values in 1998, was that privatisation of the 314 companies under Law 203 was unlikely to continue offering the spur it had been a year earlier, unless

Exhibit 5.4
The 10 most profitable privatised companies, 1998–99 (E£ million)

Company	Profit			Share price		
	1997	1998	% change	31/1/98	31/1/99	% change
Nasr Dried Agricultural Products	(169)	221	230.77	29.78	24.47	(17.83)
Giza Contracting	932	3,043	226.50	54.86	58.65	6.91
Misr Chemical Industries	1,236	3,631	193.77	8	4.52	(43.50)
Industrial and Engineering Products	17,704	35,874	102.63	54.44	56.45	3.69
Eastern Company	70,590	140,166	98.56	72.56	106.90	47.33
Upper Egypt Contracting	1,054	1,901	80.36	83.20	112.62	35.36
Bisco Misr	15,016	26,197	74.46	14	14.01	0.07
Nasr Company for Civil Works	10,441	17,684	69.37	33.25	27.72	(16.63)
Egyptian Financial and Industrial	25,257	42,332	67.61	96.30	71.41	(25.85)
Alexandria Spinning and Weaving	7,199	11,870	64.88	27.89	37.32	33.81

Source: Financial Securities

Exhibit 5.5
The 10 least profitable privatised companies, 1998–99 (E£ million)

Company	Profit			Share price		
	1997	1998	% change	31/1/98	31/1/99	% change
Nile Match Company	7,294	5,348	-27.22	21.96	15.07	-31.38
Arab Cotton Ginning	5,548	7,058	-28.02	52.50	67.90	29.33
Nasr Clothes and Textiles (Kabo)	16,037	11,544	-28.02	49.44	65.79	33.08
Middle and West Delta Flour Mills	14,302	9,844	-31.17	51.32	38.72	-24.55
Paints and Chemical Industries (Pachin)	35,331	23,922	-32.29	96.91	87.26	-9.96
Misr Aluminum	210,786	140,485	-33.35	71.25	40.52	-43.13
General Silos and Storage	26,016	17,062	-34.42	63.04	56.04	-11.10
United Arab Shipping & Stevedoring	2,216	1,188	-46.39	31	12.86	-58.52
Egyptian Chemical Industries (Kima)	6,567	2,952	-55.05	17.50	12.57	-28.17
South Cairo and Giza Flour Mills	5,555	1,198	-78.43	39.50	20.70	-47.59
Telemisr	-1,011	-6,565	-549.36	16.04	11.58	-27.78

Source: Financial Securities

major privatisations also take place.

Retaining investor interest in the stock exchange as a means of bolstering the privatisation process and thereby activating domestic savings, has led to a variety of strategies on the part of brokers and fund managers operating in the Egyptian market. Funds are currently being retained by several of the largest fund managers, in anticipation of bank, insurance and utilities privatisation, at the expense of the 'Law 203 industrial and commercial companies' which still remain to be privatised. By December 1998, 100 of these companies had been privatised, or 32 per cent of the total. Despite 17 formerly family-owned private sector companies now being actively traded, the private sector's role has not compensated for the slow pace of public sector privatisation. However, fund managers investing in the Egyptian market are expecting earnings growth in the best privatised public sector companies to improve over time as a result of private sector competition.

Dominating the future success of privatisation, aside from the record of companies already privatised, will be the pricing mechanism employed. While the government sees itself essentially as a seller, which has earned E£12.36 billion in proceeds from privatisation since 1994, it is also expected to price sensibly to make a success of sales which are regarded as vital to creating a liquid stock market. The 62 companies earmarked for privatisation between January–July 1999 are regarded by some investment bankers as better-suited as private placements rather than IPOs. Criticism has mounted against the ongoing sale of minority stakes, which has diluted the value of companies without increasing market liquidity because of the unlikelihood of major restructuring and earnings growth in companies which remain largely in government hands. Liquidity and the development of the secondary market remain priorities for market players, and only the sale of the public sector utilities will energise the market sufficiently to draw in the foreign investors who are essential to making such sales a success.

New products to enhance savings

Accelerating the growth of the Egyptian capital markets is as dependent upon an expansion in the range of products offered by institutions as it is upon attracting more people to invest, to use their savings for investment, and to increase the overall level of savings by opening up new avenues to investment. So far, investor interest has been determined by the pace of privatisation and the issue of shares in private sector companies. This pattern has in turn been influenced by the character of the companies coming to market, their earnings growth, and the consequent impact on the liquidity of the market. Retail demand in Egypt has been primarily through participation in new offerings. With the decline in the quality of offerings, coupled with rigidity in the pricing terms set by the government for privatisation issues, the primary market has declined.

The result of this decline in investor interest has been to try and find alternative ways of generating market activity by enhancing savings. A potential alternative now being considered is to broaden the availability of capital guaranteed products, redeemable after between three and five years, which would give the investor a guaranteed return of the full principle sum, whatever level the stock market had reached, plus profit if there had been a gain. In late 1998 the CMA approved the formation of a capital guarantee portfolio to be managed by Egyptian Portfolio Management Group, the first of its kind in Egypt. The capital guarantee portfolio is specifically designed for the low-risk investor and will have a minimum investment of E£100,000 with fixed management fees. In January 1999, Delta International Bank became the second financial institution to offer such a product when it launched the first capital mutual fund of E£50 million, in which capital is guaranteed.

Ways are now being sought to create money market funds and market-makers in the bond market as well as convertible bonds, as means of creating a variety of fixed-income savings instruments. The first of these was created by Lazard Asset Management Egypt in May, with the launch of a E£100 million American Express Bank money market fund, investing in T-bills. Introduction of funds offering a variety of contributions and maturities would allow movement away from the T-bill market, which has a E£25,000 minimum bill, which is widely regarded as too high for use as a savings instrument by individual investors.

Banks are expected to lead the way in offering the broadest and most readily accessible range of new products. The obvious need for a mortgage market is only likely to be met by banks that are able to establish a firm enough footing with real estate developers through whom it may become possible to offer mortgages, despite the absence of adequate legislation allowing lenders to seize property upon which borrowers have defaulted in their payments. The retail banking operations of Middle East banks are extremely cautious, owing largely to an unfavourable legal environment. Research by Nomura puts the proportion of retail lending in the region at 10–20 per cent of total lending. Expanding the variety of products available through insurance companies is an aim of both the insurance companies and banks now seeking to expand the take-up of provision of insurance products. Government policy-makers take as their basic assumption, the view that investment can only be increased by increasing savings. But the success of this view depends upon being able to divert savings from the traditional bank deposits. This has been actively pursued by mutual fund managers. Since 1994, 21 local funds, five country funds and one Arab fund have been established. The local funds have since become a major vehicle for investing individual savings, and currently have E£3.8 billion under management.

Insurance and pension reform

A major challenge for the architects of Egypt's capital markets is to adapt existing sources of investment income, and to direct these sources in new ways to both increase their profitability and to allow such changes to take the place of the existing system. Dominating all areas of government policy reform is a strategy of creating parallel systems. The government is reluctant to dissolve what exists until an alternative has been put in place and the people affected by the change have drifted naturally towards the new system. This strategy is evident throughout the government's reform programme, and is intended to ensure political stability while new measures are introduced.

The pressing need for change remains a major influence on government thinking. In many areas, there is no choice but to change, and at some point in the future the wish to retain control over the pace of that change will inevitably weaken. Reform of the insurance and pension plans currently on offer, are two cases in point.

With the reduction in the size of the public sector there is a reduced need to invest pension funds in the public sector. Equally, with privatisation the number of employees who have moved from the public sector with companies in which the government has sold a majority stake now stands at 102,000. The shrinking of the public sector ought to create a larger pool of employees to whom the new private sector employers can offer private company pension schemes. Creation of such schemes is viewed as vital to reforming both the insurance and pension systems, thereby generating a higher savings level, greater resources for the insurance companies and a consequent rise in investment levels. The total assets of Egypt's social insurance schemes, along with the private pension funds and the insurance companies themselves, stands at 40 per cent of GDP, though the return on investment of these assets was marked by losses of 12 per cent of the original investment during 1980–90. Consequently, the real value of the sector's assets fell by 78 per cent in 10 years. With reform, the potential for a reversal of this situation has appeared.

Administratively, the government has linked the previously separate ministries of social insurance and social affairs, with a view to creating an interlinked system of benefits which also acts to invest the income from contributions more effectively. The first step in this direction was to create the Egypt International Fund, Egypt's E£1 billion investment fund financed by the four state-owned banks but with a E£200 million stake taken by the state pension fund, which has assets of E£77 billion. The government accepts that, as in many developed and developing countries, Egypt faces the prospect of the assets of the welfare system failing to cover the value of claims. Egypt has in one sense overcome this by retaining both a low level of contributions as well as a low level of benefits. Low inflation of 3.6 per cent has assisted in deflecting pressure for a rise in the level of benefits. However, it is also widely accepted that with a growing private sector, and a growing need for highly trained workers who can become the engine of economic growth, wages will need to rise. Consequently, the social insurance and pension systems will be forced to adapt, both to higher wages and the demand for higher benefits by contributors.

Currently, the state has four pension schemes, covering old age, disability, unemployment and health, two with a minimum and maximum contribution. A third system is offered to Egyptians working abroad, and a fourth is for casual labourers. All are designed for an economy in which wages are extremely low, with minimum monthly contributions ranging from E£1–E£50. It is intended that the government schemes will be retained to provide for people on lower wages, which is the majority of the population. According to the figures of the Ministry of Social Insurance, 65 per cent of Egyptians are considered poor, meaning they earn E£4,168 (US$1,225) per annum per household, or E£814 (US$239) per capita per annum.

As a consequence of the limited economic power as contributors of those most in need of benefits, the benefits are low, and barely reflect the needs of a growing private sector workforce, in which wages are likely to grow. There are, however, limitations on this anticipated wage growth. Despite the reform programme having led to 102,000 workers having being transferred from government employment to majority private sector owned companies, employment law has hindered restructuring of the companies once they have moved into private sector hands. As a result, the size of workforces and wages have not changed perceptibly in newly privatised companies. This has been an impediment to the development of new insurance and pension schemes, and consequently to the development of the sector as a whole, as the growth of the private sector would not appear to have increased the number of workers in a particular sector to whom an insurance company could offer viable group insurance policies. The model for such policies exists in both the public and private sectors. In addition to the four established insurance schemes, the state social insurance system has, since 1980, offered alternative schemes to individual companies where the minimum monthly salary is E£525. The higher average level of contributions to the alternative schemes means that fewer people need to join the schemes to make them economically viable. Currently eight such schemes are in operation – seven with banks and one with a company. The schemes receive contributions from a total 5,754 people, with 746 people now receiving pensions based on their contributions. These schemes have their own boards of directors, responsible for investing the funds, while the accounts are overseen by the Ministry of Insurance and Social Affairs.

A third area of social insurance currently in operation is the complementary schemes, run by companies, ministries or unions. Individuals contribute to these as well as one of the main government schemes. There are currently 560 complementary schemes in operation, receiving contributions from three million individuals.

Demographics and extremes of wealth and poverty are the key factors influencing the character of reform in the insurance and pensions sectors. Reform will create an amalgam of benefits and contributions, while taking into account the social aspects of the pensions and the economic viability of the system as a whole. The aim will be to both simplify the system, which is currently structured on the basis of Law No. 79 of 1975. As economic circumstances change, so the proportions paid by employers and employees will alter. Currently employers pay 76 per cent of the total contributions, which is regarded as a deterrent to increasing the gross level of contributions as the employers generally opt for the lowest level to minimise costs. As the aim is to increase the amount being paid into the system, a more equitable distribution of contributions is likely to be found, with private insurance companies likely to play an increasingly important role. The private insurance companies already operating in Egypt regard the best way forward as being the development of group life insurance offered to companies. Mohandes Insurance, one of Egypt's private insurance companies, currently offers such a scheme to 500,000 employees of the Ministry of Health. In addition, 50 private sector companies are offering their employees similar policies from the company. However, increasing this number to cover all private and public sector employees is regarded within both the insurance industry and the companies, as an uphill task. Absence of experience of insurance, as well as cultural resistance among more conservative sections of the population which hold the view that in Islam it is inappropriate to make provisions against fate, are recognised within the industry as the main hurdles to the sector's expansion. However, the probability that these inhibitions can be overcome is borne out by the fact that the state schemes have always attracted high levels of support. It is likely that the main objection to reform of the system will lie in popular suspicion of a growing private sector role, which is only likely to be overcome when average wages start to rise and the benefits of individual or group private schemes begin to be felt. It will be at this point that the contractual savings of the insurance and pension schemes can begin to play a meaningful role in developing the capital markets.

Private pensions and social security: the Latin American model?

Egypt has sought examples of pensions and social security reform from several countries which have pursued similar policies, while also continuing to provide for a large pool of low wage-earners whose combined incomes would not be adequate to provide an attractive business proposition for private sector insurance companies. The assets of the pension funds and insurance companies in most Latin American countries are below 10 per cent of GDP, with the exception of Brazil, Colombia and Chile. The Chilean example is the one most often cited as a potential model for Egypt, owing to the size of its pension fund's assets. Following the reform of its social security system in the 1980s, Chile saw the total assets of its contractual savings institutions expand from less than 1 per cent of GDP in 1980, to 31 per cent in 1990, and 52 per cent in 1993. This has been explained as being mainly due to the expansion of coverage and high investment returns during the 1980s. Egypt had achieved a similar assets/GDP ratio without this radical reform, with assets now standing at the equivalent of 40 per cent of GDP. The expanding assets of the Chilean insurance sector resulted from pension funds investing heavily in government, mortgage and corporate bonds and bank deposits. Investment in corporate equities for the privately managed pension funds was less than 20 per cent of total assets in the late 1980s, because of tight restrictions on their investment portfolios, a study by the Egyptian Centre for Economic Studies states. However, the gradual relaxation of investment rules allowed the investment in equities to be raised to 30 per cent of assets in 1990, while investment in foreign assets was also permitted. It is this example that Egypt has partially followed, in its reform of the resources of the state pension system.

From the Egyptian perspective the increasing role of the private sector in the Chilean system is not regarded as a model for a change of management of the entire system, as it was the management of the fund's money rather than the money itself, which was placed into private hands. Moreover, Egyptian reformers remain acutely aware that the successful overhaul of the Chilean system has derived ultimately from the fact that contributions are larger than is likely to be the case in Egypt for the foreseeable future.

6 The stock exchange

Statistical summary

The Egyptian Stock Exchange (ESE) is both the engine of Egypt's capital market growth, as well as being the most technologically advanced institution within the capital markets and consequently a model which other areas of the markets are likely to follow. This growth from 1996–99 has taken place in the face of shocks which have tested the resilience of the Egyptian economy as a whole and the capital markets in particular. The Asian financial crisis led to US$1 trillion being withdrawn from all emerging markets.

Egypt's share of total emerging market capitalisation is now around 8 per cent. This proportion has increased with the growth of the Egyptian market's capitalisation, which stood at E£83 billion at the end of 1998 (see Exhibit 6.1) and E£91.0 billion as at May 1999. The ESE lists 891companies on an official list and two unofficial lists. There are 17 preferred shares, 116 government bonds and 19 corporate bonds (see Exhibit 6.1). The ESE's 10 most active stocks accounted for 57.7 per cent of total volume traded in January 1999, and 62 per cent of value traded. The yield on 91-day Treasury bills was 8.81 per cent, while on average the interest rate on three-month deposits was around 8.5–9 per cent. Earnings yield reached 10.1 per cent in January 1999, a yield gap of 1.28 per cent.

The capitalisation of the ESE is dominated by the financial sector, which has a 24.45 per cent share at E£22.1 billion. Second is the cement industry, at E£10.8 billion and third the food and beverage industry, at E£9.1 billion. Trading by type of securities in terms of value is dominated by shares, with a 94 per cent share of trading activity, with the balance made up by bond trading. Listed shares accounted for 88 per cent of the value traded in January 1999 whilst

Exhibit 6.1
Capitalisation of the Egyptian Stock Exchange 1990–98, (E£ million)

	1990	1991	1992	1993	1994	1995	1996	1997	1998
Value of trading	341.5	427.8	596.6	568.6	2,557.2	3,849.4	10,967	24,219	23,363
Listed shares & bonds	206.2	233.9	371.4	274.9	1,214	2,294.2	8,769.2	20,282	18,500
Unlisted shares & bonds	135.3	193.9	225.3	293.7	1,343.2	1,555.2	2,198.3	3,937.4	4,863
Market capitalisation	5,071	8,845	10,845	12,807	14,480	27,420	48,086	70,873	83,140

Source: Capital Market Authority

THE STOCK EXCHANGE

Exhibit 6.2
The 20 largest listed companies by market capitalisation, end-1998

Ranking	Company	Market value (E£ million)
1	Abu Qir Fertilizer	2,807
2	Suez Cement	2,389
3	Mobinil	2,079
4	Misr Aluminium	2,013
5	Eastern Tobacco Co	1,957
6	Comm Int Bank	1,754
7	Gas Misr	1,518
8	MIBank	1,488
9	Portland Tourah Cement	1,383
10	Misr Eldeda for Housing and Reconstruction	1,326
11	Helwan Portland Cement	1,208
12	El-Canal Shipping Agencies	1,199
13	Delta for Suger	1,197
14	Holding for Financial Invest	1,150
15	Alexandria National Iron & Steel	1,149
16	Commercial Int. for Investing	1,147
17	Misr Exterior Bank	1,116
18	Orascom for Projects and Tourist Development	1,050
19	Oriental Textile	1,025
20	Ameryah Cement	1,020

Source: Capital Market Authority

12 per cent were over-the-counter trading. The 30 most heavily traded stocks, accounted for 85.81 per cent of the absolute liquidity of the market. Trading by foreigners has seen a steady rise since the liberalisation of the economy began in earnest in 1996. Between January 1998 and January 1999, foreigners engaged in a total 61,488 transactions as buyers (9.18 per cent of the total) and 59,701 as sellers (8.92 per cent). In terms of traded volume, foreigners accounted for 16.59 per cent of purchase transactions and 21.6 per cent of sales, while in terms of value traded foreigners accounted for 18.14 per cent of purchases and 22.38 per cent of sales.

At the end of 1998 equity holdings by foreigners stood at US$1.25 billion. The patterns dominating stock market activity in

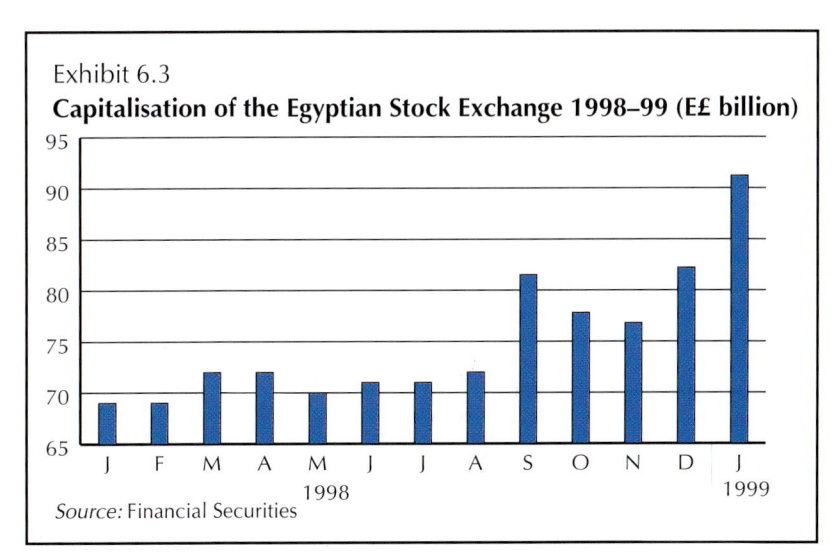

Exhibit 6.3
Capitalisation of the Egyptian Stock Exchange 1998–99 (E£ billion)

Source: Financial Securities

1998 reflected the condition of emerging markets worldwide. During 1998, the ESE experienced a decline in initial flotation prices for privatised companies. By December 1998, 65 per cent of the 34 public sector companies which had been majority sold during the privatisation programme had seen their share price fall by an average 36 per cent, while the remaining companies had seen their share price rise by an average 99 per cent on the initial flotation price. Amid the global market turbulence, the ESE saw an inflow of E£51 billion against an outflow of E£80 billion in 1998.

Modernisation of the ESE

The modernisation of the ESE has evolved on several interconnected fronts. The reformers of the exchange realised very early that without introducing technology it would be impossible to either cope with the volume of trade or conduct business with a degree of transparency which only an electronic surveillance system could provide. Equally, the growth in volume necessitated a rapid improvement in the skills level of brokers, as well as in the management skills of those running the exchange itself. Technological advances have been the most rapid, while regular training programmes are being held for all brokers, as a means of raising both knowledge levels and standards of practice. The goal of the ESE is to use its electronic power to create a private communications network which will tie in all the participants in the capital markets. Brokers will have direct telephone lease lines to the exchange and the depository, and computer terminals on the trading floor will accommodate 145 members. There will also be up to 400 workstations from which other brokers can operate, with a total of 145 in the exchange, 70 at the ESE training centre in Cairo, and others for access by remote users. To facilitate ease of access by clients to brokers, there will eventually be 600 telephone lines feeding into the ESE building, as well as two telephone networks, one directly chargeable to the floor traders, and another passing through the ESE switchboard.

There is widespread acceptance of the fact that increasing the client base cannot be done purely by brokers based at the ESE. Consequently, the next stage of the ESE's modernisation will involve linking bank branches around the country to the ESE system, allowing remote users in banks to trade. It is estimated that by using 40 per cent of the 1,250 bank branches around the country, the market size could increase by up to 100 per cent. In evolving these development plans, the ESE has examined systems elsewhere, in which nationwide systems have assisted in the rapid acceleration of market activity.

Communications are regarded as the key to making a quantum leap which allow the ESE to move from its current level of 500,000–600,000 shareholders, up towards a target of several million. It is not expected that this target can be reached from within the domestic market, and the ESE is looking to attract regional investors by facilitating transactions electronically, as well as many of the four million Egyptians who live abroad, many of them in the Gulf and North Africa. The exchange is currently negotiating with NileSat, an Egyptian satellite launched in 1998, which has communications channels to rent. The ESE intends to beam information by satellite to other exchanges and individual investors. Banks throughout the region will also receive the information.

A major hurdle to establishing a regional trading system, is the absence of uniform regulation, surveillance and due diligence in regional capital markets. Alongside the technological advances in the Egyptian market have been major improvements in the quality of personnel, training and adherence to regulations governing the practices of the capital markets. The ability to improve these standards is inextricably linked to the introduction of the technology, which is now allowing surveillance on a much more sophisticated level. An advanced surveillance system introduced to the ESE in April 1999, has both on-line and off-line capabilities, with a range of alerts and the ability to freeze transactions. The system allows complete market control on-line, and validation of share ownership and position monitoring. On-line surveillance is at the order level, and offers the capability of either suspending trade automatically or allowing the surveillance department to be alert to potential illegality before the trade takes place. The ESE is responsible for on-line surveillance, while the regulatory body, the Capital Market Authority (CMA), possesses the off-line function, although the facilities will be available to both if necessary. The ESE is also establishing a data depository, to allow both off-line surveillance and statistical analysis, to enhance these control and supervisory powers, by providing access to background material. The aim is for the system to play a leading role in the region, though this will require the harmonisation of listing requirements across the region.

Electronic trading and the new settlement system

The installation of a new electronic trading and settlement system in 1999 equipped the ESE with an integrated solution system providing automated trading, exchange management, clearance and depository systems, as well as an advanced surveillance system. Many of Egypt's brokerage companies are human resource heavy and technology light by international standards, and have had to move rapidly towards automation to keep pace with the development of the market. The development of technology, automated settlement, and back and front office operations have all dominated the development strategies of the larger brokerage firms, though automation and preparation for use of the fully automated Misr Clearing and Settlement Depository (MCSD) system, and the ESE automation, have been the priorities.

The aim of the ESE integrated solution system, built and provided by EFA Software Services of Canada at a total cost of E£14 million, was to both enhance the liquidity of the market, as well as improve the system's fairness and transparency. To achieve this, the system provides a strong back-office facility for the exchange itself, equipping it with the variety of risk management tools. As a central component the system also provides the exchange with a shareholding registry, and facilities whereby accounts can be validated to prevent short-selling by sellers who don't own the full number of shares they have offered for sale. The system has been adapted to the needs of the Egyptian market for automated bookkeeping, certificate handling, regulatory reporting and controls, interfaces, and Arabisation. It also has detailed logging and audits, to expose insider trading. By linking trading, settlement and clearing, the exchange hopes to eliminate deliberate and unintentional short-selling. There is no pre-settlement facility, and the clearing and settlement system will be part of the back-office of the ESE, though the system will be open-ended, and capable of incorporating new methods of trading as the market develops. The automated OTC trade and trade in unlisted stocks began in April 1999. The entire system, customised for the Egyptian market, was expected to be fully functional by the end of 1999. Major investment is also expected to be made in the training of ESE staff, particularly in the area of surveillance.

Foreigners on the ESE: consolidation among local brokers

Opinions vary widely as to how best local brokerage firms should react to the presence of foreign-owned companies operating on the ESE. Dominating this reaction is a blunt assessment of how effective the foreign companies have been in the past three years. In the immediate aftermath of the initial acceleration of the economic liberalisation process, the flurry of activity in Egypt and in particular in Cairo led to a great deal of attention being paid to the role that foreign firms might play. There was certainly a degree of anxiety on the part of the local firms, who feared losing their way in the face of well-resourced, highly skilled players with a global reach of potential clients and an unmatchable access to research. The assessment of the major local companies is that the market has worked very much in their favour. From the global perspective, foreign participation has accounted for around 20 per cent of stock market transactions. Using their own resources, the leading local firms have pursued these investors themselves, drawing many from the Gulf. It is difficult to establish the exact geographical pattern of foreign portfolio investment into Egypt, but 40 per cent or more is estimated to originate in the Gulf states. This proximity, as well as the advantage of a common language, has served the local firms well when seeking to generate business in the region. In so doing, it has allowed them to take on the foreign competition, and has diminished the advantage of global reach that foreign companies had enjoyed over local brokers.

In the domestic market, local firms have been far more successful in establishing client bases, which have become the envy of the foreign firms seeking business. Until February 1999, the key foreign companies operating through joint ventures on the ESE were ING Barings, through its 29 per cent stake in Intercapital Securities, Robert Fleming, through its 50 per cent stake in Fleming Mansour Securities, and HSBC, which has established its own brokerage operation with no local partner. The character of the market changed radically in March 1999, when ING Barings sold its stake in Intercapital Securities to the company's other main institutional shareholder, the local investment bank CIIC. At the same time Fleming Mansour and CIIC merged their brokerage operations to form Fleming CIIC Securities, which now has 16 per cent of the brokerage market. The company's main rival is EFG-Hermes, which has a similar market share. EFG-Hermes is now in the position of being the largest brokerage

THE STOCK EXCHANGE

company to have no foreign partner. Fleming CIIC was created in part with the aim of broadening both companies' activities to include a much larger share of regional business. The merger clearly revealed the need for foreign companies such as Flemings to create successful local partnerships, as a means by which to establish themselves in the Egyptian market. The strength of the local players has been bolstered by the partnerships, and has further diminished the anxieties felt two years ago, when the local companies had not fully realised the real strength of their positions.

Local brokerage companies cite placing power rather than an attachment to a famous name as being the key to success in brokerage in the Egyptian market. All the local companies are ready to acknowledge that the presence of foreign firms is vital to the improvement of their own services, which have suffered from poor standards which have in turn in the past tarnished the reputation of the stock exchange at times when it was vital to prove that the institution was indeed a sound place to invest. By learning from foreign partners, local brokers have established increasingly high standards, which have improved the reputation of the ESE in the eyes of investors. A further necessary measure in this direction will be to increase the capital for brokerage firms, from E£250,000 to E£2 million, as a means of streamlining the industry. Local firms have achieved much of the consolidation that is likely to take place, leaving the market with one large wholly local player, in the form of EFG-Hermes, one local-foreign partnership in Fleming CIIC, and several smaller companies. The only possible further element of consolidation will be the establishment of a partnership between EFG-Hermes and a foreign partner. If such an arrangement were to take place, it would probably lead to a major restructuring of that company, which has advanced its interests in asset management and investment banking as much as in brokerage. The evolution of the market now means that 10 firms have 85 per cent of the total brokerage markets, leaving the remaining 15 per cent to 136 small companies. It is expected that the smaller firms are more likely to merge or go by the way as the

The cement industry is the second largest by market capitalisation on the ESE

The Stock Exchange is the engine of Egypt's capital market growth

Exhibit 6.3
Foreigners trading on the Egyptian Stock Exchange 1998–99

	Number of transactions				Traded volume (no. of shares)				Traded value (E£)			
	Buyer	% of total	Seller	% of total	Buyer	% of total	Seller	% of total	Buyer	% of total	Seller	% of total
1/98	2,179	3.18	2,864	3.35	2.6m	16.6	2.8m	18.32	178m	21.24	196m	23.37
2/98	3,585	6.72	4,120	7.72	2.8m	11.56	4.3m	17.71	258m	14.24	368m	20.35
3/98	6,855	9.31	4,885	6.64	4.6m	18.79	5.8m	23.43	419m	24.08	499m	28.68
4/98	4,669	10.43	3,386	7.57	3.5m	25.46	3.3m	23.81	260m	26.21	275m	27.76
5/98	5,106	9.42	4,771	8.8	5.7m	23.66	4.7m	19.4	289m	20.69	271m	19.4
6/98	4,755	7.97	6,009	10.08	4.5m	11.95	4.8m	12.83	266m	17.45	265m	17.4
7/98	4,781	12.54	3,921	10.29	3.4m	7.43	29.2m	62.55	209m	19.48	480m	44.65
8/98	6,447	13.01	5,462	11.02	6.6m	14.67	5.3m	11.69	269m	15.57	273m	15.84
9/98	7,466	12.32	5,738	9.47	7.2m	22.92	6.2m	19.65	355m	20.41	359m	20.68
10/98	4,435	9.45	6,081	12.96	3.9m	15.61	6.1m	24.42	178m	15.26	307m	26.33
11/98	4,776	8.90	7,406	13.81	5.3m	13.65	7.2m	18.66	189m	17.26	311m	28.34
12/98	5,894	11.88	5,058	10.2	21.8m	20.38	14m	13.16	463m	14.14	509m	15.52
Total	**61,488**	**9.18**	**59,701**	**8.92**	**72.5m**	**16.59**	**94.3m**	**21.6**	**3,338m**	**18.14**	**4,119m**	**22.38**
1/99	8,635	11.88	6,564	9.03	12.2m	22.68	10.1m	18.8	484m	17.81	456m	16.78

Source: Financial Securities

demands for technological upgrading exceed their capacity, rather than disappear in the face of foreign competition.

Broker regulation and codes of conduct

At the heart of regulations governing the conduct of brokers on the ESE is the practice of self-government. Brokers' representatives on the ESE board of directors, as well as their presence on committees within the exchange, have assisted in making the ESE a cohesive and internally regulated institution with a very clear set of rules with which its members are strictly forced to comply. The 146 members of the exchange must establish and enforce written procedures which will enable the member-company itself to enforce compliance with the rules of the exchange by each of its employees. Responsibility for supervision of the employees lies with the member companies, each of which has a designated employee whose task is to ensure that ESE rules are complied with. While it is the responsibility of the companies to enforce member compliance, it is the exchange itself which has disciplinary jurisdiction and powers to investigate and prosecute members who break the rules. The powers of the ESE are drawn from the rules and regulations of the capital markets Law as well as the ESE's own rules. The exchange itself thus has powers to expel, suspend, limit the activities, functions and operations, fine, censure or bar from association with other members, any member of the exchange which is found to have broken the rules.

THE STOCK EXCHANGE

The rules of the ESE extend both to the relationship between the member companies and the exchange, and the relationship between the companies and their clients. For the former, if a member gives false information to the exchange regarding transactions, or gives insufficient information on an issue which has come to the attention of the exchange board or the surveillance committee, the company can be prosecuted. But it is the second provision, governing the relationship between company and client which in many ways reflects the preoccupation of the CMA to ensure a steady flow of accurate information.

The CMA regards its role as being that of both regulator and educator of the evolving system. As part of this strategy, it is concerned to ensure that new investors to the market are assisted in their investment decisions by the brokers through whom they deal. In this way, the CMA hopes to encourage brokers to foster a climate of popular trust in the stock exchange, as it emerges into a new era at a time when many potential investors have little knowledge of how it works or remain distrustful of financial intermediaries. Where action is taken by the ESE board or the chairman against companies, the aim is to ensure a swift and accurate conclusion of a case. Respondents must answer any charges against them within 15 days of the accusation being made. Cases against brokers are heard by officials of the exchange, or by a subcommittee of exchange officials and members, excluding any individuals with a possible involvement in the case. Details of a case are considered in writing, a judgement delivered, and appropriate action taken. Where a case is minor and a fine is imposed, the fact of the fine remains confidential.

Market indices and their constituents

As a key part of the growing volume of information available to investors and capital markets institutions, indices tracking the progress of shares on the ESE have provided a regularly updated picture of market trends. The main index is the CMA Index, which covers all 891 listed companies on the ESE. The CMA issues a total of 27 indices, in addition to its general index. These indices cover the rise and fall of share prices in specific sectors of the economy. The weakness of the CMA General Index is that it incorporates the stagnant condition of the more than 700 companies that are not actively traded on the ESE, and whose dead-weight tends to have a negative effect on the apparent performance of those which are actively traded. In particular, the General Index fails to give an accurate impression of the condition of blue-chip stocks, notably the 10 most actively traded stocks which represent an average of around 50 per cent of trade. The single index has been criticised for giving an impression of stability, due to the vast majority of companies remaining at par value, as witnessed in 1998 when the market slipped by 32 per cent, distorting the real direction of the market. Consequently, fund managers opted to use the International Finance Corporation Index of 60 Egypt companies, which are tracked by the IFC when it draws up its global composite index of emerging markets, to which Egypt was added in 1997. EFG-Hermes maintains two indices to measure the performance of the Egyptian stock market. The Hermes Fianancial Index (HFI) is a broad-

Exhibit 6.4
Hermes Financial Index, 1992–1999

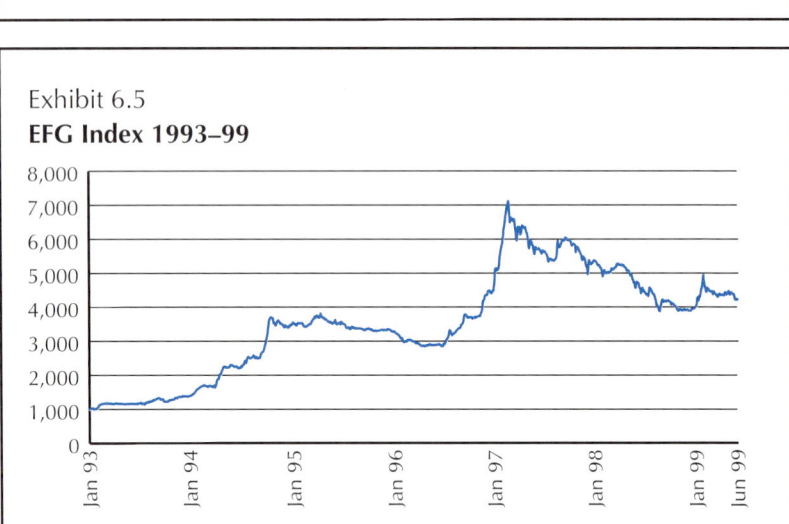

Exhibit 6.5
EFG Index 1993–99

based index tracking the most actively traded companies. It currently has 57 constituents. The index is designed to show general market trends. EFG Index is a large cap index and only includes actively traded companies with a sufficint market capitalisation to interest investors who are focused on large transactions. The EFG Index currently includes 22 companies.

To remedy the obvious need for a more select index, the CMA is to create a FT-CMA Index, with the *Financial Times*, which will track the 15 most active companies.

Progress of the new Capital Markets Law and its effects

The new Capital Markets Law, which will build upon Law No. 95 of 1992, is intended to modify and update the existing legislation by addressing in much greater detail the issues of corporate governance, insider dealing, shareholder minority rights, trading laws, penalties, and the structure of the ESE. It is not expected to be written in draft until the end of 1999. Legislation is expected to be introduced in the meantime, to clarify many of the outstanding legislative shortcomings within the current operations of the Egyptian capital markets. Among these are measures now being considered by the government for the establishment of a fast-track settlement process for commercial disputes, which would create courts presided over by three judges and two experts in the relevant field. The intention would be to avoid complex cases being heard by juries and legal officials with little or no knowledge of the issues being discussed.

Further to the Capital Markets Law will be a new and separate Central Depository, Central Registry, Clearance and Settlement and Securities Law, expected to be put before parliament in 1999 and to be applicable before the new Capitals Market Law itself. The introduction of new securities law will supersede the limited references made to these areas of capital markets activity in the current legislation, and clarify their function within the system as a whole. The current law refers only briefly to these elements of the capital markets, and is regarded as providing little definitive guidance as to how the increasingly sophisticated institutions relate to each other. The existing Capital Markets Law covers both joint-stock companies that offer shares to the public, as well as companies that deal with securities, underwriting, company formation, venture capital, clearance and settlement, the management of securities portfolios and investment funds, mutual funds and book-keeping. Several other laws have been introduced since 1992, which have implications for the capital markets, notably investment and companies legislation. As well as modifying the existing law, the new Capital Markets Law will also clarify trading laws and penalties to be applied when companies fail to abide by the rules of the CMA.

7 Fund management

A new business for Egypt

The rapid evolution of Egypt's investment climate has brought with it an investment superstructure now able to offer a sound alternative to the banking system. The extensive change in mentality which was necessary to create a critical mass of approval for the liberalising measures of the early to mid-1990s, followed by the privatisation, was all the more necessary if the non-bank financial intermediaries were to succeed in offering alternatives. The first hurdle was the history of such intermediaries. The losses incurred by the Islamic investment companies (ICCs) of the 1980s had exposed the regulatory shortcomings of the financial sector. The Capital Markets Law of 1992 was as much an attempt to redress the legislative shortcomings of the past, as it was a move towards creating the foundations for future development of the financial sector. A key result of the law was the emergence of mutual funds, as a secure form of investment managed by private companies but launched in concert with leading banks with which individual investors were familiar. As a means of ensuring their credibility in the eyes of investors, the law stated that the mutual funds must have professional management, and that the banks must hold 5 per cent of the total assets. Added to this, the banks had to remain investors for the life of the fund. Consequently, the main sources of finance for the funds are banks as underwriters, as well as insurance companies and government pension funds.

By early 1999, there were 21 local closed and open-ended funds and six offshore country and regional funds operating in Egypt (see Exhibit 7.1). The character of the Egyptian funds reflects well the potential and limitations of such investment vehicles in emerging markets. The ultimate success of the funds depends on several factors, all of which have in part already been put in place. While individual investors on the Egyptian Stock Exchange (ESE) have continued to invest despite the market downturn of 1998, the mutual fund managers are aware that their investors are likely to be the most reluctant to see the value of their investments fall. While the mentality in Egypt may have changed, it is still the case that losses are regarded with suspicion rather than resignation, in part due to many privatisation stocks having originally been overpriced.

Taken as a whole, the Egyptian fund management business has indeed become a business. The 21 local funds now have E£3.8 billion under management, with around 300,000 investors. However, the size of this business remains relatively small. As an example, the first of two funds operated by Banque Misr and managed by Concord International Investment

FUND MANAGEMENT

Exhibit 7.1
Fund managers, fund capital and market share, 1999

Funds	Capital (E£ million)	Total managed (E£ million)	% of all funds under management
Managers			
Concord International Investments Group		1,580	41.26
Banque Misr I	500		
Banque Misr II	300		
MIBank	280		
Egypt International Fund	500		
Al Ahli for Investments		500	13.05
NBE I	200		
NBE II	300		
Hermes Fund Management		550	14.36
Delta	50		
Banque du Caire	100		
Egyptian Gulf Bank	100		
American Express Bank	300		
Egyptian Fund Management Group		400	10.44
EAB	200		
BoA	200		
Egyptian Anglo		200	5.22
Suez Canal Bank	100		
Allied	100		
Prime Investments		250	6.53
SAIB I	100		
SAIB II	100		
SAIB III	50		
Egyptian Investment & Finance Co.			
Orient Trust	50	50	1.31
Cairo Portfolio Management			
Export Development Bank	100	100	2.61
Lazard Asset Management		200	5.22
Misr Exterior Bank	100		
Misr Iran Development Bank	100		
Total	**3,830**		

Source: IBTCI

initially attracted subscriptions from 17,000 people within nine days of opening in February 1995. Around 65 per cent of these subscribers were Banque Misr clients. Within 18 months there had been an 80 per cent turnover of shares, taking the number of investors down to 8,000, as larger investors remained and small investors redeemed.

With nine fund managers, 21 funds and 300,000 investors, the market is regarded by some fund managers as saturated more by funds than investors. The relatively low ratio of investors to funds has limited the liquidity in the market, which is the crucial element necessary to energising the market as a whole. From the perspective of mutual funds, this shortcoming has been caused by inadequate distribution of the securities on offer. Only Egypt's banks have the nationwide networks capable of allowing fund managers to reach the mass of the population. To fully exploit this network requires close coordination between banks and fund managers, who are capable of explaining to bank customers the benefits of investing in the funds. This has yet to happen on a meaningful scale.

Even before they have resolved the problem of securities distribution, some fund managers are pursuing the creation of a variety of products in the hope that breadth rather than initial depth will grow the market. While it is generally reckoned that the funds are fulfilling their role as stable investments, it is also the case that while the breadth is lacking they are failing to offer investment vehicles which reflect the necessary spectrum investors should be able to expect. As at May 1999 Egypt had only one money market fund, had no aggressive funds seeking capital appreciation, and no Egyptian management of regional funds in other countries. All the funds are essentially conservative, while nine are growth funds, two income funds, and the rest a combination. Consequently a distinction between them is the choice of managers, most of whom follow roughly similar strategies, though with undoubtedly different results. Equally, they compete in the form of the fees charged, with a significant variety in terms of the redemption, incentive and custodian fees charged. Likely to strongly influence the development strategies of the fund managers from now on is the difficulty faced in raising new funds.

Of the 21 funds now operating, 19 were in operation by the end of 1997, when the attraction of the Egyptian market was still strong despite the downturn in emerging markets. Only three were created in 1998. There is little doubt that the funds raised between 1996 and 1997 would be difficult to find now. Consequently, some fund managers have retained substantial funds in expectation of utilities privatisation. In the meantime, there is a degree of uncertainty as to how to regard the recent privatisation stocks, most of which have not seen management changes since they were sold, 29 per cent of them having seen reduced profits since privatisation. While the market is cheap and dividend yields are attractive, some fund managers are currently faced with a degree of uncertainty as to whether they should hold onto their remaining funds, or invest small amounts in companies with relative promise.

The pattern of investment by the funds has reflected the nature of the companies managing them. It is this variety which is perhaps the most promising aspect of the fund management business, as it has revealed the potential for vastly different strategies if only the market itself would grow. The larger companies have tended to invest large amounts in large projects, from which they can earn higher fees profits. This approach is criticised by other managers, who see

FUND MANAGEMENT

a conflict between fund size and innovation and regard one of their roles as being to provide expansion financing for smaller companies, through direct investment funds.

The funds established so far

The 21 local mutual funds under the management of nine fund managers established in the past five years now manage E£3.8 billion (see Exhibit 7.2). The number of investment funds is likely to increase in the near future, as banks establish and manage their own investment funds. Established funds have been managed through joint-stock companies established for the purpose. The banks, insurance companies and state pension fund which have established 20 of the funds now operating, are regarded as having both a key role in the acceleration of investment levels, while also being regarded as slow to take up the opportunities on offer. Managers of the investment funds, while having successfully established ties with the banks as underwriters, have certainly had to cajole the four public sector banks which have 65 per cent of total bank assets, into taking a more active role in the area of investment funds. The growth of the industry can be almost entirely attributed to the managers, rather than the banks which have invested in the funds.

Egypt's 21 local mutual funds include nine growth funds, three income funds, and nine income/growth funds. Six of these funds, valued at a total E£1.6 billion, were launched by Egypt's state-owned banks. By the end of 1994, 66 per cent of the mutual fund market was dominated by four banks. A further 13 were created by the joint-venture banks, one by an insurance company, and one, the Egypt International Fund, by the state-owned banks and the state pension fund. Eighteen of the funds are open-ended. In addition there are five offshore country funds and one regional fund investing primarily in Arab countries.

The skills with which the established funds have been managed has played a major part in the evolution of the Egyptian financial sector. Despite the limits of the market, fund management has attracted a significant concentration of highly skilled individuals with extensive experience in global markets.

Four funds managed by Concord International Investments have secured the company 41.26 per cent of all funds currently under management in Egypt. Two Banque Misr funds, with funds of E£500 million and E£300 million respectively, as well as a MIBank fund of E£280 million and management of the Egypt International Fund, have given Concord a leading position in the fund management business. A further four funds are managed by Hermes Fund Management, the fund management arm of EFG-Hermes. The company has 14.36 per cent of total funds under management, with management of a E£300 million American Express Fund, E£100 million each in funds managed on behalf of Banque du Caire and Egyptian Gulf Bank, and a E£50 million fund managed on behalf of Delta International Bank. Third in the market is Al Ahli for Investments, which now manages two funds on behalf of the National Bank of Egypt, of E£200 million and E£300 million, giving it 13.05 per cent of the all funds now under management. Fourth in the market as

FUND MANAGEMENT

Exhibit 7.2
Egyptian local mutual funds

	Launched	Size (E£ million)	Type	Nominal value per certificate (E£)	Certificate price on 24/12/98
NBE 1	3/9/94	200	Growth	500	710
NBE 2	3/10/95	300	Income	100	78.25
EAB	15/10/94	200	Growth	100	92.11
BoA	1/12/94	200	Growth	100	101.21
Banque Misr 1	1/2/95	500	Income	1,000	106.85
Banque Misr II	17/9/95	300	Growth	1,000	82.35
Allied Insurance	3/10/95	100	Growth	500	433.75
Banque du Caire	9/11/95	100	Growth	100	165.44
SAIB I	12/5/96	100	Growth/semi annual	500	699.77
Export Development Bank	6/8/96	100	Income	100	91.31
Suez Canal Bank	17/11/96	100	Income/growth	500	405.02
American Express Bank	25/2/97	300	Income/growth	100	78.22
Egyptian Gulf Bank	23/3/97	100	Income/growth	100	77.56
SAIB II	23/9/97	100	Income/growth	100	96.44
Misr Exterior Bank	11/12/97	100	Income/growth	1,000	911.99
MIBank	15/1/98	100	Growth	100	80.68
Misr Iran Development Bank	5/7/98	100	Income/growth	100	100.28
SAIB III	20/12/98	50	Income/growth	100	n/a

Closed-end fund established by state-owned banks, insurance companies and pension fund

| Egypt International Fund | 10/12/97 | 500 | Growth | 1,000 | n/a |

Private companies' closed-end funds

| Delta International Bank | 26/5/96 | 50 | Income/growth | 100 | 116.16 |
| Orient Trust | 27/11/96 | 50 | Income/growth | 1,000 | 978.8 |

Source: IBTCI

manager is the Egyptian Fund Management Group, also part of EFG-Hermes, managing two E£200 million funds for Egyptian American Bank and Bank of Alexandria, which account for 10.44 per cent of the market total. Fifth with a 6.53 per cent market share is Prime Investments, managing three funds for Société Arab Internationale de Banque, two of E£100 million and one of E£50 million. Equal sixth ranking with 5.22 per cent market shares are Egyptian Anglo, managing the Suez Canal and Allied funds each of E£100 million, and Lazard Asset Management, also with E£100 million each invested in funds created by Misr Exterior Bank and Misr Iran Development Bank. Seventh ranking is Cairo Portfolio Management with a 2.61 per cent market share, managing E£100 million on behalf of the Export Development Bank, with the eighth ranking Egyptian Investment and

Finance Company holding 1.31 per cent of total managed funds with a E£50 million fund managed on behalf of Orient Trust.

Fund fee structures

A key distinguishing factor between the mutual funds is the fee structure. The significance of this aspect of their business is greater in a relatively small market, where the opportunities for investment are relatively narrow. When the local industry was launched, the fees were on average a great deal higher than the average on global markets, with some as high as 25 per cent. Competition has brought these fees down, with fees on the NBE funds having dropped by 50 per cent. Other bank fund manager's have also reduced fees, though they generally remain high. This cost is explained by the shortage of experienced fund managers in the market, and with the top five currently managing 85.64 per cent of all funds under management. On the specific costs, 12 of the funds charge subscription fees of an average 0.95 per cent per certificate, 16 charge redemption fees of an average 0.89 per cent of NAV, all charge management fees of an average 0.86 per cent of NAV, 14 charge incentive fees of an average 10.4 per cent, 16 charge bank fees of an average 0.79 per cent of NAV, seven apply bank incentive fees of an average 7.5 per cent of net profit, and 10 charge custodian fees of an average 0.285 per cent of the securities' value.

Fund performance

The mutual funds did not escape the 33 per cent overall decline in the value of the Egyptian market in 1998. This decline was largely brought about by the divestment trend affecting all emerging markets, which saw their share of total world market capitalisation fall by US$1,000 billion to around 8 per cent. All the Egyptian local funds declined in 1998, only three of them by less than 10 per cent. On average the funds declined by 15.5 per cent, four of them by more than 20 per cent.

Against the background of the 33 per cent decline in Egyptian stock prices between March 1997 and June 1988, it is clear that the funds remained a safer investment than non-fund investments. The average annual return earned ranged from between 8 per cent and 21 per cent, while the steepest decline for a fund in this period was 22 per cent, a full 11 points less than the market as a whole. In response to the decline, fund managers have asked to be permitted to retain a proportion of profits as reserves against further decline.

Aside from mutual funds, Egypt now has two capital guaranteed funds, established following the approval in 1998 of the Capital Market Authority that such funds could be created. In December 1998 the Egyptian Portfolio Management Group established both a capital guarantee portfolio and an index portfolio tied to the performance of the stock market index. The capital guarantee portfolio was aimed at low risk investors, and launched in light of the overall turbulence in world stock markets. The minimum investment will be E£100,000. The launch was followed by a similar fund in January 1999 created by Delta International Bank, which launched the first capital mutual fund, of E£50 million, in which capital is guaranteed. Launched at the same time was the Misr Insurance Company Investment Fund of E£100 million, in which the state-owned Misr Insurance retains a 5 per cent stake while the rest is to be offered for public subscription. The fund has a total capitalisation of E£100 million, with certificates to be offered to both retail and institutional investors. The creation of two other investment funds intended as market-makers has also been announced. A E£300 million fund launched by National Bank of Egypt, Banque du Caire and four insurance companies, as well as a E£300 million fund launched by Banque Misr, Bank of Alexandria and four insurance companies, are both planned to begin operations in October 1999.

Lessons from other emerging markets

Egypt's ability to draw upon a pool of highly-skilled financial sector practitioners with wide experience of global financial markets, put it at a distinct advantage when formulating the criteria by which it intended to develop the capital markets institutions. Equally, many of the institutions which the government's strategists knew would have to play a vital role in attracting investment and ensuring the success of privatisation, were already in place and to an extent needed simply to be kick-started. This was particularly true of the ESE, founded in Alexandria in 1881 and in Cairo in 1903. During 30 years of dormancy skilled practitioners had gone abroad. But what has been remarkable is that a number of those who left while the stock exchange was mothballed, have now returned. This reverse brain-drain has had an impact on the speed with which Egypt's financial sector has developed and matured in the past few years. Instead of seeking extensive guidance from the experience of similar markets, Egypt has sought guidance from the most sophisticated markets. To this end, the ESE has an advisory panel comprising members from the most developed stock markets. The same approach to development of the financial sector applies to fund managers. There are few models sought in the other emerging markets. Meanwhile, the main Egyptian players have returned with the skills which are now strongly influencing the direction that the market is taking. These participants are themselves more skilled in the practices of the developed markets than they are in the emerging markets. There is a frank acknowledgment that as Egypt is in a position where it is competing with overseas fund managers who are viewing it as one among several emerging markets, there is regard paid to how to make Egypt appear attractive among its emerging market peers.

From the institutional point of view, Egypt's reformers have looked at the ways in which popular awareness of investment opportunities has been raised and widened. While the impact of this influence is minimal, Tunisia's television and media campaign, as well as the creation of investment clubs, has led to calls for a financial news channel to be launched in Egypt which will teach people about the purpose and technicalities of investing in funds. Lessons from Malaysia and Kenya were also taken on board, particularly in the areas of awareness. From the investment perspective, the rapid move towards liberalisation undertaken in Poland is regarded as a model for Egypt, but one which no fund managers expect the government to adopt. Any assessment of the potential lessons learned from other emerging markets by practitioners within any area of Egyptian reform – capital markets, privatisation, foreign investment – tends to be seen against the background of the macro reform process. The relatively slow though steady pace of reform in Egypt, has been matched by the relatively slow pace at which the capital markets are moving towards reaching a level of sophistication which will allow them to increase their reach. Only when the major banks are in private hands, will there be the real opportunity for fund managers, for example, to take full advantage of having a banking sector run on market lines by bankers and financiers determined to widen banking practice and maximise returns by offering a real variety of products and services. The lessons from other emerging markets tend, therefore, to be strongly influenced by a sense of waiting for the government to withdraw from economic activity to an extent which will give impetus to the private sector.

Cairo as a regional investment centre

Capitalising on local strengths and pursuing regional ambitions are the twin elements in the strategic vision of Egypt's economic reformers. What is still being formed is a method of marrying these two elements into a cohesive foundation, which will see direct investment in Egypt accelerate on the back of portfolio investment, thereby creating the investment momentum and company growth necessary to raise regional interest in the Egyptian market. It is widely accepted among Egyptian financiers that significant growth in the domestic market is the key to selling the Egyptian story abroad. Foreign direct investment in 1998 stood at US$989 million, while foreign portfolio investment saw US$248 million withdrawn. Clearly the interconnection between the health of the domestic market and the role of a particular market as a regional centre is not always vital. But in the current climate it is necessary for Egypt to prove that the commercial banking base of Bahrain, which lacks the capital markets base that Egypt is attempting to build up, as well as the capital markets skills present in Beirut – a market which lacks the variety of stocks available from the Egyptian domestic market ñ are reason for Cairo to take the lead. A critical mass of people, companies, financial intermediaries and regulatory measures, are the major requirements. In the meantime, it is a matter of Egypt raising its head above the parapet to ensure that the region's financiers are aware that the market is here and growing.

Against the background of a need to ensure that Egyptian companies themselves are offering a sound investment as a means of raising the profile of the Egyptian market, two other vital areas are necessary to develop if Egypt is to emerge as the investment centre of the Middle East. The first is the setting of standards of accounting, listing requirements and due diligence in the Egyptian market which mirror global standards. Vital to the development of the Egyptian market as a financial centre is the level of expertise. Despite the presence of well-trained players in the market, it remains the case that the foreign companies now operating in brokerage, asset management and investment banking are those responsible for injecting the high standards by which all the players in the Egyptian market now judge themselves and each

FUND MANAGEMENT

other. Egypt's moves towards establishing international standards of practice as its benchmark have been steady, if not rapid enough. To create a favourable investment climate within the country, a greater consistency in accounting procedures will be required. While all companies were required in 1997 to adopt the International Accounting Standards, enforcement has been inadequate. In 2005, when Egypt becomes a full member of the World Trade Organisation, Egyptian companies will have to abide by these standards. Enforcement of these standards is regarded as a vital element in the transformation of the Egyptian market into an attractive investment for regional institutions.

Closely connected to this accounting change is the broader achievement of potential by the privatised companies. Their earnings' growth is regarded as a vital element in the growth of the stock exchange. The profitability of many of these companies since privatisation has on average been varied, with 29 per cent of them showing lower profits since their sale, and 9 per cent showing no change.

The second vital change necessary for Egypt to establish a regional role drawing its fundamental strength from the foundation of its relatively large domestic market, is the extension of the global standards of practice on a regionwide basis. Beirut, Abu Dhabi and Kuwait all form considerable competition to Cairo on the basis that they have long-term regional and global financial institutions with a critical mass of funds under management, while the Egyptian market is still relatively small and dominated by retail trade. While needing to

Exhibit 7.3
Private company initial public offerings

	Offer date	Number of shares	% of total shares	Offer price E£	Closing price 1/2/99	Change %
Arabian International Construction	7/97	1,500,000	43	14.26	30.03	110.66
Egyptian Real Estate	9/97	1,400,000	56	80	138.89	73.61
Olympic Group	3/98	7,500,000	27	12.10	17.53	44.88
Oriental Weavers	2/98	2,500,000	19	58.4	84.00	43.84
Egytrans	10/97	120,000	4	18.25	22.89	25.42
Orascom Hotel Holdings	6/98	12,500,000	95	11	12.02	9.27
Cairo Precision Industries	1/97	300,000	17	85.50	90.01	5.27
Savola Sime Foods	11/98	6,250,000	25	22.75	22.75	0.00
El Ezz Gemma Porcelain	12/98	12,054,682	35	8.10	8.10	0.00
Miraco	9/97	24,168	1	75.60	72.71	-3.82
International Electronics	5/98	2,943,000	27	53.00	48.63	-8.25
Mena Tourist & Real Estate	3/98	300,000	22	35	27.48	-21.49
Alexandria Real Estate	6/98	600,000	23	153.9	121.92	-20.78
Shorouk Press	5/98	571,000	22	35	27.48	-21.49
International Foods	6/97	1,066,670	71	60	44.81	-25.32
OPTD I	9/97	10,661	3	59.86	38.67	-35.40
OPTD II	3/98	12,793	3	66.94	38.67	-42.24

Source: Financial Securities

develop the depth of its market, Egypt must simultaneously contend with the absence of regional harmonisation over transaction settlement periods, which will remain a considerable challenge in the absence of cross-listed securities. There is a need for standardisation of rules for new issues – to avoid creating a disparity which would allow issuers to take advantage of markets with the most limited listing requirements, which would in turn reduce information and lead to competition between stock exchanges. Uniformity is also required in the flow of information about companies, in which Egypt is generally regarded as lagging behind markets such as Oman and Jordan.

To develop as a regional leader will also require offering products not available elsewhere. Aside from the electronic and communications infrastructure, a regional market would require a facility for electronic payments, forward exchange, interest rate and currency swaps, as well as index-linked derivatives. These developments are some way off in the Egyptian market. Of more immediate concern, a shortage of foreign exchange in late 1998 and into 1999 caused anxiety among bankers, as it revealed the government's main priority as being to ensure that its macro target of maintaining the exchange rate was given precedent over the need of banks to service their clients in the face of the impact on liquidity. Equally, on the practical side, the need for adequate office space, a larger pool of experts, and a rigid system of surveillance fostering a transparent environment, are all vital. As a long-term strategy, a vital component necessary to offering products so far unavailable, but which are now envisioned by financiers in Cairo, is the creation of an offshore financial zone which would target multinational corporations, banks, insurance companies and accounting firms, whose activities would also complement the Egyptian domestic market. In the Egyptian context, strides are undoubtedly being taken firmly in this direction. What is now required is to ensure that the domestic market continues and provides the base which is Egypt's singular advantage over its potential regional rivals.

8 The insurance sector

History of the Egyptian insurance and reinsurance industry

In many ways the Egyptian insurance sector symbolises all the phases through which Egypt's economy has passed through in the twentieth century. From being created essentially for the benefit of foreign nationals living in the country, the industry expanded through joint ventures. In 1957, in the wake of the Suez crisis, the entire industry was Egyptianised in response to the souring of relations with Britain in particular. This was followed in 1961 with the nationalisation of the industry. In 1974, with the introduction of the *Infitah* open-door policy of President Anwar al-Sadat, the market was reopened to joint ventures within the free zones. In 1995, foreign companies were permitted to own 49 per cent of Egyptian insurance companies. In 1998, this was increased to 100 per cent.

The first insurance company to be established, the National Insurance Company, was created in 1900. Its establishment followed the arrival in Egypt of agents for European insurance companies in the late nineteenth century, notably Gresham of the United Kingdom and Assicurazioni Generali of Italy, which provided life and property assurance for foreign nationals living in Egypt. The industry grew both with the creation of new companies incorporated in Egypt, and with the arrival of foreign companies offering insurance. In 1920 the Alexandria Insurance Company was established, followed by the Al Chark Insurance Company in 1930 and the 25 per cent British-owned Misr Insurance Company established by Banque Misr in 1934.

It was only in 1939 that the first regulations governing the conduct of insurance companies were introduced, with the passing of the first insurance law. At the time of the revolution of 1952, over 150 other companies were operating in the Egyptian market. During the 1956 Suez crisis, British and French assets were seized, and the following year the assets of all foreign insurance companies were transferred to Egyptian companies. Two new national insurance companies were created, Al-Muttahedah, which incorporated the previously joint-venture companies L'Union, and Al-Goumhoureya replacing The Prudential, La Paternelle and Assicurazioni Generali. In 1958, the Egyptian Reinsurance Company was established, to which all the insurance companies then operating had to cede reinsurance business amounting to the reinsurance of 30 per cent of their premiums. The remaining 70 per cent could be reinsured with a foreign company, or be retained.

In 1961, all the companies were nationalised, a process which was followed by a drastic restructuring of the industry. Mergers between the 14 largest companies resulted in the creation of three state-owned companies, Misr Insurance, Al Chark Insurance, and National Insurance

THE INSURANCE SECTOR

or Al Ahly. The three companies' domination of the industry lasted until 1974, when the open-door policy allowed the creation of two new joint-venture companies to operate in the free zones. These were Arab International Insurance, established in 1976 with a 65 per cent foreign shareholding, and Egyptian American Insurance, established in 1977 as a 50-50 joint venture between the state-owned Al Chark Insurance company and AIG of the United States, and in which Al Chark is now selling its share.

The protection of the non-free zone market was confirmed in Law No. 10 of 1981, governing insurance supervision and regulation, and allowing the creation of new insurance companies with a minimum of E£2 million in paid-up capital. A freer environment prevailed in the 1980s, following the passing of Law 10, which saw the creation of four public-private companies. One, Suez Canal Insurance, had been created in 1979. This was followed by the creation of Mohandes Insurance in 1980, Delta Insurance in 1981, in which the state-owned Al Chark Insurance had a 16 per cent stake, and the 100 per cent privately-owned Pharaonic Insurance and Allied Investors Insurance companies in 1993.

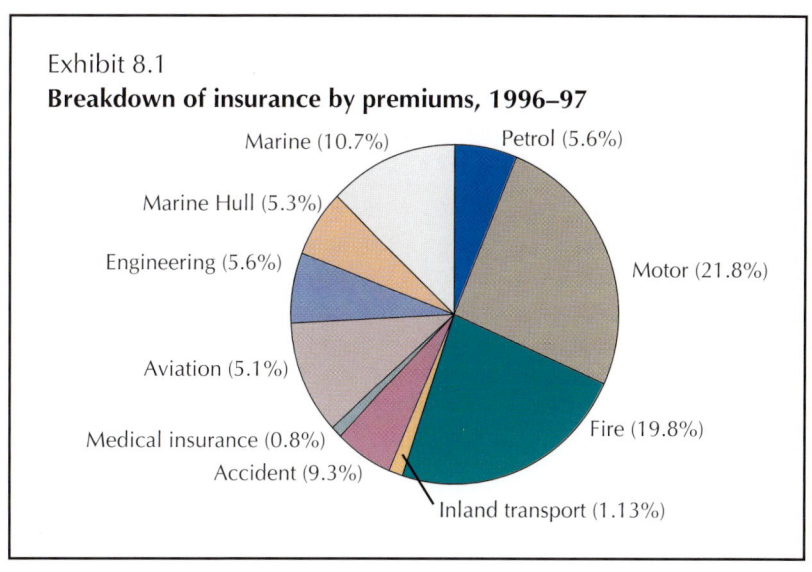

Exhibit 8.1
Breakdown of insurance by premiums, 1996–97

- Marine (10.7%)
- Petrol (5.6%)
- Marine Hull (5.3%)
- Engineering (5.6%)
- Motor (21.8%)
- Aviation (5.1%)
- Medical insurance (0.8%)
- Fire (19.8%)
- Accident (9.3%)
- Inland transport (1.13%)

The performance of the state and private companies

Ten direct insurance companies and one state-owned reinsurance company now constitute the Egyptian insurance sector, plus two operating solely in the free zone areas. Of the largest, three public sector companies have a 76 per cent share, with Misr Insurance having 37 per cent of the total market, followed by Al Chark with 26 per cent and National Insurance or Al Ahly with 13 per cent. Five joint-venture companies have a total market share of 24 per cent, with Suez Canal holding 7 per cent, Mohandes 6 per cent, Delta 5 per cent, Pharaonic 4 per cent and Allied Investors 2 per cent. In the free zones, Arab International Insurance has 85 per cent of the market, while Egyptian American has the balance.

The Insurance Federation of Egypt estimates that the insurance sector represents an average 1 per cent of GDP in Arab countries, compared with 6-12 per cent in G7 countries. In 1996–97, gross premiums experienced 1.9 per cent growth of E£1,76 billion, or E£955 million after reinsurance. Between 1993 and 1997 the industry experienced significant fluctuations in the value of premiums and the cost of claims. Income from premiums has seen a 595 per cent decline, from E£765 million in 1993 to E£110 million in 1997. Claims have risen by 97 per cent in the same period, from E£350 million to E£690 million. In 1996–97, the total income from premiums was E£1.76 billion (see Exhibit 8.1).

Exhibit 8.2
Direct premiums and net premiums by class of business, 1992–97 (E£ million)

	Direct premiums					Net premiums				
Class	1992–93	1993–94	1994–95	1995–96	1996–97	1992–93	1993–94	1994–95	1995–96	1996–97
Fire	211,878	252,963	285,863	284,243	278,100	89,053	109,826	138,719	140,185	110,561
Marine cargo	141,152	156,158	177,306	186,688	158,501	49,179	63,776	63,993	63,835	61,259
Inland transport	10,143	11,805	15,081	13,737	14,166	5,629	6,207	7,948	6,701	7,950
Marine hull	48,534	62,824	76,088	70,439	65,062	10,394	14,616	19,247	15,904	12,072
Aviation	66,918	60,299	58,255	54,032	54,827	37,776	26,513	25,668	24,752	28,747
Accident	89,969	107,250	122,780	146,662	135,095	48,849	57,741	63,008	63,730	72,852
Health	0	0	15,957	15,009	19,630	0	0	6,981	5,929	7,157
Engineering	94,861	121,040	82,554	84,479	94,585	11,297	12,615	11,980	14,814	12,592
Oil	0	0	88,859	92,179	76,836	0	0	8,296	4,570	6,896
Motor Act	65,178	68,528	83,956	95,546	101,637	45,288	47,348	61,540	73,776	76,148
Motor comprehensive	144,372	202,400	307,077	284,821	322,217	101,827	147,082	221,346	201,001	222,734
Total	**873,005**	**1,043,267**	**1,313,776**	**1,327,834**	**1,320,656**	**399,292**	**485,724**	**628,726**	**615,197**	**618,966**

Source: Egyptian Insurance Supervisory Authority, *Annual Report 1998*

Exhibit 8.3
Insurance and reinsurance companies consolidated balance sheet, 1992–97, (E£ million)

	1992–93	1993–94	1994–95	1995–96	1996–97
Assets					
Investments	5,508	6,538	7,561	8,635	9,598
Cash & deposits	67.2	77.9	103.5	143.2	131.7
Debtors	1,097	1,236	1,578	678.4	1,761
Other assets	42.9	49.8	61.4	1,022	84.3
Total	**6,715**	**7,902**	**9,305**	**10,479**	**11,576**
Liabilities					
Shareholder - rights	698.1	882.2	1,241	1,198	1,442
Policyholder - rights					
- Life	1,441	1,760	2,110	2,444	2,882
- Non-life	2,416	2,805	3,253	3,586	3,905
Commercial reserves	783.6	864.5	948.1	1,048	1,118
Creditors	1,375	1,589	1,751	2,202	2,228
Total	**6,715**	**7,902**	**9,305**	**10,479**	**11,576**

Source: Egyptian Insurance Supervisory Authority *Annual Report 1998*

The performance of individual companies has to be seen against the background of the industry being greatly underdeveloped. The Insurance Federation of Egypt estimates that the industry could grow by a factor of 10 within 10 years if privatisation takes place and the

THE INSURANCE SECTOR

industry succeeds in expanding the market by overcoming popular ignorance and cultural resistance to its products. Currently the federation estimates that the market in fire insurance is 5 per cent of what it should be, that less than 1 per cent of the population is insured against accident liability, and only 7 per cent of cars are insured.

Of the state-owned companies, Misr Insurance saw its annual net profit rise by 24 per cent, to E£141 million in 1997–98. This included a 1.2 per cent increase in profit from investments, most of which is in government and other securities. Al Chark Insurance saw net profit from non-life insurance increase by E£10.5 million or 8.66 per cent to E£132 million. For the private sector companies, profits have risen by between 10 per cent and 20 per cent. Dominating the strategies of the private sector companies is the need to expand their range of products in advance of both the privatisation of the state-owned companies, and the liberalisation of the industry, in accordance with Egypt's membership of the World Trade Organisation, which will take effect in 2002. Delta Insurance reported a net profit after taxes in 1998 of E£13.7 million, an 11 per cent annual increase. In 1997–98, Delta saw profits increase in all classes of business, and Mohandes Insurance saw a 24 per cent rise in net profit,

Total investments of the insurance sector amounted to E£10.4 million as at mid-1998

The Insurance Federation of Egypt estimates growth of the industry by a factor of 10 within 10 years

83

from E£8.6 million to E£10.7 million. For all the companies, the small size of the market remains the key hurdle to growth.

Legal reform in the insurance sector: prospects for international control or ownership

Legal reform of Egypt's insurance sector has evolved over almost a decade, since the need to revitalise the private sector's role in the highly underdeveloped industry became clear. The main turning point in the legal reform of the industry came with the introduction of Law No. 156 of 1998, which had the effect of updating and clarifying a variety of amendments introduced to Law No. 10 of 1981. Prior to the introduction of Law 156, the status of the state-owned insurance companies had been similar to those of the state-owned banks, although owing to the history of the insurance companies the process was less complicated, as amendments had already opened the market to foreign involvement prior to the decision to allow full privatisation. Law No. 156 of 1998 was essentially designed to bring the public insurance sector into parity with the provisions affecting the public banks. The law amended Law No. 10 of 1981, the Law for Insurance Supervision and Regulation, which had been amended in 1991 to allow foreigners to own 49 per cent of the state-owned insurance companies. Law 156 increased this proportion to 100 per cent. The legal change in 1998 also allowed foreigners to take all the seats on the boards of directors of the insurance companies. It also stated that if a single individual or institution wanted to buy 5–9 per cent of the company it must notify the insurance industry regulator, and that permission must be sought if a stake were to reach 10 per cent or more.

Two decrees issued by the Ministry of Economy followed the introduction of Law 156, and were intended to improve the practical framework for the sector, which has been accused of inefficiency. Decree No. 356 of 1998 explains how investors should go about notifying the regulator of the intention of buying the 5 or 10 per cent stakes in the insurance companies. The second, Decree No. 45 of 1999, was intended to address the problems of claimants in receiving payments from the insurance companies. The decree was an amendment to the executive decree, Decree No. 362 of 1996, and created a framework for policy holders' rights and claims from the companies.

Further to the legislative changes affecting the industry, the three public sector insurance companies and the Egypt Reinsurance Company have employed A.M. Best of the United States, the international insurance rating agency, to assess their condition in advance of their valuation, as one step towards privatisation. Misr Insurance was awarded an A rating, while Al Ahly and Al Chark were both awarded A- ratings. Egypt Reinsurance was awarded a B++ rating. The Ministry of Economy has asked seven international investment banks to submit proposals for the valuation and privatisation of the four companies, while one of the banks will evaluate the proposals. Meanwhile, all of Egypt's insurance companies will become subject to internationally recognised Insurance Accounting Standards.

The prospect of international control or ownership of Egypt's insurance companies has certainly increased with the passage of laws allowing this to take place. The key question facing foreign insurers will be whether the Egyptian market is one which, given the degree of underdevelopment, is worth trying to expand. From the perspective of the companies now operating, two issues are regarded as vital to determining the future growth of the industry: income levels, and the distribution of national wealth. As with the provision of social insurance, the growth of the commercial insurance market will take place against a 5.1 per cent to 5.3 per cent GDP growth rate which has yet to break the cycle of poverty in which large numbers of Egyptians continue to live, and which deem the government-run social insurance schemes both viable and vital. According to the figures of the Ministry of Insurance and Social Affairs, 65 per cent of Egyptians are considered poor, meaning they earn E£4,168 per annum per household, or E£814 per capita per annum.

These figures will severely limit the expansion prospects of the commercial insurance market. Equally, they provide a background against which competition with the established companies will be launched. With 224 branch offices, competition against Al Chark insurance, for example, will be a formidable task, particularly in the area of life insurance. The state companies know the market, and it will take a major effort to unseat them from their dominant position. However, the state sector is itself reckoning on expansion possibilities, stemming from the growing realisation among the population that religious objections to insurance are misplaced. In advance of a broadening of the market, state interference in the setting of rates has now been abandoned, and the state-owned companies are themselves looking to expand their market in advance of any competition.

Clearly there is certainty that competition will arrive, and that with the legal changes foreign ownership or control will become a major factor. Already, Egypt's leading private sector bank, Commercial International Bank (CIB), has entered into a partnership with Legal & General of the United Kingdom to establish an insurance service based on the CIB branch network. Other banks and financial intermediaries are planning to do the same, further pressuring the state-owned companies to modernise and streamline, so that by the time their privatisation looms they will be well placed to tap a market which currently attracts around 5 per cent of the people insurance industry practitioners estimate are potential clients.

Valuing the state sector for privatisation

The first moves towards the valuation of the state sector insurance companies was made in 1998, when discussions were opened with seven international investment banks with experience in the privatisation of the insurance sector, with a view to their submitting proposals for the valuation and privatisation of the four companies, Misr Insurance, Al Chark Insurance, National Insurance and Egypt Reinsurance. Misr Insurance, the largest of the four, is expected to be privatised first, on the grounds that selling the most successful company would have the greatest benefit to the market. Merrill Lynch and Morgan Stanley have been contracted to carry out the evaluation, and HSBC is acting as adviser to the government. Merrill Lynch is expected to work on the assessment of Misr Insurance and National Insurance, while Morgan Stanley is expected to work on Al Chark Insurance and Egypt Reinsurance Company. The valuation is expected to be completed by the beginning of 2000. The insurance companies are to retain specialised accountants to work alongside the investment banks on the actuarial analysis, which relates the value of the assets to the provisioning policy used. Central to the analysis of asset value will be an assessment of the value of real estate assets held by each company. As the real value of property is difficult to assess, due to the difficulties faced by landlords in the definition and enforcement of property rights, the evaluation procedure is expected to be lengthy, lasting as long as six months for each company. Misr Insurance puts its market capitalisation at around E£5 billion. Al Chark, which is expected to be privatised last, estimates its value at around 10 times its capital of E£250 million, so at around E£2.5 billion. The government is examining several options as to the most suitable method of evaluation, and has yet to state whether it will be an insurance company or Egypt Reinsurance which will be the first to be privatised. By June 1999 none of the four state-owned companies had been privatised.

Domestic savings and the capital markets: the role of insurance funds

Most financial intermediaries now conducting business on the Egyptian capital markets regard the funds available to the insurance companies as a vital and lucrative resource for overall growth of the market. Total investments of the insurance sector amounted to E£10.4 billion by mid-1998, a 10.6 per cent rise on the previous year. This figure has subsequently increased with the launch of a E£100 million investment fund by Misr Insurance. The Egyptian securities market accounts for 29 per cent of insurance company investment. Pressure for this figure to be increased has mounted. Law No. 10 of 1981 states that not more than 50 per cent of policy-holders money can be invested in bank deposits, and not more than 30 per cent can be invested in the stock market, while free reserves can be freely invested. Some insurance companies themselves believe the amount able to be invested on the stock market ought to be increased to 50 per cent of their profits. Already the proportion of securities represented in the investment portfolio of Misr Insurance is 38 per cent. However, other companies regard the most appropriate forms of investment as being long-term Treasury bills, and prefer the creation of new investment companies in which they have a controlling stake, to investment in securities. The variety in investment strategies is marked. During the stock market downturn in 1998, when the Egyptian Stock Exchange (ESE) lost 34 per cent, Misr Insurance continued to invest in shares, regarding itself as a national investment institution as much as being an insurance company. The private sector Mohandes

THE INSURANCE SECTOR

Exhibit 8.4
Insurance companies' investments, 1992–97, (E£ million)

	1992–93	1993–94	1994–95	1995–96	1996–97	1997–98
Government bonds	2,755	2,743	2,839	2,825	1,877	2,301
Securities and shares	428.5	1,302	1,327	1,483	2,781	3,276
Real estate	168.5	180.3	313.9	479.3	521.5	535.9
Mortgages	1.7	28.1	27.1	0.9	0.9	
Loans to policyholders	31.6	34.9	36.4	41.3	45.3	515.5
Other loans	92.1	87.6	95.4	113.2	100.5	825.1
Fixed deposits	2,029	2,161	2,921	3,691	4,271	4,207
Total	**5,507**	**6,538**	**7,561**	**8,635**	**9,598**	**10,472**

Source: Egyptian Insurance Supervisory Authority *Annual Report 1998*

Insurance Company, on the other hand, stopped buying shares altogether. It had been buying across 45 sectors, and had invested in 67 companies, and nine mutual and equity funds. These investments had brought its portfolio up to E£261 million, E£80 million of which is in shares, the balance in bonds and T-bills.

The investment patterns of the insurance companies are clearly a key factor in determining the strength and weakness of the Egyptian capital markets (see Exhibit 8.4). In 1996–97 E£4.2 billion (44.6 per cent of the total invested) of the insurance sector's investments was in fixed deposits, while E£1.8 billion (19.6 per cent) was in government bonds, E£2.7 billion (29 per cent) was in securities, E£521 million (5.4 per cent) in real estate, E£45 million (0.4 per cent) in loans to policy-holders, E£930,000 (0.1 per cent) loaned in mortgages and the balance of E£100 million (1 per cent) in other loans. Private insurance fund investments amounted to E£4.5 billion in 1997, of which E£2.5 billion (55 per cent of the total invested) was invested in government bonds, E£1.3 billion (31 per cent) was in deposits, E£236 million (5 per cent) was in securities and shares, E£185 million (4 per cent) was in real estate, E£122 million (3 per cent) was issued as loans to members, and E£70 million (2 per cent) was in other investments. The scale of investment by each company reflects the relative size of the 10 companies, as well as the greater investment power of the state sector. Misr Insurance accounts for 42 per cent of total investment by the insurance sector, with total investment of E£4 billion (see Exhibit 8.5). Al Chark has a 21 per cent share, with E£20 billion invested, and the third state company, National Insurance, has a 13 per cent share with E£12 billion invested. The total investments of the private sector companies amount to E£899 million. Mohandes is the

Exhibit 8.5
Investments by companies, 1996–97

- Misr (42%)
- Al Chark (21%)
- National (13%)
- Suez Canal (2%)
- Mohandes (3%)
- Egyptian American (1%)
- Delta (2.7%)
- Pharonic (1%)
- Allied Investors (1%)
- Arab International (1%)

Source: Egyptian Insurance Supervisory Authority, *Annual Report 1998*

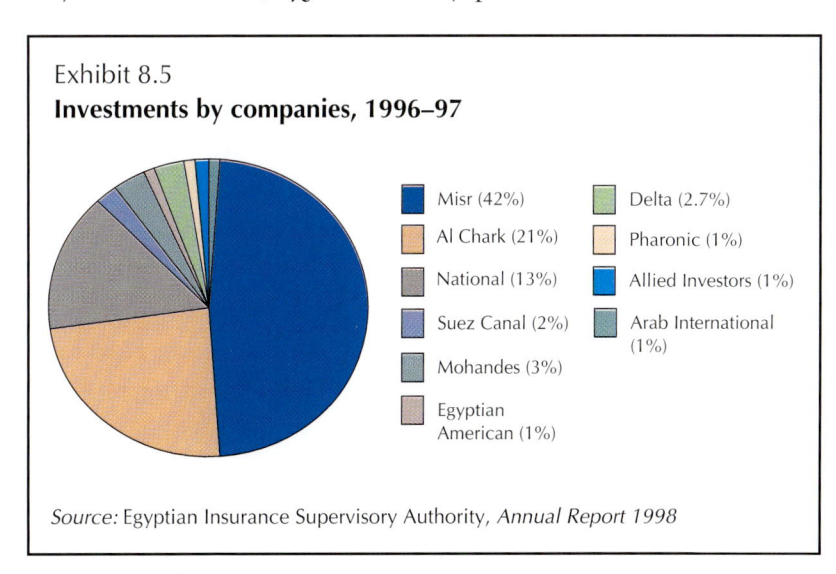

most heavily invested, with a total portfolio valued at E£261 million, or a 3 per cent share of the total sector. Next is Delta with a portfolio valued at E£227 million (2.7 per cent of the total), followed by Suez Canal Insurance with an investment portfolio of E£166 million (2.02 per cent).

Opinion varies greatly as to whether the 30 per cent limit on the investment in the stock market should be raised. It is already higher than the limit in many G-7 countries. Within the more conservative state-owned companies, there is a strongly held view that the insurance companies are not responsible for the success of the capital markets, and that the opportunity to invest in the capital markets should be viewed entirely from the perspective of potential profits for the insurance sector rather than as an obligation. This view is not shared by others within the industry, in particularly within Misr Insurance, which is the fifth largest financial institution in Egypt, and regards itself as a major player in the broad economic development of the country. The call from investment bankers, that this limit should be raised, stems in part from the history of the companies' investment strategies.

Before the 1974 *Infitah* or open-door policy, the state insurance companies had no discernible investment strategy. Consequently, their substantial funds were put in deposits. This led to the accumulation of substantial funds, the size of which was essentially revealed when the Open Door policy allowed for their investment. In the meantime, the creation of private sector insurance companies exposed the disparity in assets between the state and private companies, and led to the initial calls for the state companies to play a greater investment role. Such calls have become a tradition among investment bankers, while being resisted among the more conservative of the insurance companies for fear that they will not be able to meet their obligations to the policy-holders. Safeguarding the interests of policy-holders is enshrined in the much-amended Law 10, which demands that all the companies present their balance sheets to the Egyptian Insurance Supervisory Authority, the industry regulator. Increasingly, however, as the insurance sector is liberalised and the state sector prepares for privatisation, discussion over whether to invest at all will be replaced by decisions as to which sector to invest in.

For the life insurance industry, the most convenient channel for investment is regarded as being long-term T-bills, which are likely to continue to dominate the portfolios of all the companies, particularly with the 10- and 15-year government securities now being offered. New companies are also likely to be established by the insurance companies, while real estate is regarded by the insurance companies as the least attractive investment, due to oversupply. All the state insurance companies have substantial real estate investments, mostly in property which is rented out. As property laws prevent rents from being increased, the attractiveness of this sector is fading, as maintenance costs for buildings now exceed rent income. In 1997 fixed-term leases were introduced for new properties, but the benefits of this legal change for established property owners is limited.

9 The banking sector

Banking sector reform: ensuring institutional stability

A major success of Egypt's wide-ranging economic reform process has been the retention of a steady pace of change without any serious banking sector problems. This is a significant achievement in the context of a sharp fiscal contraction-led reduction in inflation, with the consequent contraction in banking sector activity. To reduce the hurdles to banking sector activity in the early years of the economic stabilisation programme, the government eliminated credit and interest rate controls, and lifted curbs on fees and commissions. It also opened the banking sector to foreign banks, which are now allowed to deal in foreign currency. At the same time significant steps were taken which would not only ensure stability during the transition, but would strengthen the banking sector as it moves into a new era of diversification and competition.

The guidelines provided by the 1975 and 1983 Basle concordats and the Basle report of 1988 on banking supervision and regulation are the foundation upon which Egypt's banking system has evolved since the early 1990s. The Basle standards were clarified in Law No. 101 of 1993. The necessity for such provisions had started to influence banking practice in Egypt earlier, however, with the creation of joint-venture banks in the mid-1970s, involving foreign banks whose operations were already conducted on the basis of the conventions. With a view to strengthening banking supervision, on and off-site supervision manuals have been revised, with technical assistance from the US Agency for International Development (USAID) and the European Union. The system includes monitoring of indicators that are furnished in a systematic way to the Central Bank of Egypt (CBE). Among the indicators monitored are provisions for capital adequacy and concentration of loans. Banks are individually monitored, and the system allows the tracking of a problem detected in one bank throughout the banking system.

The three areas of prudential supervision dealt with in the Basle conventions – liquidity, solvency and foreign currency positions – have been increasingly rigidly applied in the Egyptian banking sector. The CBE has made it clear that it will not allow banks to enter into new activities if they lack adequate capital. All banks operating in Egypt, with the exception of local branches of foreign banks, are now required to respect the minimum 8 per cent risk ratio laid down by Basle.

Between 1991 and 1993, a total of six sets of regulations were issued by the CBE to ensure that prudential measures were observed. In December 1990 the banks were ordered to maintain a liquidity ratio of 20 per cent of local currency and 25 per cent of foreign currencies.

THE BANKING SECTOR

In January 1991, the requirement of an 8 per cent capital adequacy ratio was ordered. In September 1991, this was followed by an order that banks classify and provision their assets and contingent liabilities in accordance with World Bank guidelines. In 1993, banks were prohibited from having claims against one client in the form of either credit facilities or ownership of capital, which exceeded 30 per cent of the bank's capital base. Further, banks were disallowed from maintaining more than 10 per cent of a short or long-term position in any single currency, while the total short or long-term currency positions should not exceed 20 per cent of the bank's capital base. In 1991 the CBE ordered all banks under its supervision to reach the 8 per cent capital adequacy ratio by, at the latest, 1995, depending upon the extent to which they were below that limit when the order was issued. This date limit was later brought forward to 1993. It was later announced that this limit would be increased to 10 per cent by 1996, though it is not the case that the banks have now reached this target.

Moves towards compliance with CBE regulations governing the internal practices of the banks have greatly enhanced the banking sector's depth and the ability to adapt to a changing climate. Several key factors have also brought a deepening of the banking sector, which have further enhanced its credibility during the era of reform. A reflection of the health of the system has been the spread between the lending and deposit rates. In its Egypt country report of September 1998, EFG-Hermes shows that following the liberalisation of interest rates, spreads initially widened to reach a peak of −5.14 per cent in 1994. By 1997 this had declined to −3.83 per cent. This decline in spreads reflected the improved intermediation of the banking sector, an improvement further enhanced by the fact that it had not resulted from any reductions in the legal reserve requirements. The stabilisation period of the early 1990s, also saw a reversal in dollarisation, from 42.69 per cent in 1992 to 19.64 per cent in 1997. This growing sense of confidence in the currency was enhanced by the increased repatriation of assets, which saw the total value of private transfers rise by 36 per cent between the period 1990–91 and 1997–98, from US$2.5 billion to US$3.5 billion. Further confidence in the banking system is reflected in the low cash/deposit ratio, which has remained relatively low and fallen by 1.85 per cent since 1992, to 13.32 per cent in 1997. The focus on fiscal restraint and external debt reduction has given banks a freer hand to develop their own strategies, despite interest rates remaining at 12.25 per cent throughout 1998. By driving inflation down to its current level of around 3.6 per cent, banks have been spared a degree of uncertainty and allowed credit to grow.

Two major developments have tested the stability of the banks against the background of reform. The introduction of Law No. 5 of 1998 affecting the profit banks could accrue from investment in government securities, caused a marked reaction within the banking sector. The Unified Tax Code limited tax exemption on Treasury bill income to T-bills bought with company or bank funds. Exemption was lifted on T-bills bought with loans above the company or bank's net worth, thereby ending the double tax exemption banks had previously enjoyed. The interest paid on these borrowings have had to have been offset against tax. This aspect of the loophole had effectively allowed double tax exemption, as the interest on borrowings for these purchases was tax free, while interest earned on T-bills and time deposits also enjoyed tax

THE BANKING SECTOR

exemptions of 100 per cent and 90 per cent respectively. Cairo banks had strongly criticised the government for announcing that changes were imminent, without providing details of the calculations which would be used to assess liability. Consequently, banks had been forced to set aside substantial provisions in advance of the new law being applied. While many banks saw profits rise in 1998, in the case of Commercial International Bank (CIB), Egypt's largest private sector bank, this had led to a 30.5 per cent drop in first-quarter results. It ultimately appeared that some banks had over-provisioned in advance of the closure of the loophole. The law does allow tax exemption up to the level of a bank's net worth, which was not expected when the law was first discussed. It assesses net worth on the basis of paid-in capital plus reserves plus related earnings, and assesses the level of the non-self-financed portion of their stock of T-bills on the basis of investments in T-bills less equity. Taxable income is assessed on the basis of total income from T-bills less administrative costs. The tax level is 20 per cent.

Ultimately, the banks weathered the storm caused by the long period between the announcement of the law and its introduction several months later. A second factor to have exposed the banks to pressure was a shortage of foreign currency in late 1998 which continued into 1999. The shortage stemmed from a 9 per cent rise in imports in 1997–98, which led to a 15.1 per cent rise in the trade deficit. The CBE and the government did not want to draw upon the US$20.3 billion in

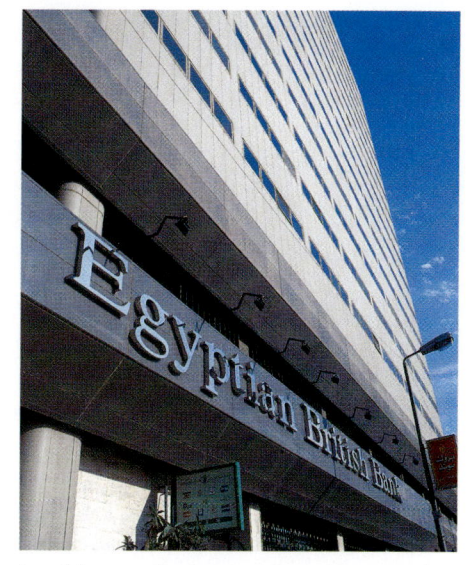

Looking to the future, Egyptian British Bank hopes to expand its retail operations and bring vital expertise to the banking sector

A major success of Egypt's wide-ranging economic reform process has been the retention of a steady pace of change without any serious banking sector problems

foreign exchange reserves retained by the CBE, interest from which is held in a special account for use in time of crisis. Consequently, banks were forced to draw upon their own foreign exchange reserves held with banks abroad. The shortage led to the growth of an informal foreign exchange market, which saw the value of the currency fall by 2 per cent, from the official rate of E£3.41 to the dollar, to E£3.48. The CBE responded in December 1998, by releasing US$1 billion of funds from the state-owned banks onto the market to meet the demand.

New competitive practices

Dominating the strategy of liberalisation in the banking sector has been the assumption that the competitive advantages enjoyed by the state banks have to be reduced. An important early step in this direction was taken in 1992, when public sector companies were authorised to deal with all banks without prior permission from a public sector bank. Further steps were then taken to generate greater liquidity in the sector in 1992 and 1993, when ceilings on bank lending to the private sector and bank-specific ceilings on lending to public sector companies were removed. The greater role enjoyed by the joint-venture and foreign banks has borne fruit, as reflected in a variety of performance measures. Based on a limited sample of asset-employee ratios, the IMF concludes that the joint-venture banks and local branches of foreign banks appear more efficient than the state commercial banks. According to the IMF, for every E£15 million of assets, the state commercial banks have five employees, compared with three for the joint-venture banks and one for the foreign banks.

Levelling the playing field in the banking sector has been most apparent in the process of divestment by the state banks of their shares in the joint-venture banks, although this process has been slower than originally anticipated. The four state-owned banks were ordered in 1996 to reduce their stakes in the 23 joint-venture banks to a maximum 20 per cent. Progress towards this target has been slow and patchy, although momentum in this direction has been maintained. By December 1998, the National Bank of Egypt (NBE) was the only one of the four state-owned banks to have reached this target, having sold stakes in the three joint-venture banks in which it had previously held more than 20 per cent. Most significantly, this involved NBE's reduction of its 42 per cent stake in CIB to 23 per cent, and the reduction of its stake in Credit Internationale d'Egypte from 51 per cent to 31.5 per cent. NBE has also reduced its stakes in five other joint-venture banks, in which it had held less than 20 per cent. NBE's stake in the 11 joint-venture banks in which had an interest has now been reduced from an average 20.1 per cent to an average 10.7 per cent.

Banque Misr, which had stakes in three joint-venture banks exceeding 20 per cent has reduced these stakes to below that level in all but one. Its average stake in 10 joint-venture banks in which it had an interest has been reduced from 23.5 per cent to 12.4 per cent, having sold its entire remaining stake in three of the banks. Bank of Alexandria while still holding more than 20 per cent in two joint-venture banks, has sold its stakes in others. The bank has reduced its

Exhibit 9.1
The four state-owned banks' holdings in joint-venture banks, as a percentage of total shares*

	NBE	Banque Misr	Banque du Caire	Bank of Alexandria	Total share
Alexandria Commercial & Maritime Bank					00.00
Commercial Arab Bank				9.75	9.75
Banque du Caire et de Paris			22		22
Cairo Barclays International Bank			40		40
Cairo Far East Bank			29		29
Commercial International Bank	19.61				19.61
Credit Internationale d'Egypte	19.50				19.50
Egypt Arab African Bank					00.00
Egyptian American Bank				35.33	35.33
Egyptian Gulf Bank					00.00
Egyptian Saudi Finance Bank	7.69		8.50	7.39	23.58
El Togarioun Bank	17.00	16.02	16.50	9.70	59.23
Export Development Bank	11.46	11.46	11.46	10.08	44.46
Housing & Development Bank	0.01			0.01	0.02
Islamic Bank for Investment & Development	19.96	20.00	20.00	20.00	79.96
Misr America International Bank			32.80		32.80
Misr Exterior Bank		19.50			19.50
MIBank		24.80			24.80
Misr Iran Development Bank				37.50	37.50
Misr Romanian Bank		33.00			33.00
National Bank for Development				0.01	0.01
National Société Générale Bank	18.00				18.00
Suez Canal Bank	4.59	0.019	0.07	0.01	4.69

* As at 30 May 1999

Source: IBTCI

average stake in the 12 joint-venture banks in which it had an interest from 20.75 per cent to 10.8 per cent, and sold its entire stake in two banks. Banque du Caire's stakes in 13 joint-venture banks have been reduced from an average holding of 24 per cent to 13.8 per cent, having sold its entire stake in four banks, and retaining more than the 20 per cent limit in four banks.

The four state-owned commercial banks have retained an average holding of 24 per cent in the 23 joint-venture banks (see Exhibit 9.1). Their combined holdings in 12 of these banks remains above the critical 20 per cent limit deemed the upper limit necessary for private sector shareholders to exercise a sufficient degree of control to make a meaningful difference to bank management. This ongoing state sector influence in the joint-venture banks, coupled with the state sector's own control of 60 per cent of bank deposits, 70 per cent of assets and 65 per cent of loans, gives the state-owned banks considerable ongoing influence in the sector, despite attempts to dilute it.

Until the privatisation of one or more of the state-owned commercial banks, competition is unlikely to be marked by a broad realignment of the sector. Instead, competition is increasingly to be seen in the expansion of the product base in both the state and private sector banks. The expansion of the capital markets, particularly in investment banking, has led banks to reassess their strategies with a view to assessing their own role in light of the expansion in the number and range of non-bank financial intermediaries. Consequently, all the banks are looking to widen their retail base, with a view to moving away from reliance on cheque accounts and deposits and to meeting demand for personal loans, mortgages, insurance products, guaranteed investments, long-term deposits, individual retirement plans and credit cards. Among some non-bank intermediaries there is the view that the growth in the corporate bond market stems from the failure of some banks to provide a follow up service for their customers. The lending patterns of banks is criticised by investment bankers for lacking a strategic vision, with short-term lending often evolving into medium-term lending, which has hampered the growth of the small businesses most in need of long-term lending by banks.

Foreign banks

The progress of activity by foreign banks operating in Egypt is set against the ongoing review of the extent to which the banking sector as a whole should be exposed to influence and control by institutions over which the CBE has limited power, and whose resources and expertise could allow them to compete successfully with Egyptian banks. The Egyptian banking sector currently comprises 64 banks, of which four are public commercial banks, and 24 are private and joint-venture commercial banks, two are real estate banks, one is an industrial development bank, one an agricultural bank, 11 are joint-venture businesses and investment banks, and 21 are branches of foreign banks. Changes within the status of the foreign banks began with Law No. 120 of 1975, which allowed foreign banks to operate in Egypt under one of three criteria. They could form a joint venture with an Egyptian bank, within which the foreign bank would be restricted to a maximum 49 per cent holding. Or they could establish a wholly-owned foreign branch, from which they would not be allowed to operate in local currency dealings, and were thereby restricted essentially to providing trade finance and letters of credit. Finally, they could open representative offices in Egypt, from which they could not operate any banking activities, and would be restricted to operating purely to represent the interests of the parent bank. This legislation was modified by Law No. 101 of 1993, which allowed foreign banks which had established wholly-owned branches in Egypt to conduct local currency business, provided they had a minimum capitalisation of US$15 million. The law was further modified with the passage of Law No. 97 of 1996, which allowed those foreign banks which had formed joint ventures with Egyptian banks to increase their shareholding to 100 per cent.

The legal status of foreign banks has yet to be fully clarified in the legislation regarding the regulatory powers of the CBE over these banks. The responsibility for maintaining the liquidity of a wholly-owned branch of a foreign bank operating in Egypt, as well as safeguarding the rights of depositors, remains the responsibility of the regulator in the country of origin of the branch's parent bank, while the general supervision of the branch is the responsibility of the CBE. The CBE is the regulatory body of the joint-venture banks.

The opportunity for foreign partners to buy majority stakes in the joint-venture banks has been the single most important aspect of their developing role in the Egyptian banking sector. Dominating the view among the more established foreign banks operating in the country, is the basic assumption that it is a mistake to bring banking personnel from abroad, and that it is far better to train local staff. Complementing the local industry, the foreign banks regard themselves as vital in bringing their knowledge of processes and procedures, risk assessment strategies, and portfolio and treasury management techniques to the Egyptian market. The assumption is that the market will become more sophisticated as it becomes more liberalised, requiring the ability to manage foreign currency exchange exposures through currency swaps on behalf of Egyptian companies.

Competition within the banking sector is likely to intensify in response to the growing role of foreign banks. In addition to those already established, Citibank is to resume operations in Egypt, a move which is certain to accelerate moves by all the banks to try and take a larger share of the relatively untested retail banking area. The strategies of the foreign banks now present in Egypt vary widely, however. Among the Swiss banks, UBS and Credit Suisse are not planning moves beyond their traditional areas of private banking, leaving commercial banking to the joint-venture foreign banks. UBS also has a mandate to manage US$100 million of CBE funds and has been managing assets of Egyptian commercial banks since it opened its office in Cairo in 1997, from which it is not permitted to engage in commercial or retail banking operations. The wholly-owned branches of foreign banks are expecting to adapt their strategies in response to the growing trade finance operations of local banks. Foreign banks have found the credit terms of local banks difficult to compete with, limiting foreign involvement to large-scale projects such as the private sector Sidi Krier power project and GSM mobile telephone systems currently being operated and expanded in Egypt. Foreign banks have looked for advisory and investment banking roles in the launch of private sector IPOs, but have generally found the volume of business disappointing. Only 17 private sector IPOs have been conducted between January 1997 and June 1999. Ten of these issues were managed by EFG-Hermes, three by Intercapital Securities, one by CIIC, one by Egyptian-Anglo, one by NBE and one by FINBI-Shawki, all of them local companies. Consequently, the foreign banks remain patiently awaiting the privatisation of the utilities, banks and insurance companies, in which they hope their extensive resources and global reach will secure them mandates.

Exhibit 9.2
Foreign banks' representative offices in Egypt

	Date registered
Al-Raghi Banking and Investment Corp.	10/93
Bank of New York	10/93
Société Générale	2/94
United Bank Limited	2/94
Kriess Bank	3/94
Bankers Trust Company	4/94
Banque Nationale de Paris	4/94
Commerz Bank	5/94
Crédit Commerciale de France	6/94
Monti dei Paschi di Siena SPA	7/94
Union de Banque Arabes et Françaises (UBAF)	8/94
Dresdner Bank	8/94
Arab American Bank	9/94
State Bank of India	10/94
Deutsche Bank AG	11/94
Habib Bank Limited	3/95
Banca Commerciale Italiana	3/95
Crédit Agricole Indosuez	7/95
Arab Islamic Bank	12/95
Chase Manhattan Bank	8/96
Arab Banking Corporation	1/97
Bank of Tokyo Mitsubishi Limited	3/97
Union Bank of Switzerland	10/97
Banque Française de l'Orient	3/98
Credit Suisse	3/98
First Union National Bank	5/98

Source: Central Bank of Egypt

Investment banking in Egypt: a new business

Intense rivalry in Egypt's financial services sector has been replaced by a growing realisation that cooperation is vital if the expected growth in the size of deals being handled is to be met with the optimum degree of talent available in the Egyptian market. A total of 200 companies are now operating under Law No. 95 of 1992, which allowed for the creation of non-bank financial intermediaries. Of these, three are operating as investment banks, while 142 are registered brokerage firms, 48 provide underwriting services and nine operate as mutual fund management companies. With the downturn in the stock market in 1998, investment banking came to the fore as a major element in the financial services sector, as it allowed the companies which had developed this sector to fall back on income which had contracted in the areas of brokerage and asset management (see Exhibit 9.3). Among financiers there is now an emerging view that the entire financial services sector must start to be regarded as an industry which, in the not too distant future, should be contributing 2–3 per cent of GDP. Investment banking is expected to play a key role in this development, as the scope of services offered by investment bankers, as well as the growing size of deals with the privatisation of utilities, mergers and acquisitions within manufacturing industry, and structural changes within the financial sector itself, will create new opportunities for the provision of investment advice and banking services.

The structural changes within the economy as a whole are the most important single element which will lead to a major growth in the investment banking sector. By 2002, Egypt will adhere in full to the directives of the World Trade Organisation. The impact on Egyptian industry is expected to be significant, leading to mergers and acquisitions. By that time, the privatisation programme is expected to be well advanced. Consequently, the role of government within industry will have greatly diminished. While the role of investment banks in private sector business has so far been limited largely to initial public offerings and private placements, this is expected to change as the newly privatised companies face the need for restructuring in the face of the competition certain to emerge from WTO membership. Similar change will result from the establishment of a partnership with the EU which Egypt is expected to sign this year following lengthy negotiations. The agreement will open up the Egyptian market to competition from EU countries, further intensifying competitive pressure on Egyptian companies.

Against a background of anticipated change in manufacturing industry, Egypt's investment banking business has sought to both consolidate and to grow. Even so, the business remains concentrated in a few hands. In 1998, EFG-Hermes, which has a leading position in Egyptian investment banking as well as having 16 per cent of Egypt's brokerage market and substantial interests in asset management, earned E£100 million from its investment banking operations, in what was considered a poor year. This accounted for 50 per cent of total company earnings, up from an expected 38 per cent, due largely to low brokerage and asset management earnings in the market generally. Research into the company by Merrill Lynch anticipates that around 50 per cent of its investment banking income

Exhibit 9.3
EFG-Hermes – revenues from investment banking, 1998–2000, (E£ million)

	1998	1999*	2000*
Transaction revenues	28.7		
Expenses	6.2		
– General administration	3.2		
– Bonuses	3.0		
Pre-tax profit	22.5	28.0	38.0
Tax	4.7		
Effective tax rate (%)	21		
Net profit	17.8	28.0	38.0

*Expected

Source: Merrill Lynch

THE BANKING SECTOR

will come from equity issues, 30 per cent from mergers and acquisitions advisory and 20 per cent from debt products. All three are expected to show growth this year and in the near future. In the wake of growing competition for the handling of privatisations, during which fees dropped, the company expanded its business in the private sector arena. Maximum fees charged by investment bankers for privatisations total 1 per cent of the value of the transaction, while in the private sector it is around 4 per cent, which is less than in other emerging market standards. This shift in company emphasis, as well as its extensive contacts within the Egyptian market, has allowed EFG-Hermes to compete favourably with foreign companies seeking business in the country. The company's reputation recently secured it a mandate in a consortium with Merrill Lynch, to lead manage the sale of minority stakes in Egypt's seven state-owned electricity generation plants. The deal will begin with the sale of 20 per cent of Cairo Electric Company, which will lead to the valuation and sale of the other companies, whose aggregate value is US$12–14 billion. The sale will be the largest single offering of state assets as part of the privatisation programme. Such prospects have encouraged EFG-Hermes to consolidate its investment banking business, and the company will rarely now accept deals worth less than US$30 million. The average size of equity deals now being handled by the company is from US$40–50 million, though this is expected to reach US$90–100 million in 1999.

EFG-Hermes' main rival in the investment banking arena is CIIC, formerly the investment banking arm of Commercial International Bank (CIB), but which now has a varied group of investors among which NBE is the largest single institutional shareholder. Investment banking income doubled for the company in 1998, mostly from fees. Most significant in the consolidation of the company was the merger in March 1999 of its brokerage arm, Intercapital Securities, with the UK-based Robert Fleming's Egyptian brokerage operation Fleming Mansour. CIIC, which is capitalised at E£600 million (US$176 million) and has handled business worth E£5.5 billion (US$1.6 billion) since its establishment in 1994, has a local client base which foreign companies have found difficult to match without a well-established local partner. The merger of the companies will allow CIIC access to Fleming's regional network. Alongside the creation of the new brokerage operation, CIIC is to spin off its asset management operations to the new Fleming CIIC operation, capitalised at US$100 million and will also develop the group's corporate finance arm.

The emergence of two strong local investment banks has overshadowed the activities of other similar institutions in the market. This has become more so since CIIC and EFG-Hermes have worked jointly on at least one IPO in recent months, heralding a new era of cooperation.

The structural changes in Egyptian industry are expected to broaden the market for other players. Currently, the market is regarded as one in which the private sector has used the investment banks simply to issue bonds and pay off debt. Financiers now expect convertible bonds to be issued in the near future, widening the expertise required of the investment banks. It is hoped by foreign banks with investment banking operations in Egypt, that with greater depth to the market there will be a greater opportunities for banks who lack the local contacts of the domestic banks to be able to play a greater role than is currently the case, by offering the more sophisticated services that are presently absent. The international reach and long experience of HSBC Investment Banking, UBS, Deutsche Bank and others now seeking business in Egypt, are anticipated by these banks to hold the promise of their future expansion. To date their role has been limited by the grip the local operations have had on the Egyptian scene. All three remain convinced that, despite their small market share, their day will come, and that in the meantime it is worth their while remaining in Egypt, as researchers into the evolving industrial sectors, allowing emerging market strategists to assess investment decisions which all remain convinced would not be correctly assessed without a permanent staff in Cairo.

The decision by the Ministry of Public Enterprise in September 1998, to employ investment banks to promote and underwrite the sale of the remaining 214 companies earmarked for privatisation, is a major potential boost to the investment banking industry in Egypt. A total of 56 companies each paid E£5,000 for application forms to qualify for the business of promoting and underwriting the shares of companies to be privatised through the stock market, as well as searching for strategic investors. Thirty-eight companies were selected, among them 12 leading global investment banks.

The prospects for privatisation and mergers

The privatisation of Egypt's four main commercial banks remains a cornerstone of government policy, despite slow progress in that direction. Major legal hurdles allowing the privatisation have been passed, albeit in the face of criticism and concern from parliamentarians. The government has pursued the policy despite the criticism, convinced that the privatisation of at least one of the four commercial banks is an essential element in the liberalisation of the economy as a whole. The intention remains for more than one of the state-owned banks to be sold, though current government strategy envisages the sale of a minority stake in one bank in the near future. The passage of Law No. 155 of 1998 allowed for a private sector stake in the state-owned banks. Executive regulations following the introduction of Law 155 have further clarified how a public sector bank would be transferred to the private sector after the sale of any part of the bank's capital. The regulations also clarify what information a potential investor will have to disclose to the government when seeking partial ownership of one of the state-owned banks. This information will have to include the investor's nationality, what holdings are held in other companies, and what secondary holdings the investor has in other financial institutions.

The privatisation of the state's banking interests has moved further ahead in the joint-venture banks in which the state-owned banks have substantial shares. The four state-owned banks were ordered in 1996 to reduce their stakes in the 23 joint venture banks to a maximum 20 per cent. By December 1998, NBE was the only one of the four state-owned banks to have reached this target, having sold stakes in the three joint-venture banks in which it had previously held more than 20 per cent. Banque Misr, which had stakes in three joint-venture banks exceeding 20 per cent has reduced these stakes to below that level in all but one. Bank of Alexandria still holds more than 20 per cent in two joint-venture banks, though has sold its stakes in others. Banque du Caire's stakes in 13 joint-venture banks have been reduced from an average holding of 24 per cent to 13.8 per cent, having sold its entire stake in four banks, and retaining more than the 20 per cent limit in four banks. Negotiations are now ongoing for the sale of public sector stakes in three joint venture banks. The sale of Banque du Caire's 32 per cent stake in Misr American International Bank is currently under discussion. The 79.96 per cent stake held in three tranches of 20 per cent and one of 19.96 by the four state-owned banks in the Islamic Investment and Development Bank remains controversial. All four banks are within the 20 per cent limit, but with their combined holdings have secured a tight state grip on the bank, which is regarded as a sign of poor commitment to the universal liberalisation of the banking sector. A similar situation prevails with the El Togarioun Bank, in which the four state commercial banks currently have a 59.23 per cent share, sale of which has been discussed only occasionally.

Bank merger remains an issue that is rarely discussed, despite suggestions that NBE may merge with CIB. The likelihood is remote. Some suggestions that the desired reduction in the number of state commercial banks to three, could be achieved by a merger of two of them, is no longer mentioned.

Competition to bank lending: the capital markets' impact on the sector

Growing private sector confidence in the institutions of the capital markets has brought with it a wide range of companies across all sectors ready to exploit this source of finance. According to CBE figures, total bank lending to the private and public business sectors in 1998 stood at E£141 billion. Of this, E£112.39 billion was with the private sector. Of the E£29.3 billion with public sector companies, 60–70 per cent is estimated by the IMF to be doubtful or bad debt expected to be settled from privatisation proceeds. The private sector accounted for 82.7 per cent of the increase in available domestic credit in 1997–98, as its use of credit increased by E£24.4 billion, bringing its credits up to E£112.39 billion, or 53.1 per cent of the total, a 10 per cent rise on 1996–97. The disparity between the public and private sector credit position stemmed largely from the government having settled the debts of many public sector companies. The credit position of some of the largest private sector companies has forced them to seek alternative sources of finance, and increasingly this need has led them to the capital markets. Between January 1997 and January 1999, 17 previously family-owned private sector companies issued shares on the ESE. A total of 49 million shares have been issued in this period by private sector companies, worth a total E£1.14 billion at the offering price, with an average 8 per cent increase in value during this period. Of increasing importance has been the growth in the corporate bond market, which is expected to grow in importance in the coming months and years. In four years the corporate bond market has grown from zero to an active market of 23 issues worth E£2.7 billion. In the first eight months of 1998, the value of trading in bonds increased by 88 per cent, from E£390.6 million in 1997 to E£734.7 million. In late 1998, six bond issuers announced the payment of coupons ranging from 8–9 per cent.

An essential element in the evolving relationship between the banking sector and the capital markets has been an entrenched mentality which has influenced perceptions of these two aspects of the financial system. The state's dominance of the banking sector has traditionally been accompanied by suspicion of private sector investment banks. This is most vividly displayed in the legislation governing the banks introduced in the 1960s and leading to nationalisation of the sector. A side-effect of state control was the engendering of suspicion of the private sector. With the launch of the *Infitah* or economic open-door policy in 1974, a partial easing of this mentality took place, as foreign banks established successful joint ventures with the Egyptian public sector banks. But it was Law No. 95 of 1992 which marked the real break with the past, by allowing wholly-owned private sector financial intermediaries to be licensed. Even so, the legacy of the historic evolution of the financial sector is reflected in the view that the banks and the private financial sector are in competition. In fact, the banking sector's share of economic activity has barely been touched by the growth of the capital markets. Banks saw their credit to the private sector grow by 10 per cent in 1997–98, despite the growth of the capital markets. Banks are regarded by the Capital Market Authority (CMA) as the short-term lending complement to the capital markets as the source of long-term finance. From the point of view of investors, the attraction of the capital markets in this context is clear. In 1998, 73 of the 100 most actively traded stocks saw an increase in profits ranging from 0.4 to 586 per cent, with 50 per cent of these stocks realising a minimum 13 per cent increase, far higher than the bank deposit rate which stood at between 9 per cent and 11 per cent for much of 1998.

Most bankers do not currently regard the capital markets as competition, though others expect it to become so over time. But the reaction of the banks will be clear. Most are now developing strategies for the broad expansion of retail banking, which will allow them to compensate for any loss in the lending services to which most currently restrict themselves. From the perspective of the CBE, there is acceptance that any strategy for developing the banking sector will be dominated by the emergence of the capital markets as the primary source of long-term finance, which banks should be prepared to support by providing working capital. This change will meet with the approval of key reformers in the market, who regard the banking sector as having for too long been the source of long-term finance, which has had a negative effect on balance sheets. In the meantime, banks are expected to establish merchant banking and other fee generating activities, which in 1998 generated 81 per cent of non-interest income for Misr International Bank, 71 per cent for CIB, 68 per cent for Egyptian American Bank, and 78 per cent for National Société Générale Bank. With extensive untapped areas still potentially open to the banks, the prospect of their activities both deepening and widening is clear, with growing capital markets engendering greater transparency and generating greater private sector activity from which the banks will undoubtedly benefit.

Exhibit 9.4
Banks' total assets and investments in Treasury bills and bonds, September 1998, (E£ million)

	Investment in T-bills and bonds	Total assets	Return on T-bills and bonds	T-bill as % of total assets
Joint-venture/private banks				
Egyptian Gulf Bank	255	2,209	26	11.5
El Watany Bank	304	2,888	24	10.5
Misr Iran Development Bank	14	1,221	2	1.2
United Bank of Egypt	30	1,646	5	1.8
Banque du Caire et de Paris	171	1,240	14	13.8
Delta International Bank	377	1,824	33	20.7
MIBank	216	9,149	62	2.4
Egyptian British Bank	627	2,735	22.9	26.5
Alexandria Commercial and Maritime	80	1,299	10	n/a
Egyptian Industrial Development Bank	n/a	2,060	n/a	n/a
Egyptian Housing Bank	n/a	5,472	1	n/a
National Société Générale Bank	527	4,089	50	12.9
Misr Exterior Bank	560	5,947	73	9.4
Egyptian Commercial Bank	40	1,396	4	2.8
Crédit Internationale d'Egypte	153	965	13	15.9
Suez Canal Bank	423	8,258	70	5.1
Cairo Barclays International Bank	236	2,213	24	10.7
Export & Development Bank	292	3,830	67	7.6
Arab Land Bank	n/a	5,421	1	n/a
Egyptian Saudi Finance Bank	284	1,809	17	15.7
Egyptian Workers Bank	n/a	n/a	n/a	n/a
Misr Romanian Bank	194	1,643	20	11.8
National Development Bank	918	5,823	n/a	15.8
Misr American International Bank	123	1,010	10	12.2
Egyptian American Bank	462	4,920	65	9.4
SAIB	n/a	n/a	n/a	n/a
Arab African International Bank	n/a	1,030*	n/a	n/a
Cairo Far East Bank	44	375	3	11.8
El Mohandes Bank	749	4,414	52	17.0
Commercial International Bank	701	13,278	103	5.3
Total	**7,907**	**99,084**	**815**	
State banks				
National Bank of Egypt	10,834	62,273	507	16.5
Bank of Alexandria	2,142	19,220	188	11.1
Banque du Caire	3,471	32,484	209	10.7
Banque Misr	7,594	51,136	523	14.9
Total	**24,041**	**165,113**	**1,427**	
Grand total	**31,948**	**264,197**	**2,242**	

* In US dollars
Source: IBTCI

The development of micro-credits: the small and micro-enterprise unit

Despite the existence of 64 banks in Egypt, with a total of 2,325 branches, the Ministry of Economy estimates that institutional finance reaches about 5 per cent of the total number of people for whom such access would create the potential for the level of business growth necessary to meet the needs of a growing workforce. By 1998, around US$560 million had been provided on preferential terms or as grants to small and medium enterprises through donors, non-governmental organisations (NGOs), and the Social Fund for Development (SFD), established to compensate for the impact of economic stabilisation and structural reform. Central to the government's calculations has been the need to create an annual economic growth rate of 7 per cent by which 550,000 new jobs will be created every year until 2017. This rate of job creation is necessary to soak up new arrivals to the employment market. It is estimated that 59 per cent, or 325,000, of these jobs will have to be created in small and micro-enterprises (SMEs). It is accepted within the government that it will not be possible to achieve this target unless existing and potential SMEs are provided with greater access to credit finance. Consequently, the development of a greater banking role in the expansion of SMEs is now regarded as vital to the success of the broader economic policy objectives. To this end, the financing of SME projects is now under scrutiny, with the purpose of matching the resources of the banks with the needs of the small businesses.

Central to any assessment of how the banks should develop their role in energising the productive capacity of the vast number of people for whom investment capital is unattainable, is an evaluation of the assets of the section of the population in question. A study in 1997 by the Egyptian Centre for Economic Studies calculated that the value of informal real estate holdings, by implication the holdings of the poorest members of Egyptian society, account for 64 per cent of the total real estate value and estimated at that time at E£241.1 billion, or 94 per cent of 1997 GDP. The scale of so-called 'dead capital' is clearly substantial. Realisation of the potential value to the economy is now emerging, and the need to formalise land and property titles creates the greater possibility of facilitating credit on the basis of fixed securities, which would allow investment finance to reach a larger population whose economic worth has been both hindered and undervalued.

To harness the potential productive power of the SMEs to the macroeconomic picture, the Ministry of Economy is now assessing first the legal impediments to alleviating this situation, and second the measures necessary to enact as a means of redrawing the relationship between creditor and lenders. SMEs are often perceived as high risk, due to the absence of feasibility studies and business plans. Meanwhile, the collateral they may be able to offer against a loan, is subject to consideration of the prohibitive expense of collateral recovery and the tortuous process of legal proceedings. Added to this, banks retain strict levels of securitisation, which SMEs are rarely able to meet. The small businesses have also traditionally suffered at the hands of a banking system which, since nationalisation in the 1960s, has favoured lending to large-scale public enterprises. The large state-owned banks, therefore, are generally ill-equipped to deal with requests for credit from SMEs, lacking as they do, the project appraisal and supervisory capacities required. Where loans are made, they are usually on a scale which is in excess of the needs of many of the SMEs, owing to the existing lending terms and conditions of the largest banks, which require collateral most SME practitioners cannot offer owing to the absence of legal title to property and the tendency to rent business premises. Credit from banks to SMEs currently stands at around 6 per cent of total lending, while 92 per cent of small enterprises have never obtained a loan from any bank, and 78 per cent have never sought to borrow from the banks. The figures are higher for micro-enterprises.

To address the needs faced by small and micro-enterprises, the Ministry of Economy is now recommending the introduction of incentives to banks prepared to extend loans to SMEs. The proposals will be to offer tax holidays and soft loans, as well as helping facilitate the establishment of new branches in close proximity to borrowers. Schemes are also being considered to cover the initial costs of investments, the establishment of guarantee funds, and to provide assistance to banks in obtaining soft loans from other sources. Legislative changes are being considered with a view to redressing the balance of banking service, which currently places small and micro-enterprises at a serious disadvantage. The conditions upon which SME loans are made are also under review, as are the supervisory requirements for such loans.

Retail financial products: personal credit, loans and mortgages

In response to the growth in the capital markets, all of Egypt's leading joint-venture and state-owned banks are seeking ways of developing retail business in advance of a contraction in long-term lending as commercial clients seek investment finance through bond and share issues. None of Egypt's banks has developed a range of retail products which in any way reflects the market potential. Hampering this growth is a legal environment which favours borrowers rather than lenders, and gives little security to banks in event of default. Until now, the determination of banks to expand operations in the face of reduced margins from corporate customers has led to the expansion of the safer areas of retail. Consequently mutual funds, private banking and a growing determination among insurance companies in partnership with banks to widen their range of services, has broadened the retail business. Egypt's 20 local mutual funds currently have US$1.4 billion under management, while CIB is developing a partnership with Legal & General of the United Kingdom to offer insurance policies. Retail banking is seen by some banks as the only area of expansion left to the banks, particularly the state-owned institutions which had in the past focused their operations on providing credit to public sector companies. But among the state-owned banks progress has been slow. As with the joint ventures, they have started their move into retail by developing plans to offer credit cards, as well as installing Automatic Teller Machines (ATM) at many branches. NBE currently has 70 per cent of the market in credit cards, and aims to have 200 ATM machines installed by 2001.

Exhibit 9.5
Commercial banks' lending and discount balances by economic activity, 1995–98, (E£ million)

	3/95	6/95	3/96	6/96	3/97	6/97	3/98
Total lending	**78,326**	**81,755**	**96,878**	**99,491**	**115,454**	**116,654**	**125,626**
Total in local currency	62,171	65,267	76,750	78,444	89,014	87,645	91,577
Agriculture	1,197	1,205	1,270	1,289	1,536	1,672	1,967
Industry	20,727	21,837	25,512	25,901	27,832	28,555	31,401
Trade	13,455	13,929	17,997	18,540	23,481	24,082	26,128
Services	11,796	12,694	15,204	15,639	17,718	18,102	20,438
Unclassified	14,996	15,602	16,767	17,075	18,447	15,234	11,643
In foreign currencies	16,155	16,488	20,128	21,047	26,440	29,009	34,049
Agriculture	124	132	156	202	171	177	256
Industry	6,649	6,468	7,795	7,977	10,435	11,182	12,614
Trade	3,395	3,443	4,556	5,040	5,934	6,709	7,342
Services	4,479	4,770	5,660	5,804	7,621	8,470	10,796
Unclassified	1,508	1,675	1,961	2,024	2,279	2,471	3,041

Source: Central Bank of Egypt

Analysts regard Egypt's public sector banks as both ideal for the expansion of retail services, as well as inappropriate institutionally to the development of these services. A lack of expertise will hamper this growth, despite the state-owned banks having a total branch network of 866, which places them in a strong position to develop a retail customer base. Imagination and energy are clearly key to making a move into retail banking a success, owing to the need for aggressive marketing.

Egyptian American Bank, which has 29 branches concentrated in northern Egypt, is about to start lending for mortgages which will entitle the developer of a property to retain the title deed until the bank has been repaid. Non-payment would give the bank the right to the property. EAB launched a car-loans programme last July, and currently has 800 loans with personal and corporate clients, as well as those arranged through car dealers. EAB also has seven ATMs and is planning to install a further 16, as well as planning telephone banking to allow customers to arrange transfers by telephone, and to launch a local currency credit card in the near future.

CIB is aiming to increase its number of retail clients, with the launch of seven credit and debit cards. Misr International Bank (MIBank) is intending to shift its strategy away from a purely corporate image, in response to the fact that its conservative reputation has attracted an increasing number of retail clients, whose deposits form around 50 per cent of total deposits. The bank responded by launching a mutual fund, installing five ATM machines, and making plans to open four sub-branches in residential areas. More aggressive in the search for retail clients is Nationale Société Générale Bank (NSGB). The bank has appointed two staff specifically responsible for retail banking. NSGB is to launch car financing, mortgages and share financing this year. The bank is also to install six ATM machines, and link its ATM network with a group of banks, whose customers will be able to use ATMs from all banks within the group.

Most banks accept that the retail sector will compensate for expected drops in earnings from areas which are likely to become incorporated into the remit of the non-bank capital markets institutions. However, the transition for the banks is not expected to be easy, owing to the lack of skills in marketing, the slow growth in personal incomes, and the leap from providing cheque and deposit accounts, to evaluating clients for personal loans and mortgages. Parliament has been debating a mortgage law, which is a crucial element in the array of retail products and will provide a boost to the real estate market. Most banks considering a move to retail, have been struggling to find viable mortgage products owing to the legal hurdles. The recent arrival of Citibank in the Egyptian market is regarded by leading bankers as a major sign of the retail potential, as well as being seen as providing a lead for others to follow.

10 Privatisation

A summary of six years of privatisation

The readiness of the Egyptian state to remove itself from the centre of economic activity has been the litmus test by which the government's commitment to broad economic liberalisation has been judged. Legislation which brought the restructuring of the public sector in advance of the current programme of privatisation, was introduced to extract 314 public sector companies from the auspices of a 1983 law which had defined their primary role as being one of providing jobs, to being a profit-oriented businesses in which private shareholders would be allowed to invest. Law No. 203 of 1991 was the government's response to an increasingly dire economic situation facing the public sector.

By 1991, the productivity of the public sector was declining by 3 per cent annually. In 1996, when the privatisation programme began in earnest, 34 per cent of the workforce was employed by the government, with four million people being employed in the central and local government and service authorities, 960,000 in public enterprises, and 500,000 in the public economic authorities.

The public enterprise sector, from which the 314 companies were drawn for privatisation, accounted for 10 per cent of GDP and employed 6 per cent of the total workforce prior to the privatisation programme being launched. Law 203 aimed to increase the commercial orientation of the public enterprise sector, initially by de-linking the 314 companies from the ministries under whose auspices they fell and grouping them into first 27 then 17 holding companies, which would restructure them in preparation for privatisation. In 1996, 100 of the 314 companies were unprofitable. Aggregate profits of E£1.2 billion in 1990 had slipped by 71.4 per cent to E£0.7 billion six years later, during which time unit labour costs rose by 16 per cent. The IMF calculated that during the period in which the public sector companies were to be restructured for privatisation, their competitiveness declined by 86 per cent in five years, a factor which had contributed significantly to the difficulty in increasing exports.

The first phase of privatisation, from 1993–96, saw six 'Law 203' companies sold to anchor investors, 15 majority stakes sold as public offerings, 10 companies sold to employees and five more companies added to the list of six liquidations which had taken place in 1991–92. In 1997, 13 majority stakes were sold, six companies were liquidated, 11 sold to employees and four sold to anchor investors. With the economic downturn beginning to bite, the pace of privatisation slowed in 1998, and government targets failed to be met, despite a further four companies being sold to anchor investors, 11 to employees, three sold as majority public

PRIVATISATION

offerings and a further 12 companies being liquidated. By the end of 1998, a total of 118 companies had been through one form of privatisation or another. A total of 46 majority public offerings had been carried out, either as public offerings or sold to anchor investors, minority stakes had been sold in 20 companies, 25 had been bought by employees and 27 had been liquidated. In the process, the government had earned E£12.36 billion from privatisation. E£6.49 billion was earned from majority sales through public offerings, E£3.04 billion from asset sales or liquidations, E£2.21 billion from minority sales through public offerings and E£613 million from sales to employees (see Exhibit 10.1).

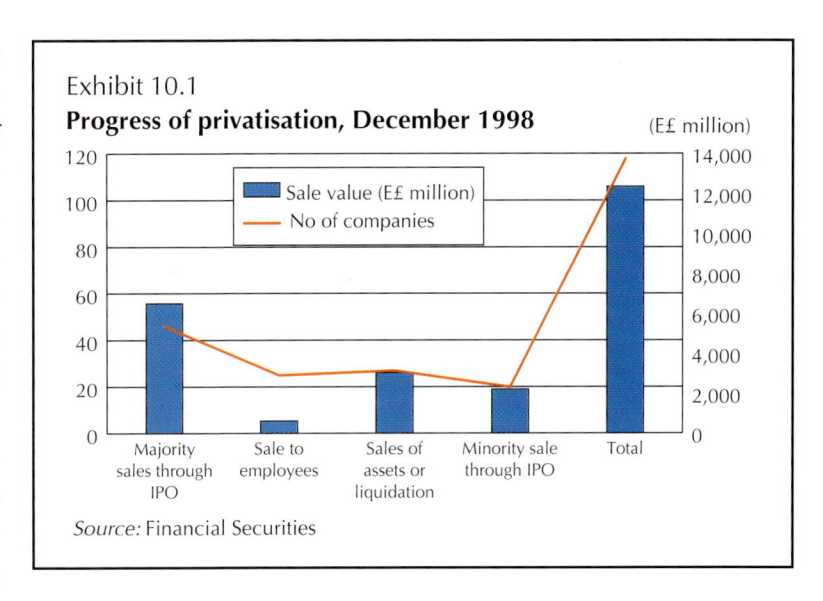

Exhibit 10.1
Progress of privatisation, December 1998 (E£ million)

Source: Financial Securities

Dominating the process of privatisation has been the evolving relationship between the pricing of the privatisation stock and the turbulent condition of the market. The ministerial Privatisation Committee took a major step towards adding further impetus to the privatisation process in September 1998, when it approved applications from 38 of a total 56 local and foreign investment banks which had responded to invitations to apply to promote and underwrite the remaining 214 Law 203 companies earmarked for privatisation. The decision to outsource the handling of the privatisations was a major step, indicating how far the government had gone towards accepting the role of capital markets institutions in pursuing its liberalisation policies. Until then, the fees charged by investment banks had acted as a deterrent. But the difficulty of privatising the less attractive stocks which are what remain of the Law 203 companies, requires greater skill and more aggressive marketing than that available to the government Public Enterprise Office. The emerging difficulty of remaining within the privatisation timetable the government set itself in 1997, is one of the factors which led to the decision to employ investment banks to handle the sales. In November 1997 the Privatisation Committee increased the number of companies earmarked for sale before the end of that year by 30, to 106. A further 50 were then slated for offerings during 1998. None of these targets was achieved. In 1998, 30 companies went through the privatisation process, but majority stakes were sold in only three companies, while four were sold to anchor investors. In 1999, a total of 66 companies are to be offered for sale, 62 of them between January and June. In 48 of these, more than 51 per cent of shares is to be offered, and in 38, 100 per cent of the shares will be sold.

By injecting a new level of expertise into the privatisation process, the government is clearly adapting in a realistic fashion to the needs of a public industrial sector from which most of the attractive stocks have already been sold. Equally, the professional advice it is now seeking is expected to hinder the temptation to overprice in the interest of maintaining broad popular support for the privatisation programme. In February 1998, the government sold a 17 per cent stake in the Egypt Aluminium Company, pricing the shares at E£71.25 per share based on the estimated future price of aluminium. The sale failed to be fully subscribed, having been deemed overpriced by investors, and the share price has fallen by 43.13 per cent since the offering. The investment bankers handling the sale had recommended a lower price, but officials insisted that at E£71.25 the sale would inject new life into the stock market. The issue highlighted the debate over the role of the government within the privatisation process, centering on whether it should be viewed as a privatisation authority committed to forming long-term relationships with investors, or as a seller wanting to maximise revenue.

The consensus among brokers is that the government is now very much acting as a seller, which has now accumulated proceeds of E£13.7 billion from sales. Pricing remains a thorny issue, and the government is regarded by brokers as having achieved a greater degree of sophistication as the process has developed. However, the process is occasionally criticised for failing to build up a total picture of a stock's value by incorporating not only account cashflow, net asset value and the multiple of earnings, but also a sense from the market of what price is accurate. Brokers want the government to establish a valuation floor, which will allow offers for discount purchases to be made. The government remains reluctant to respond to offers at discounts to the floor, and consequently has not encouraged such a floor to be established. The slackening pace of privatisation in the last quarter of 1998, during which no sales took place, is regarded by some investment bankers as having exposed ongoing shortcomings in the valuation process, leading to the conclusion that there remains little commitment to selling at whatever going price the market dictates.

Privatisation in the financial sector

With the passage of the Banking Law (Law No. 155 of 1998) the private sector is allowed to own shares in the public sector banks, heralding a new chapter in the privatisation programme by opening the state-run financial sector to the prospect of private sector ownership.

This major change had been prefaced by an instruction in 1996 to the public sector banks that they must sell their shares in the public-private joint-venture banks, so they would no longer hold more than 20 per cent of the shares in these banks. Despite this being a cornerstone of the privatisation effort in the financial sector, by December 1998, only National Bank of Egypt (NBE) had reached this target, having sold stakes in the three joint venture banks in which it had previously held more than 20 per cent. Most significantly, this involved NBE's reduction of its 42 per cent stake in Commercial International Bank to 23 per cent, and the reduction of its stake in Crédit Internationale d'Egypte from 51 per cent to 31.5 per cent. NBE has also reduced its stakes in five other joint-venture banks, in which it had held less than 20 per cent. NBE's stake in the 11 joint-venture banks in which it had an interest has now been reduced from an average 20.1 per cent to an average 10.7 per cent.

Banque Misr, which had stakes in three joint-venture banks exceeding 20 per cent has reduced these stakes to below that level in all but one. Bank of Alexandria still holds more than 20 per cent in two joint-venture banks, though has sold its stakes in others. Meanwhile, Banque du Caire's stakes in 13 joint-venture banks have been reduced from an average holding of 24 per cent to 13.8 per cent, having sold its entire stake in four banks, and retaining more than the 20 per cent limit in four banks. The four state-owned commercial banks have retained an average holding of 24 per cent in the 23 joint-venture banks. Their combined holdings in 12 of these banks remains above the critical 20 per cent limit.

Changes to the legislation governing the public insurance sector, were designed to bring the sector into parity with the provisions affecting the public banks. Law No. 156 of 1998 allowed the private sector to buy up to 100 per cent of shares in the state insurance companies. It also amended existing laws, to allow foreigners to control up to 100 per cent of the currently state-owned companies, as well as allowing them to take all the seats on the boards of directors of the insurance companies.

The next big challenges: infrastructure and telecommunications

Consistent with the broader economic policy target of increasing exports by 11 per cent, as an essential element in the drive to achieve sustainable economic growth of 7–8 per cent, the government has sought ways of improving transport infrastructure. Ambitious schemes for the private sector to build new motorway links, which would offer rapid transport between major cities, are currently under consideration. More advanced, however, are plans to increase the number of provincial airports by a further six being offered to the private sector on the build-own-operate-transfer system. Four of these projects are advanced to various stages at El Alamein, Marsa Alam, Ras Sidr and Dahab. The construction of these private sector airports has been accompanied by pressure for the liberalisation of domestic and international air routes. The monopoly currently enjoyed by Egypt Air has remained in place, and there are no plans for the state-owned airline to be privatised. Attempts by private carriers to offer alternatives have had limited success. The Cairo Air Company, a private company operating regular and non-regular passenger and cargo flights, has a licence to operate on routes which had until recently been served only by Egypt Air.

The pace of liberalisation within infrastructure sectors heretofore dominated by the state, has been determined to a large extent by the specific ministries charged with their reform. While the electricity sector has, in consequence, seen rapid and transparent reform, the same has not been the case in the transport and communications sector. Even so, the monopoly once enjoyed by Telecom Egypt (formerly ARENTO), has started to crack. First came Telecom Egypt's issuance of two licences in 1997 to establish and operate nationwide public payphone systems of 20,000 lines each to be established within five years. Telecom Egypt, 20 per cent of which may be sold on the stock exchange at an as yet unspecified date, has simultaneously sought a private sector role in its bid to achieve a 50 per cent increase in the number of fixed telephone lines to 10 million by 2002. It now has agreements with three foreign companies to improve infrastructure. Contracts for the improvement of services in specific areas of the country have also been awarded, with a view to a nationwide upgrade. NEC of Japan is currently installing 81,000 lines in Upper Egypt, and is expected to install digital public switching systems on the Red Sea and Mediterranean coasts.

Spreading the benefits of private sector participation nationwide has also led the government to invite bids for private sector ports, airports and roads. A private sector built and operated hub container port capable of handling one million units a year is now being negotiated for a site east of Port Said. The port is likely to lead to private sector management of Damietta and Port Said ports in concert with the new hub. In 1998, the government substantially reformed the legal environment governing port and maritime activities. Law No. 1 of 1998 allows for private sector participation in the maritime transport sector. Reform of the sector will complement the planned expansion of Egypt's port facilities, where the private sector is playing an increasingly important role. A E£500 million 20 million square metre port is to be established at Ain el-Soukhna, on the western coast of the Red Sea south of Suez. The Specialised Ports Law of 1996 was also amended and new decrees regulating maritime transport activities and licensing were issued to facilitate private sector competition. Plans to offer the Damietta and Port Said Container Handling Companies for privatisation, as part of the same process of liberalisation in the industry, were postponed in January 1999, to allow multinational operators to begin operations at several ports in Egypt in advance of their possible sale.

How have privatised companies benefited from privatisation?

The process of privatisation has raised many questions as to how the specific details of the programme have affected the fortunes of the 314 companies earmarked for sale, of which shares in 118 have now been offered. Strictly speaking, many have not been privatised, as the proportion of shares sold was small, and even in many majority sales the state remains the largest single shareholder in around 50 per cent of the companies. Of the 118 companies to have gone through the privatisation process, majority stakes in 46 were sold as initial public offerings, while 20 were sold as minority IPOs. The remaining 52 were either sold to employees or liquidated. Of the 118 sold, shares in 56 were being traded on the Egyptian Stock Exchange by February 1999. Of these 56 companies, 33 had reported increased profits by the end of 1998. The increases in profit varied widely, ranging from a 0.47 increase for the Alexandria Cement Company, in which the government had sold 21 per cent of its shares, to a 230 per cent rise in profits for the Nasr Dried Agricultural Products Company, in which the government had sold 61 per cent of its shares. The average increase in profits among those companies which saw a rise was 45.9 per cent. Among the 23 privatised companies which saw a decline in profits in 1998, the average profit/loss ranged from 0.55 per cent for the Upper Egypt Flour Mills, in which the government had sold 61 per cent of its shares, to a fall in profits of 549.36 per cent in Telemisr, in which a 66 per cent government stake had been sold. Analysis of the profit and loss of privatised companies does not reveal any clear pattern as to whether companies in which the government reduced its stake significantly, necessarily benefited from a proportionately greater private sector role, compared with companies in which the government retained a majority stake or was the largest single shareholder. Of the 46 companies sold as majority IPOs, 23 showed a profit in 1998 ranging from 3.04 per cent to 230.77 per cent, with an average increase of 26 per cent. Among those in which a majority stake was sold, 14 showed a decline in profits in 1998, of between 0.55 per cent and 549.36 per cent, an average decline of 56 per cent.

The privatisation programme has moved through stages which have seen the pricing strategy alternately dominated by the government's wish to make money from sales, to it having regarded its role as that of a creator of the market to which the privatisation can contribute vibrancy and liquidity. Recently, the government has decided that its role is that of a seller, to which the E£13.3 billion proceeds so far from privatisation are a key source of income allowing the restructuring of companies earmarked for sale. Cairo brokers generally expect a continued slow down in the pace of privatisation, as the condition of the companies remaining for sale becomes less attractive. The government intends to seek management contracts with private sector companies to allow the restructuring of these companies prior to sale.

The impact of privatisation on the private sector

The general health of the private sector, assessed in view of the impact of the reduced public sector role and the varied performance of the formerly public sector companies once they have joined the private sector, has been one of steady growth. The wealth of the private sector measured in terms of deposits is one indicator of the impact of the changing private-public relationship. In mid-1996, a month after the landmark sale of Nasr City Housing, total local and foreign currency deposits of the private business sector stood at E£22.6 billion, while those of the public sector stood at E£17.8 billion. By October 1998, private business sector deposits stood at E£38.7 billion, and those of the public sector at E£17.3 billion, a private sector increase of 71 per cent. The private sector, including those Law 203 companies which have joined its ranks, now accounts for 65 per cent of GDP, a steady rise which suggests that the impact of privatisation on the private sector has been absorbed by private business with little shock. Between 1995 and 1998, a total 3,811 new private sector companies were established in Egypt, with a total investment of E£15.8 billion. The rise in total investment has been marked – with a 52 per cent rise in 1995–96, a 217 per cent rise in 1996–97, and a 3 per cent rise in 1997–98. The new strength of the private sector is a clear sign of its new-found energy, only a relatively minor proportion of which is accounted for by the mixed fortunes of the newly privatised companies themselves.

11 Infrastructure and project finance

The implementation of build-operate-transfer projects, 1995–99

Economic and demographic imperatives drive Egypt's need to radically reform the methods by which infrastructure is upgraded to meet both current and future needs. To secure the project finance necessary for the implementation of the large-scale infrastructure projects necessary to meet these needs, the government has moved rapidly towards extensive use of the build-own-operate-transfer (BOOT) and build-operate-transfer (BOT) systems. Legal moves to allow BOOT and BOT concessions to be granted were a major element of the 1998 legislative programme. Law No. 18 of 1998 allowed for the creation of BOT contracts for electricity distribution companies and distribution stations, as well as allowing for the valuation of the assets of the generating stations and the grids, while also setting up a regulatory authority to supervise operations. Subsequently, Law No. 22 of 1998 allowed for general and specialised ports, as well as quays on existing ports, to be established and run through BOTs and concessions, which could be granted to both foreign and local investors. Both systems allow the private sector to construct and earn a profit from projects, which then revert to the government after an agreed period of up to 50 years. Extensive use of this method of project development in the construction of airports, roads and power generation facilities is now well developed, covering a wide geographical range and lying behind the launch of numerous projects of various sizes.

The attraction for the government of the BOOT and BOT schemes needed to be balanced by the wish of the private sector to become engaged in sectors which had traditionally been dominated by state-owned industries, but which broadly remain state controlled. Key to engineering the success of the BOOT and BOT schemes has been the need to create financial packages which lure investors. Egypt has evolved its use of the schemes on the basis of financing packages which include indemnities from the state, as well as political risk insurance. Egypt's investment-grade ratings from two international rating agencies has facilitated the creation of the financial packages by private sector business on terms reflecting the favourable attitude towards Egypt among investment bankers.

As a key example, private sector involvement in airport construction and management has not raised the possibility of Egypt Air's monopoly being withdrawn. Consequently, the success of the airports remains ultimately subject to the ability of Egypt Air to earn itself a profit from the new routes which will be on offer. Other airlines have lobbied to be allowed to operate regular scheduled flights to and from foreign airports served by Egypt Air, which they are currently not permitted to do. They also want to be able to serve destinations abroad which the state airline does not service, despite having agreements allowing flights. Strong resistance to the liberalisation of the skies over Egypt has come from within the management of the state airline.

Such resistance has been less pronounced within the other areas to which the government is developing BOOT and BOT projects. Sidi Krier II, Egypt's first venture into private sector BOOT power generation, attracted wide interest from foreign investors. Intergen, a subsidiary of Bechtel of the United States, was awarded the US$400 million project to generate 650MW of electricity from two turbines it will build at the site.

As the real value of finds of up to 40 trillion cubic metres of natural gas off the Nile Delta has come to be realised, both the increased use of gas and the extension of the domestic distribution network have become key features of Egypt's evolving energy policy. In a US$220 million deal, signed by British Gas International (Egypt) in 1998 to build a 500-kilometre gas pipeline from south of Cairo to Asyut. A total of 15 BOOT power projects are planned to be offered to the private sector in the coming two decades, intended to meet an annual 7–8 per cent increase in demand for electricity.

Power generation and airport construction are the key areas in which the BOOT schemes have borne fruit. Since the passage of Law No. 229 of 1996, plans have been under way using this method for road building projects. Plans are currently being drawn up for a major motorway linking Alexandria, Cairo and the towns of southern Egypt, which would be built by the private sector. Six BOT road projects have been offered – for the construction of roads between Saloum and Natroun, Alexandria and Fayoum, Dayrout and Fayoum, Aswan and Dayrout, Dayrout and Farafra and, Kharga and East Oweinat. The government has also recently revived plans for the construction of a third terminal at Cairo International Airport, using the BOOT method. BOOT power and airport projects requiring a total investment of E£6.4 billion have now been agreed between private sector companies and the government. The scale of the investment heralds a major expansion in the role of the private sector, but also raises expectations of major improvements in the availability and efficiency of services which two years ago were very much in the hands of the state.

Mega-projects of the future: Toshka and the South Valley; East Port Said

Guiding the ongoing re-evaluation of Egypt's future needs has been the growing realisation that vast potential exists in the as yet uncultivated areas of the country. Until the very recent past, the financial resources necessary to tap this potential have been absent. A mixture of growing

INFRASTRUCTURE AND PROJECT FINANCE

The metro system in Cairo has played a critical role in reducing traffic congestion in the city

need and private sector ambition is now increasingly driving the policy of expanding land-use, and exploiting the 96.5 per cent of Egypt's area which barely sustains more than 1 per cent of its 65 million population. The narrow strip of inhabited land along the Nile has been the traditional centre of the country for five millennia. The economic, political, agricultural and social fabric of the country are bound up in the organisational imperative required to sustain a population in a country which has an average rainfall of 80 millimetres a year, but where rain may not fall in some areas for up to three years.

Vast projects are now under way which are intended to increase the inhabitable area to 25 per cent of Egypt's land area. This plan will increase by 40 per cent the area under cultivation, from 3–5 million hectares. Two projects are now being planned which will engineer this transformation. The most ambitious is the South Valley project, at Toshka on the western bank of Lake Nasser. The first phase of the project is intended to bring 500,000 hectares under cultivation. The major investor in the agricultural project, Prince Al-Waleed bin Talal bin Abdelaziz Al-Saud and the Kingdom Agricultural Development Company (KADCO), plans to establish a US$1 billion agricultural business on 50,000 hectares of land, on which it is planned to grow wheat, barley, alfalfa, citrus fruits, cotton and vegetables. In October 1998, KADCO signed a contract for the purchase of the land, and has now drawn up plans for projects worth US$600 million. The lure of the project to investors is multifold.

The government in 1998 awarded a US$436.6 million contract to the UK-Norwegian Kvaerner Construction Company, Hitachi of Japan and Arabian International Construction of Egypt, to build the world's largest pumping station, on the western shore of the lake. Powered by electricity from the Aswan Dam to the north, the pumping station's 21 pumps will lift 300 cubic metres of water per second 52 metres into the 30-kilometre long, 30-metre wide and 7-metre deep Sheikh Zayed Canal and its four spur canals, to irrigate the 500,000 hectare area. The completed canal and spurs will be 168 kilometres long. The Egyptian government has so far spent US$176 million on the construction of the canal, for which a substantial amount has also been received from Shiekh Zayed of the United Arab Emirates, after whom it is named. Potential developers have asked the government to extend the main canal to a length of 50 kilometres. Three Arab agencies – the Arab Fund for Economic and Social Development, the Kuwait Fund for Arab Economic Development and the Saudi Fund for Development – have together provided US$100 million towards the cost of the pumping station.

The government has committed itself to providing infrastructure for the valley, but will seek a major private sector role in developing industry and agricultural projects, of which KADCO is one major example. Research by Robert Fleming, the UK investment bank, assesses the total investment required for the South Valley as being US$88 billion by 2017. The government will meet 20–25 per cent of this cost, while local and foreign private sector investors are expected to invest in agriculture, infrastructure, industry, tourism and construction. To facilitate the involvement of private sector investors, extremely favourable incentives have been offered. Investors will benefit from 20-year tax holidays, exemption from customs duties on imported capital equipment, the transfer of ownership of land to Egyptian companies at US$34.5 per hectare, and land lease for companies with foreign majority ownership at US$7 per hectare.

Similar advantages have been put in place at the so far less developed agricultural project of East Oweinat, south west of Toshka close to the border with Sudan. In this area, substantial quantities of subterranean water are estimated to be capable of irrigating up to 5.8 million hectares of land for agriculture. The government is intending to invest US$1 billion to cultivate an initial 84,000 hectares, which it will then expect private sector developers to further exploit. One company, Sagric International of Australia, has signed an agreement with the Egyptian PICO group, to provide farm development services in Toshka and East Oweinat. PICO has already secured a 40,000 acre site for agricultural development in East Oweinat.

Redirection of the water resources available to Egypt is also playing the key role in the

INFRASTRUCTURE AND PROJECT FINANCE

British Gas International (Egypt) is the first private sector company to become involved in providing gas to areas which currently have no supply

development of areas in the extreme north of the country. At the heart of plans to develop the area to the east of Port Said is the 200-kilometres El Salam Canal, pumping water from the Nile west of the Suez Canal, which will pass through pipes before re-emerging in the Sinai and irrigating land for agriculture as far east as El Arish. The evolution of the East Port Said project has seen a vast grouping of interlinked infrastructural projects, intended to harmonise needs, potential and ambitions to develop the north Sinai.

The pressing need to transform Egypt's port facilities has led to consideration of various schemes allowing private sector involvement. The East Port Said project will provide Egypt with a modern container terminal which is intended to become a hub for shipping in the eastern Mediterranean. A management agreement with a foreign private sector company to operate the port was expected to be confirmed in 1999. The new port will also be served by an adjacent 5,000 hectare industrial free-zone, which will be designed to attract export industries in the engineering, food processing and textile sectors. The potential for expansion will be created with the reclamation of 1,680 hectares of land alongside the Suez Canal. The East Port Said development will also be served by one of two BOOT power projects recently awarded by the government. Electricité de France secured contracts to build two power stations, one at Suez and the other at Port Said. The East Port Said project – known as El-Chark el-Tafriaa – is for a gas and oil fired steam unit capable of generating 350MW of electricity to Port Said.

As the real value of gas finds off the Nile Delta has come to be realised, the extension of the domestic distribution network has become a key feature of Egypt's evolving energy policy

Power generation and distribution

The government's strategy of creating private sector investment opportunities outside the privatisation programme has led to the creation of infrastructure projects which have so far brought more than US$1.2 billion in investment. Private sector power generation, gas distribution, airport construction and management, as well as projects for road building, port construction and private telecommunications are well advanced.

Sidi Krier II, Egypt's first venture into private sector BOOT power generation, attracted wide interest from foreign investors and was highly regarded for the exemplary transparency of the tendering process which led to a contract being awarded to Intergen, a subsidiary of Bechtel of the United States. The US$400 million project to generate 650MW is now one of two power generation plants under construction, intended to raise electricity output from the current 14,800MW to 23,800MW by 2006 and to 43,000MW by 2018. Intergen's bid was based on a price of US$0.26 per kWh of electricity, making it the cheapest electricity in the world. The project, expected to be running by 2002, is the first stage in the government's extensive reorganisation of the electricity generation network, and is a precursor to the partial privatisation of the system. The Sidi Krier II deal was followed by the signing of a US$1.2 billion contract with Electricité de France and the Egyptian Electricity Authority (EEA), for the construction of two further 650MW BOOT power stations in the Gulf of Suez. EDF will provide power to the EEA for 20 years.

While the national electricity grid will remain the property of the EEA, seven power generation zones, supplied by private sector power stations, have now been created. Each is a joint-stock company, whose overall value is put at US$12–14 billion. Parliament approved the sale of up to 49 per cent of each company in March 1998. The first sale, to be lead managed by Merrill Lynch and EFG-Hermes, will be for a 10–20 per cent stake in the Cairo Electricity Company (CEC). The valuation of CEC will set a benchmark for the valuation of the six other companies.

Adding value to raw materials has opened new horizons for power generation, as Egypt assesses the real value of up to 40 trillion cubic metres of natural gas finds in the Nile Delta. One example is the US$220 million deal signed by British Gas International (Egypt) in 1998 to build an initial 500-kilometre gas pipeline from south of Cairo to Asyut. The franchise was the first of its kind in Egypt to offer private sector companies the role of providing gas to areas which currently have no supply. BG Egypt, with its partners Edison International, Orascom and Middle East Gas Association, will construct a high pressure gas transmission pipeline linking towns along the Nile valley, and create a low pressure network for supply to factories and homes. The project's first US$50 million phase will carry gas under pressure from Kuriamat, near Cairo, to an estimated 20,000 potential consumers in the town of Beni Suef. BG Egypt puts domestic and industrial demand in the area of the first phase at around 240 million cubic feet per day. A similar demand is anticipated in the Asyut area.

A total of 15 BOOT power projects are planned for offer to the private sector in the coming two decades, intended to meet an annual 7–8 per cent increase in demand for electricity. Research by the Middle East Economic Survey suggests this will require investment totalling US$7.2 billion. The power plants will increase Egypt's generating capacity by 12,750MW by 2002, 17,000MW by 2007 and 27,500MW by 2017. Two plants planned for Sharm el-Sheikh and Toshka with a planned capacity of 1,300MW will be put out to tender in 1999, with two new plants offered every other year until 2003 and existing plants being earmarked for upgrading.

Egypt's increased generating capacity will make it a major player in the Mediterranean Power Pool (MPP) project, planned to be completed by 2015. The project links the electricity grids of most of the countries of the Mediterranean, allowing shortages in some countries to be met with increased generation within the pool by those with spare supply. In March 1999, Egypt and Jordan achieved a major step forward in advancing the link with the inauguration of an 8-mile undersea cable linking their national grids. The link comprises four undersea cables which will carry an initial 130MW between the two countries. Generation from Syria, Turkey and Lebanon will allow this to be increased to 350MW. The US$229 million cost of the cabling and installations has been met by the Arab Fund for Economic and Social Development. The link between the Egyptian town of Taba and the Jordanian town of Aqaba now connects Jordan, Egypt and Libya in an unbroken supply line. Libya and Egypt have been linked by a cable capable of transmitting 100MW of electricity per hour since May 1998. Tunisia is expected to become part of the grid by November 1999, while the construction of infrastructure in Syria is intended to upgrade the existing system capable of carrying 220kV between Jordan and Syria, to allow the transport of 400kV. Syria's connection with Turkey is also expected to be in place before the end of 1999. The final shape of the grid will incorporate all North African states, with Jordan, Syria, Lebanon, Turkey Spain and Italy, forming a circular grid which will allow all the connected countries to contribute power to the system to compensate for low generation in states which face shortages.

Ports, airports and other transport; concessions and foreign involvement

Legal changes to the status of Egypt's transport infrastructure have allowed significant strides to be taken towards both facilitating a greater private sector role in large-scale projects, while also attempting to make good on a commitment to raising exports by the 11 per cent necessary to achieve its targeted 7–8 per cent GDP growth rate. The government fully accepts that a major hindrance to the expansion of export industries is the dire state of the country's port facilities, which are inefficient and expensive for users. In October 1997, a 30-year state maritime monopoly was ended when private sector shipping companies were given permission to export from Egyptian ports. The move was a first step towards a radical reform of export-related services and institutions. The state-owned Egyptian Maritime Navigation Company (EMNC) now faces competition from four partnerships, which Egyptian companies have established with foreign shipping companies. EMNC has traditionally dominated exports, and been given priority as an importer, unless its ships are unavailable. Both areas are now to be open to the private sector. The need for competition had been clear for years, as Egyptian maritime transport costs had been around 27 per cent higher than those of neighbouring countries. Liberalisation measures in 1997, allowed the private sector to bid for contracts for port services such as handling. In April 1998, 4.5 per cent of the shares in the state-owned United Arab Stevedoring were sold on the Egyptian Stock Exchange (ESE), as a first step towards the privatisation of the sector. However, shares in the company have seen a 46.39 per cent decline in value since the initial public offering, despite its dominant position in the sector at the ports of Alexandria, Abu Qir and El Dekheila. Other shipping agencies were expected to be privatised subsequently, but by March 1999 all nine state-owned maritime agencies listed on the ESE had retained their original ownership structure.

While the government has been attempting to restructure existing facilities, private sector companies have shown growing interest in securing project finance for the creation of entirely new port installations. The construction of the East Port Said project was originally offered to the government on the basis of a BOOT scheme by P&O Ports of Australia. The

INFRASTRUCTURE AND PROJECT FINANCE

port will be designed to handle one million 20-foot container units per year in a terminal expected to cover 22.5 million square metres. The government has also sold land within a 54.2 million square metre area within the perimeter of the port at a rate of E£20 per square metre for industrial projects and E£5 per square metre for non-industrial use. P&O's bid has been met with rival bids, notably from ECT of the Netherlands, and in January 1999, the government postponed the offerings in the Damietta and Port Said Container Handling Companies, to widen the foreign interest in port management in advance of selling the state's interest in the two companies. In addition, a planned new port at Ain el-Soukhna, south of Suez intended to serve the new 80 million square metre Suez industrial zone, is expected to require investment totalling E£500 million.

Legal changes to the status of Egypt's transport infrastructure have allowed significant strides to be taken towards encouraging a greater private-sector role and raising exports

The passing of Law No. 19 of 1998 confirmed a trend in the telecommunications sector which has brought extensive private sector involvement

INFRASTRUCTURE AND PROJECT FINANCE

The move towards creating new facilities alongside what is already established has also been central to the strategy pursued in the development of airport facilities. Four private sector airport projects are currently under way, and a further two are being considered. In the north of the country, El Alamein airport will be offered on a 50-year concession to Kato Investments, which will invest an initial E£60 million in the project and will start operations in 2001 with the advantage of a three-year tax holiday. The three stages of the airport's development will see passenger capacity rise from 600 per hour by 2002 to 2,000 per hour by 2028. Marsa Alam airport on the southern Red Sea coast, to be built and managed by EMAK construction, will have a 40-year concession period and a five-year tax holiday on a one million square metre site which it intends to develop both for the airport and for tourism. Ras Sidr airport, on the Red Sea coast of western Sinai, is to be built and managed by Delta Gulf, without the benefit of a tax holiday but with a 50-year concession period. The company plans for capacity of 1,000 passengers per hour by 2010 and 2,000 per hour by 2038. Plans for the airport of Dahab, on the cost of eastern Sinai, remain uncertain due to the potential impact on safari tourism of an airport at the location currently planned by the developer, NESCO. Two further airports are planned on the basis of BOOT, at Bahariya and Farafra, two oasis towns in the Western Desert.

Foreign involvement consequent to the liberalisation of the maritime transport sector has been substantial, though this has not been the case in the air transport sector. Aside from P&O Ports and ETC's bids to develop the East Port Said project on the BOOT basis, the largest contracts involved so far in the sector have been for dredging and construction. A US$70–90 million contract to build quay walls for the Ain El-Soukhna port facility attracted six foreign consortia involving nine foreign and two Egyptian companies. The US$130–150 million dredging contract for Ain El-Soukhna later attracted bids from six foreign consortia involving 10 companies. As with the East Port Said project, Ain El-Soukhna will attract government financing for infrastructure and dredging, while the port will be operated as a BOOT Scheme. Three international groups bid for the US$200–220 million contract for the dredging and breakwater construction for the East Port Said project. Three consortia involving nine foreign companies bid between US$315 million and US$356 million for the contract, prompting the government to consider cancelling the project owing to the cost being way over its budget.

Communications: the future of Egypt Telecom and the boom in mobile telephony

Security issues have dominated the passage of legislation affecting Egypt's telecommunications network, and have revealed a great deal about the changing mentality at work as the government seeks not only to realign the economy but also reform popular attitudes towards economic activity. Stiff resistance among parliamentarians hampered the passage of Law No. 19

of 1998, which sought parliamentary approval for a radical overhaul of the National Telecommunications Authority (NTA). The authority, previously known as the Arab Republic of Egypt National Telecommunications Office (ARENTO), and now called Telecom Egypt, was widely regarded as being a strategic industry which should be excluded from the possibility of privatisation, and should remain a public service. In response to the force of conservatives, the government announced in March 1998, that it would retain 80 per cent of Telecom Egypt and may at some point in the future offer 20 per cent to the Egyptian private sector. Law 19 transferred the NTA from the direct control of the Ministry of Transport and Telecommunications, to that of a joint-stock company under Law No. 203 of 1991, which allowed public sector companies to be grouped into holding companies, which could sell shares in the constituent companies as part of the privatisation programme. At the same time, Presidential Decree No. 101 of 1998 was issued, creating a regulatory body for telecommunications. The regulatory body was given the power to assign frequencies, set rates, provide rights for interconnection, and settle disputes. As part of the battle the government fought to have Law 19 passed, it agreed to demands by parliamentarians that there would be a mandatory extension of the telecommunications service into rural areas, that fee increases would be limited, and a new telephone company would have to assume the potential liabilities from judicial cases which were pending. With the passage of the legislation, estimates as to Telecom Egypt's market value placed it at E£28.1 billion.

The passing of Law No. 19 of 1998 confirmed a trend in the telecommunications sector which had brought extensive private sector involvement, either on a contractual or on a concessional basis. Telecom Egypt's issuance of two licences to establish and operate nationwide public payphone systems of 20,000 lines each to be established within five years brought strong foreign interest. France Telecom, which won the first contract, will pay the government 66 per cent of revenues, estimated at around US$590 million during the 10-year period of the contract. Landis and Gyr of Switzerland will operate the second system, also over 10 years. The appearance of an array of brightly coloured pay phones in the streets of Cairo is a promising sign. Meanwhile, Telecom Egypt has pursued a programme of modernisation in other areas, including offering the Iridium global mobile and satellite service to both domestic and international users.

The awarding of licences and the introduction of two mobile telephone systems are now operational in many parts of the country and have been a soaring success. Alcatel of France installed a 70,000 subscriber Global System for Mobiles cellular telephone system in late 1996 on behalf of Telecom Egypt. In April 1998, the government announced the sale of a licence for a rival GSM system, which was bought by a consortium led by Vodafone of the United Kingdom, Air Touch of the United States and local partners – trading under the name MisrFone – on payment of US$516 million. The success of this sale prompted the government to announce the privatisation of the established system, which was bought on payment of the same amount by a consortium grouping France Telecom, Motorola and Orascom Technologies, trading under the name Mobinil. By January 1999, six months after taking over the network established by Telecom Egypt, Mobinil had almost doubled its number of subscribers, and exceeded its 1997 year-end target by 7 per cent experiencing a 93 per cent rise in subscriptions, from 83,000 to 159,850. Analysts predict the company will have 320,000 subscribers by the end of 1999.

In November 1998, Mobinil's rival MisrFone started operations with plans for a sevenfold increase in the total number of subscribers within two years. A variety of sales strategies have been introduced by MisrFone, intended to lure customers and achieve around one million total subscribers for the two companies by mid-2000. Chief among these is a system of pre-payment for up to 45-minutes of calls, intended to prevent subscribers from amassing bills which they cannot afford to pay. By February 1999, MisrFone had secured 50,000 subscribers.

Egypt's generally flat terrain means up to 85 per cent of the country can be covered with as few as a quarter of the US$60,000–100,000-apiece base stations needed to provide a nationwide service to geographically varied countries. MisrFone estimates it will have to make a US$100 million investment in infrastructure by the end of 1999, to match the Mobinil network. Both companies estimate that beyond current subscribers who comfortably afforded connection fees of up to E£2,000 (US$589), there are an estimated six million people awaiting a drop in prices. Industry analysts estimate the potential size of the market as being anything up to 12 million subscribers or 20 per cent of the population.

12 Other forms of fixed foreign investment

Joint ventures

The growth in opportunities for investment in Egypt has been accompanied by a growing array of methods by which foreign investment has been committed. As the Egyptian market has become more familiar to potential foreign investors, so the character of investment has been determined by what the newly arrived foreign business community has learned. The great need to accelerate this process is made clear when Egypt is viewed against the background of similar emerging markets. Among the larger emerging markets, Egypt in 1998 ranked 23rd in the league table of countries receiving foreign direct investment (FDI). Of the US$136 billion total received by these 23 markets, Egypt received 0.58 per cent or US$0.8 billion. Other indicators assessing Egypt's strengths and weaknesses relative to other emerging markets seeking to increase their share of FDI are much more favourable. According to the United Nations Conference on Trade and Development (UNCTAD), US companies which have invested in Egypt show an average rate of return of 22 per cent, which is higher than the average rate of return of affiliates of these companies located in developing regions which have attracted higher FDI, and twice as high as rates of return in Europe. By the end of 1998, the FDI stock amounted to US$4.2 billion in manufacturing (52 per cent of the total), US$3.02 billion in agriculture (37 per cent), and US$193 million in other sectors (2 per cent).

In a relatively short period of time, since 1995–96 when foreign investment started to pick up, there has been a major growth in the provision of information on companies and investment opportunities. Whereas in 1996 foreign investors generally sought information on sectors, they now seek detailed analyses of individual private and public sector companies. A trend that has emerged subsequent to this growing familiarity with Egyptian business practice has been the tendency towards establishing joint ventures in which Egyptian partners play a key role with foreign investors. Of the US$989 million of FDI into Egypt in 1998, at least 60 per cent was for investment in joint-venture projects, in particular the purchase from the government of two licences to operate mobile telephone systems in the country. Total FDI into Egypt in 1998 breaks down as US$441 million in agriculture and construction, US$243 million in manufacturing industry, US$203 million in tourism, and US$41 million in the financial sector and services. In addition, US$61 million was invested in Egypt's free zone areas (see Exhibit 12.1). The attraction of joint ventures as key vehicles for FDI has been well established, particularly in the banking sector. Of the 23 joint-venture public-private commercial banks, 12 have foreign shareholders. In December 1998, Barclays Bank

OTHER FORMS OF FIXED FOREIGN INVESTMENT

International of the United Kingdom agreed to buy a majority stake in the joint venture it had established in 1975 with Banque du Caire. Joint-venture partnerships are also to be found in metallurgy, software manufacture, and the food and confectionery sectors.

Licensing agreements

Although most new foreign investment in Egypt has been in the form of direct investment, licensing agreements are still significant. The strength of global brands has lured a number of Egyptian companies to seek licensing agreements, both on the basis of purely financial relations, as well as creating the opportunity for technology transfer. Brands such as Coca-Cola, Pepsi-Cola, Cadbury Schweppes and McDonalds, are well-established. In 1997, the privatisation of Egypt's state brewing monopoly effectively launched a new phase in licensing agreements. Al Ahram Beverages Company (ABC), which was sold to an anchor investor as part of the government's privatisation programme, drew up a licensing agreement with the Danish brewer Carlsberg, both to produce Carlsberg beer in Egypt and benefit from technology by agreement with Carlsberg's consultancy arm, Danbrew. Subsequently, ABC signed agreements with RC Cola of the United States, Guinness of the United Kingdom and took control of the rival Nile Brewery, which had licensing agreements to produce other foreign brands.

Despite the wide use of licensing agreements, the system is hampered by inadequate patent protection, the inconsistency of quality controls for licensed products, and a weak legal and judicial framework. A study by the EIU concluded that significant strides had been taken to improve the protection of intellectual property rights in Egypt, largely through police swoops on the production facilities of software pirates. Piracy in video has dropped as the profits in the legal market have become more attractive, while computer software piracy has been reduced largely in response to an agreement between the government and Microsoft of the United States to allow local companies to incorporate Microsoft software into their computers if the government cracks down assertively against piracy. Vital to facilitating the launch of a new era in licensing, which could in turn mark a great leap towards accelerating the rate of technology transfer into Egypt, is the improvement in judicial procedures. Piracy cases can take up to two years, trademark cases up to five years, and with appeals up to 15 years. The capacity of judges to deal with complex commercial cases has been exposed as inadequate, as it has in other areas and in particular with regard to capital markets-related litigation. The shortcomings of the

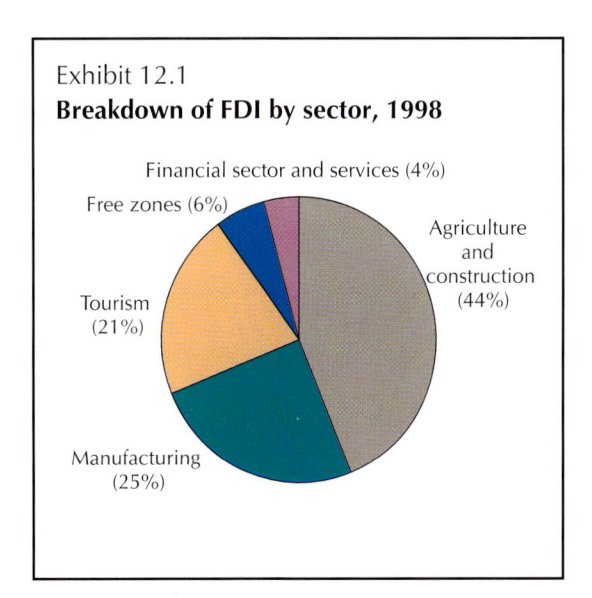

Exhibit 12.1
Breakdown of FDI by sector, 1998

- Financial sector and services (4%)
- Free zones (6%)
- Tourism (21%)
- Manufacturing (25%)
- Agriculture and construction (44%)

legal system have been recognised by the government, and there is now acceptance of the need for change as being essential to the creation of an investor-friendly environment.

Mergers and acquisitions

Foreign investment in the form of mergers and acquisitions has been less significant than the practice of creating joint ventures or establishing licensing agreements. In the past year, the Egyptian private sector companies which have perhaps been in the strongest position to conduct mergers or acquisitions have opted for stakes in privatised companies as anchor investors. However, the growth of the financial sector has required mergers as a means of both widening market presence and meeting the local demand for skills and technology transfer. The merger of Fleming-Mansour – a joint-venture brokerage company established in 1997 by Robert Fleming of London and the local Mansour Group – with the local CIIC and its Intercapital Securities brokerage arm, was a significant step for the UK company. Its declared aim in going ahead with the merger was to both strengthen its position in the Egyptian market, but also use Egypt as a regional base. The newly created Fleming-CIIC is now a key player in the market, through a joint venture which then became a merger.

Mergers require the permission of the Ministry of Economy if they fall within the Companies Law 159. The traditional concern for safeguarding the security of workers plays an important role in the legislation governing mergers, particularly if the merger is likely to lead to redundancies. However, a new Labour Law is expected to greatly ease the restrictions, and introduce a greater flexibility. In the meantime, for foreign companies keen to broaden their presence in Egypt, the process has effectively been one of creating a joint-venture partnership which then acquires a controlling stake. This is effectively what happened with the acquisition of the state-owned mobile telephone company, which was bought under the name Mobinil by a joint-venture partnership involving foreign and local partners. Where a full acquisition has taken place, it has usually been done by companies well-established in Egypt. An appropriate recent example was the US$117 million takeover of Amoun Pharmaceuticals by Glaxo Wellcome Egypt (GWE). With the purchase, GWE, a wholly-owned subsidiary of the UK parent Glaxo Wellcome, become Egypt's leading manufacturer of pharmaceuticals and raised Glaxo Wellcome's investment in Egypt to US$184 million. The purchase increased GWE's 6 per cent share of the Egyptian market to 9 per cent. The deal bought GWE 30 generic brands produced by Amoun, and was the largest acquisition by a single company in Egypt in recent years. Such a large acquisition is unlikely to be repeated soon.

Setting up a manufacturing operation in Egypt

In 1998, approval was given for the creation of 2,187 new companies, including 95 in the free zone areas of Egypt, a 731 per cent increase in the number of new companies established in

1995. While it is clear that the increasingly liberalised business environment has encouraged the creation of new ventures, much of the increase is explained by the steady if slow streamlining of the procedures necessary for the establishing of new companies. A major step in this direction was the introduction of Ministerial Decree No 354 of 1996, which scrapped the demand that companies must seek security clearance before registration. Meanwhile, Ministerial Decree No. 178 of 1996 introduced the practice of offering the registration services free of charge. The Companies Law (Law No. 159 of 1981) governs the process by which new Egyptian companies are created, and it is possible for foreign companies to be established under the law's auspices. However, more appropriate to the establishment of business operations by foreign companies is Law No. 8 of 1997, the Law of Investment Guarantees and Incentives. The law applies to all companies created after its introduction and its remit is wide, covering: the reclamation and cultivation of barren or desert land; animal, poultry and fish farming; industry and mining; hotels, motels, hotel flats, tourist resorts and tourist transportation; refrigerated transport, and the refrigerated transport of agricultural crops, industrial products, and foodstuffs, as well as the establishment of container depots and grain stores; aviation and related services; overseas maritime transport; oil sector exploration and drilling, as well as the distribution and installation of natural gas services; residential housing projects; infrastructure projects concerning drinking water, sewage, electricity supply, roads and communications; hospitals and medical centres; financial leasing; underwriting and the distribution of securities; venture capital operations; the production of computer software and systems, and projects funded by the Social Fund for Development. Petroleum refining and cinema production were later added.

All these areas of activity benefit from the ownership conditions which have become the foundation upon which the government has built its efforts to accelerate the level of FDI. Under Law 8, the investor applies to the General Organisation for Industrialisation (GOFI) for an industrial licence authorising the establishment of the factory housing production facilities. The investor then requests the approval for production of the Companies Department of the Ministry of Economy, after which the same procedures are applied to foreign investors as they are to local investors. After licensing by the GOFI, investor requests are processed by the General Authority for Investment (GAFI), which automatically approves requests as long as they are within the remit of Law 159. Law 8 requires that investors must provide the following details: the names of the contracting parties; the legal structure of the company; details of its activities; the company name and the length of time it has engaged in its business activities; the percentages of Egyptian and non-Egyptian participation, and the form of that participation, as well as details of the partners' obligations and equity. Under Law 159, the majority of company directors must be Egyptian, and the workforce must be represented on the board of directors, while under Law 8, none of these conditions apply. Equally, companies incorporated under Law 8 can benefit from a provision allowing land ownership by foreigners for the purpose of establishing and expanding the business. Foreigners are also allowed to own residential property, although restrictions apply on their ownership of historic buildings. Services provided by the GAFI are charged at a rate of 0.25 per cent of the project's capital, up to a limit of E£500, or its equivalent in foreign currency. Law 8 companies can also announce their incorporation in the 'Investment Journal' for a E£1,000 fee, whereas Law 159 companies must do so in the 'Official Journal', which is a longer process and costs between E£25,000-40,000. The GAFI is also responsible for investment in the free zones, which were established by Law No. 43 of 1974. The provisions of Law 8 regarding the free zones, are the same as those of Law 230 of 1996, thereby giving local and foreign investors the same procedures and conditions. To accelerate the approval process for investments in the eight public free zones, Law 8 allows applications to be routed through the directorial boards of the free zones themselves.

Incentives for investment have been incorporated in the law, and the government is steadily if unevenly attempting to ensure that the bureaucratic hurdles to investment are dismantled in practice. Law 8 takes the incentives further in Article 9, by protecting investments against nationalisation, confiscation or administrative sequestration. The same law also offers guarantees against seizure, requisitioning, blocking, confiscation, and placing under custody or sequestration and against full or partial expropriation of real estate and investment project property. Companies established under Law 8 are free from stipulations in Law 230 of 1996 regarding capital inflow and the repatriation of funds. Under Law 230 of 1996, investors may import foreign currency, but must place it in a special account. The repatriation of funds is guaranteed under Law 230 of 1996, but is not specified in Law 8. Equally, Law 8 does not address the issue of the repatriation of profits. However, companies established under Law 159 are subject to restrictions on the amount which can be transferred if the company is liquidated, up to a maximum of E£20,000. Law 230 guarantees the repatriation of profits provided the amount remitted does not exceed the balance of the companies, foreign currency operating account. This issue is not addressed in Law 8, while companies established under Law 159 have no restriction on profit repatriation.

As a signatory to multilateral conventions on the settlement of investment-related disputes, Egypt is bound by the same international criteria which have in part been incorporated into its own legislation. Egypt is a signatory to the Convention on Recognition and Enforcement of Foreign Arbitration Awards (1958), the Convention on the Settlement of Investment Disputes between States and Nationals of other States (1965), and accedes to the authority of the International Centre for the Settlement of Investment Disputes (ICSID). Law 8 stipulates that investment disputes may be settled through conciliation, mediation and arbitration, as well as through the domestic judicial system, while acknowledging the right of disputants to settle within the framework of the agreements to which Egypt is a signatory. In addition, Prime Ministerial Decree No. 64 of 1996, established a committee for settling investment disputes between investors and public authorities.

13 Egyptian industry in figures

Statistical summary of Egypt's GDP by sector

The value of Egypt's GDP has seen an average year-on-year increase of 14.5 per cent in the period 1989–99. From E£76.8 billion in 1989, GDP now stands at E£305.2 billion. In the same period, real GDP has seen an average growth of 4.25 per cent. In the period 1999–2003, the IMF expects an average GDP growth rate of 5.46 per cent, reaching 6 per cent in 2003.

Exhibit 13.1
Composition of GDP 1990–98, (E£ million) and as a percentage of total GDP

	1990–91	1991–92	1992–93	1993–94	1994–95	1995–96	1996–97	1997–98
Total GDP (E£ million)	111,200	139,100	157,300	162,967	191,010	214,185	239,500	262,220
Commodity sector (%)	50.8	49.9	49.8	49.6	49.1	48.9	49.5	49.8
Agriculture (%)	17.6	16.5	16.7	16.9	16.8	17.3	17.7	17.5
Industry/mining (%)	16.6	16.6	16.7	17.2	17.5	17.7	18.1	18.6
Petroleum/products (%)	10.1	9.9	9.5	8.2	7.9	6.9	6.6	6.4
Electricity (%)	1.4	1.7	2.0	2.1	2.0	1.9	1.8	1.7
Construction (%)	5.2	5.1	4.9	5.2	5.0	5.2	5.3	5.6
Commodity sector (E£ million)	56,489	69,410	78,335	80,880	93,750	104,684	118,532	130,509
Production sector (%)	31.2	33.3	32.9	32.3	32.6	32.6	32.4	32.2
Transportation (%)	10.4	11.3	10.9	10.8	10.3	10.0	9.5	9.3
Trade, finance, insurance (%)	20.0	20.1	20.2	20.2	20.8	21.1	21.3	21.6
Hotels, restaurants (%)	0.8	1.8	1.8	1.4	1.5	1.5	1.6	1.2
Production sector (E£ million)	34,694	46,320	51,751	52,710	62,250	69,850	77,552	84,336
Social services sector (%)	18.0	16.8	17.3	18.0	18.3	18.5	18.1	18.1
Housing/real estate (%)	2.0	1.8	1.8	1.7	1.8	1.8	1.8	1.9
Utilities (%)	0.3	0.3	0.3	0.4	0.4	0.4	0.4	0.4
Social insurance (%)	0.1	0.1	0.1	0.1	0.1	0.1	0.1	0.1
Government services (%)	7.6	7.1	7.4	7.8	7.9	8.0	7.9	7.9
Social/personal services (%)	8.0	7.5	7.7	8.0	8.2	8.2	8.0	7.9
Social services sector (E£ million)	20,016	23,368	27,212	29,377	35,010	39,655	43,416	47,375

Source: Central Bank of Egypt

GDP can be divided into three sectors: commodities, production services and social services. The commodity sector accounts for 50 per cent of GDP, and itself can be divided into: industry and mining (37.4 per cent), agriculture (35.2 per cent), petroleum and products (12.9 per cent), construction (11.2 per cent), and electricity (3.4 per cent).

The contribution of the commodity sector to overall total GDP has remained stable for the past decade. Accounting for between 47.6 per cent and 50.8 per cent of total GDP. The production services sector has remained similarly consistent in the past decade, varying from 31.8 per cent to 33.3 per cent of GDP. In 1998, trade, finance and insurance accounted for 21.6 per cent of the sector's output as a percentage of GDP, while transportation accounted for 9.3 per cent and hotels and restaurants 1.2 per cent. Social services, the third constituent part of GDP, accounted for 18.1 per cent of the total in 1998, having fluctuated by 3.3 per cent during 1989–99. Of this, government services and social and personal services both accounted for 7.9 per cent, housing and real estate 1.9 per cent, utilities 0.4 per cent and social insurance 0.1 per cent. Listed according to their relative significance to total GDP, the constituent parts of the three sectors have a different weight. The 13 constituents' individual contributions are: trade, finance and insurance (21.6 per cent); industry and mining (18.6 per cent); agriculture (17.5 per cent); transport (9.3 per cent); government services and social and personal services (each 7.9 per cent); petroleum and products (6.4 per cent); construction (5.6 per cent); housing and real estate (1.9 per cent); electricity (1.7 per cent); hotels and restaurants (1.2 per cent); utilities (1.4 per cent); and social insurance (0.1 per cent).

Trade flows

Essential to increasing its real GDP growth rate is the need to increase exports by up to 11 per cent. Many measures have been instigated with the aim of achieving this target, in particular measures to improve port and transport facilities for Egyptian exporters. The pattern of exports has yet to benefit from these new measures, and the current composition of export sales has remained generally stable since the economic liberalisation programme was launched. The overall value of exports has risen by 20 per cent in 1990–98, from US$4.2 billion to US$5.12 billion, despite a 53 per cent drop in earnings from crude oil in that period.

Overall, exports of industrial commodities have remained stable, with a 2 per cent drop in value from US$3.49–3.41 billion between 1990 and 1998. An increase in the export of petroleum products has partially compensated for the fall in receipts from crude oil, seeing a 40 per cent rise in 1990–98. The spinning and weaving industries have seen the most significant export fluctuations in the period 1990–98 of all the commodity groups, despite an overall increase in the value of exports from the sector of 43 per cent, from US$529–759 million. The fluctuation has been particularly pronounced in the export of cotton textiles, which has seen its value drop by 73 per cent in 1990–98, from US$75–20 million. Where the spinning and weaving sector may have lost, the agricultural sector has gained by increased earnings from raw cotton exports, which saw a 24 per cent rise in 1990–98, from US$83–103

Exhibit 13.2

Exports by commodity groups 1997–98, (US$ million)

Total	**5,128**
Agriculture	243
Industrial	3,143
Petroleum & petroleum products	1,728
Spinning & weaving	759
Engineering	286
Foodstuffs	147
Chemical	173
Metal	159
Mining	32
Materials	46
Other	1,146

Source: Central Bank of Egypt

EGYPTIAN INDUSTRY IN FIGURES

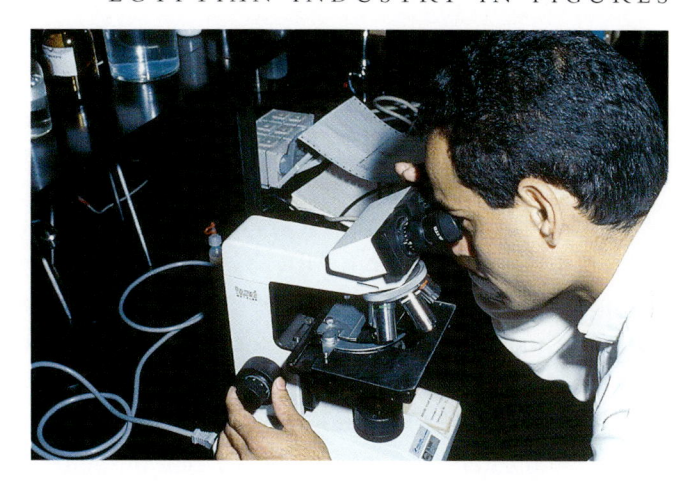

Egypt is the largest pharmaceutical producer and exporter in the Middle East, accounting for 20 per cent of total regional production

The transformation of the agricultural sector has become a cornerstone of the government's long-term policy

million. Despite a marked rise in the mid-1990s, the value of agricultural exports has seen a mere 7.5 per cent rise in 1990–98, from US$226–243 million. As the drive to increase exports has accelerated, non-traditional exports have begun to play a more significant role. A wide variety of engineering industry exports is now beginning to make a more significant contribution to GDP, with a 257 per cent rise in the value of these exports recorded in 1990–98, from US$80–286 million.

Growing Egypt's exports will require a diversification from its traditional export markets and products. Dominated by oil exports, the United States is the destination of 32.7 per cent of Egypt's exports, closely followed by the EU, which attracts 30.5 per cent. Steps have been taken to find markets elsewhere, in which Egyptian goods may be more competitive. Egypt in 1998 joined the Southern and East African economic grouping COMESA, with a view to increasing trade within Africa. African and Asian markets currently account for 14.6 per cent of Egypt's exports, the Arab countries a mere 13.9 per cent, non-EU Europe 5.7 per cent, Russia and the CIS 1.3 per cent, and other markets 1.4 per cent.

Egypt's level of imports continues to be a major source of concern, having increased the trade deficit to US$11.7 billion in 1998, with imports reaching US$16.89 billion in 1998

Exhibit 13.3
Imports by commodity groups 1997–98, (US$ million)

Total	16,899
Agricultural	2,506
Oil/products	2,188
Chemical	1,840
Wood/textiles	1,566
Machinery	4,530
Metals	1,414
Others	904
Unclassified	805

Source: Central Bank of Egypt

(see Exhibit 13.3). The value of imports from the EU rose by 104 per cent in 1991–98, from US$3.29 billion to US$6.73 billion. In the same period, imports from the United States increased 200 per cent, from US$1.12 billion to US$3.36 billion. A similarly large rise is apparent in imports from Arab countries, though of a much smaller scale. Between 1990 and 1998 Egyptian imports from its Arab neighbours rose by 160 per cent, from US$281–732 million, while imports from African and Asian countries excluding Arab states rose by 147 per cent from US$1.2–2.98 billion. Dominating Egyptian imports are machinery and transport equipment, accounting for 26 per cent of the total import bill in 1998, with imports valued at US$4.5 billion. Second are livestock and animal products, which in 1998 amounted to US$2.5 billion, or 14 per cent of the total. Oil products and fuel imports accounted for US$2.1 billion or 12 per cent of the total. The 120 per cent rise in the value of machinery and other capital goods imports has been the major element in the changing nature of Egyptian imports, and is regarded as a sign that the investment climate the government is intent upon creating is emerging, evidenced by the growing proportion of imports that are expected to be used for production rather than consumption.

Exhibit 13.4
Proportion of imports and exports by region, 1998–99, as a % of total

	Africa/Asia	Arab world	EU	US	Other European	Russia/CIS	Other
Imports (% of total)	17.3	4	42.7	18.9	10.8	1.8	4.5
Exports (% of total)	9.2	10.9	32.2	40.4	5.8	0.3	1.2

Source: Central Bank of Egypt

Exhibit 13.5
Balance of payments by region, 1997–98, (US$ million)

	Export proceeds	Import payments	Trade balance
Total	5,128	16,899	-11,771
EU countries	1,564	6,735	-5,171
Other European countries	292	1,821	-1,529
United States	1,675	3,368	-1,693
Arab League	712	732	-20
Africa/Asia*	750	2,988	-2,238
Russia/CIS	65	379	-314
Australia	4	166	-162
Other countries	66	710	-644

* Excluding Arab states

Source: Central Bank of Egypt

The growth of tertiary industries: pharmaceuticals and electronics

Among the 26 major transnational companies (TNCs) present in Egypt, some of the most successful are eight pharmaceutical giants whose expansion has been steady for almost 40 years. Their operations were ultimately strengthened by the state control of the economy during the 1960s, when limited patent protection of imports was a major incentive for them to establish production facilities in Egypt. Aside from the TNCs, the Egyptian pharmaceutical industry also comprises 11 public sector companies. Twenty year's ago the public sector controlled 69.9 per cent of the market according to industry analysts Prime Investments, but had seen its share reduced to 47.9 per cent by 1998. Until 1995 the public sector companies were 100 per cent state owned, though this stake has been reduced to a minimum of 60 per cent. The Egyptian private pharmaceutical sector now comprises 13 companies. The market capitalisation of the entire pharmaceutical industry now stands at E£2.7 billion, or 3.9 per cent of GDP. The largest single company is the private sector Egyptian International Pharmaceutical Industries (Eipico), which has a 12 per cent share of the local market and 30 per cent of Egypt's pharmaceutical export market. Among the public sector companies, the largest market share is that of Arab Drugs and Chemical Industries, which has 20 per cent of the market. The largest TNC is Glaxo Wellcome Egypt, which has 9 per cent of the total Egyptian pharmaceutical market.

The growth of Egypt's pharmaceutical industry has been dominated by a high degree of concentration on the activities of the largest companies. The top 10 companies control 44 per cent of the market, and the top five companies 27 per cent of the market, according to a survey by UNCTAD. In the decade 1985–95, the growth of the industry was dramatic, despite fluctuations in the market share of the three sectors operating within the industry. The public sector companies saw the value of output increase by 221 per cent, from E£304–976 million during this period.

For the transnational corporations, the value of output leapt by 118 per cent between 1984 and 1991, while for the Egyptian private sector the increase was dramatic, rising by 4,300 per cent, from E£28 million in 1984 to E£1.2 billion in 1995. The value of total output has risen by 407 per cent, from E£435 million to E£2.2 billion during 1985–95, according to UNCTAD. A significant cause of this rapid rise has been the growth of both the domestic and export markets.

Local pharmaceutical production is tailored for end-use consumption, relying upon raw material imports which in 1995 were valued at US$221 million. A second feature of the Egyptian market is the impact of the patent law, Law No. 132 of 1949, governing pharmaceutical products. Patents expire after 10 years, and this has had the effect of encouraging the production of generic drugs, which now account for 66 per cent of the public and local private sector output. The production of the generic drugs accounts for 67.1 per cent of public sector output and 68.2 per cent of local private sector output, while the TNCs now produce only licensed products. As with other growth areas of the economy, the pharmaceutical industry relies heavily upon the large domestic market, which accounts for

EGYPTIAN INDUSTRY IN FIGURES

The spinning and weaving industries have seen an increase in the value of exports of 43 per cent since 1990 (see also opposite page)

94–95 per cent sales and meets 91 per cent of local demand. This demand is projected to grow in terms of value by 27 per cent between 1999 and 2005, from E£3.5 billion to E£4.5 billion. The export market despite its current size is growing more rapidly than the domestic market, having increased by 422 per cent since 1990, reaching E£208 million by 1996 and establishing Egypt as the largest pharmaceutical producer and exporter in the Middle East, accounting for 20 per cent of total regional production.

Attempting to match the competitiveness of the regional pharmaceutical industry, Egypt's electronics industry has moved through several important phases, with the strategic aim of attracting foreign technology and competing effectively in the regional market. Central to this strategy has been the robust pursuit of greater efficiency within the industry. Productivity per worker increased by 767 per cent in 1992–96, rising from US$10,600 earned per worker to US$92,000 per worker in 1996. During this period, the number of people employed in the industry dropped by 91 per cent, from 16,000 to 1,350, as greater efficiency and automation were achieved, and despite a doubling of the number of electronics companies to 200. Total production subsequently increased by 636 per cent, from US$117 million to US$861.2 million, increasing the sector's proportionate contribution to GDP from 0.3 per cent to 1.8 per cent.

Tariff structures encouraged the establishment of production facilities by foreign companies in Egypt. An 80 per cent duty on imported consumer electronics such as television sets, which account for 48 per cent of the total market, was effective until 1997. This had the effect of promoting local production, encouraged by a 10 per cent tariff on imported components. The tariff structure has since been revised, with the introduction of a 5 per cent tariff on imported goods. The changing tariff regime has intensified competition and led to a rise in the quality of locally produced goods, with local production of major global brands now being carried out under licence. The rise in quality has allowed for some growth in the export market, though this represents only 5 per cent of the total market.

The future for agriculture and the prospects of land reform

The transformation of Egypt's agricultural sector has become a cornerstone of the government's long-term policy, as it seeks not only to increase food output but also to redraw the political geography of the country by extending habitable areas away from the Nile valley. With only around 3 per cent of Egypt's 0.38 million square mile area arable, half the country's food needs are met through imports. Consequently, 14 per cent of Egypt's imports are accounted for by food, amounting to imports worth E£2.5 billion in 1997–98. Meeting the food needs of 65 million people has required reform on several fronts. Prior to announcement of plans to extend the arable area of the country, the government sought ways of making more effective use of the land which was already available. In 1992 it amended Law No. 178 of 1952, which had frozen the rents imposed upon tenant farmers. The impact of the 1952 law had been to discourage land owners from renting land for which they could not charge a market rent. Consequently, land had been underused. The 1992 amendments came into effect after a five-year grace period, on 1 October 1997, when Egypt's 904,000 tenant farmers saw rents fixed at seven times the value of land tax and allowed inheritance. Average annual rents of E£600 per *feddan* – a measure just less than one acre – more than doubled to E£1,300. Since the introduction of the amendments in 1992, rented agricultural land has diminished from 24 per cent of the total farmed to 13 per cent. Rented agricultural land now amounts to 1 million acres, as farmers bought land from landlords in preparation for the change. The legal amendments allowed landlords to reclaim possession of the 13 per cent of Egypt's agricultural land which is rented, but over which they had little effective control despite their ownership. A side-effect of the new law has been a fall in land prices as more has come onto the market, with the price of land falling recently by 15 per cent to around E£2,500 (US$737) per acre. The strengths and weaknesses of market forces are viewed as the main determinant of the tenant farmers' fate. A key factor will be the temptation of landlords to sell land altogether, either for agriculture in bigger units or to developers. Up to 60,000 acres a year of agricultural land is lost to building developments, according to the Ministry of Agriculture.

Critics of the reform predicted the law would fail to assure the basic food security, by gearing production towards high-value export crops. In fact, CBE figures show that the value of fruit and other high value exports fell during 1992–96, from US$58 to US$23 million, while the value of rice exports rose from US$5 million in 1990 to US$71 million in 1996. According to the Ministry of Agriculture, 95 per cent of the crops grown by tenant farmers deemed them the effective guarantors of national food security by growing 'strategic' crops, namely cotton, wheat, rice, maize and onions. Overall, wheat production also rose by 29 per cent in 1994–97 and vegetable production by 16.9 per cent in the same period. The government estimates agricultural incomes will rise overall, from E£56.4 billion in 1997 to E£68 billion in 2002, caused in part by increased output and the contribution made by fully exploiting production from the 1.6 million acres of land reclaimed since 1986 from desert areas. The increased output is intended by the government to meet domestic needs for staple crops, in particular wheat. In 1997 Egypt produced 6 million tonnes of wheat, meeting 55 per cent of annual needs. The aim of land reform is to increase production to meet 70 per cent of needs, through expanding the land area and increasing yields.

The rural social instability predicted by some critics of the legal changes did not materialise, as most tenant farmers had either bought the land they tilled or had reassessed their level of rent before the law came into effect. The increased yield expected from existing land is intended to be complemented by the addition of 2 million acres to the arable land mass by 2017. To achieve this feat, three large-scale land reclamation projects are under way, with several other projects also advancing, which will increase the inhabited areas of Egypt to 25 per cent of the total area. Most ambitious in this area is the development of North Sinai, where the Al-Salam canal will bring Nile water to irrigate a 620,000 acre area between the Suez canal and Al Arish. Most challenging is the Toshka project, which is intended to bring 500,000 acres of desert land west of Lake Nasser under cultivation. This project will be complemented by the planned irrigation of East Oweinat, an area south-west of Toshka, where 84,000 acres is intended for cultivation. Other land reclamation projects are also under way, in the Eastern and Western Deserts, which will ultimately lead to Egypt's cultivable land area growing to around 5.5 million acres.

With the liberalising of rents, the incentive to tenant farmers to maximise land use to pay market rents, and the incentive to landlords to use their land more effectively, the agricultural sector is expected to emerge from the years of stagnation dominated by price controls and state marketing of products. Agriculture accounts for 17.3 per cent of GDP, represented 4.74 per cent of total exports in 1997–98, and employs 33 per cent of the entire workforce. The contraction of the arable land area in the Nile valley, which will be more than compensated for when the reclaimed areas start production, has been caused by the expansion of the industrial, mineral and tourism sectors, but has not led to a decrease in production. With greater concentration on mechanisation, more productive land use, and easier access to credit for farmers, the sector is expected to move steadily towards reducing the agricultural trade deficit and provide a greater diversity of products, for local consumption and the larger export market which will emerge when Egypt reaches agreement with the EU in 1999 or in early 2000, establishing a trade partnership agreement guaranteeing access to goods.

14 Taxation and incentives for foreign investors

KPMG Hazem Hassan

Taxation

The main taxes in Egypt are: salary tax, withholding taxes on certain categories of income, unified personal income tax, corporate profit tax, real estate taxes, customs taxes, sales tax, stamp tax, and social insurance contributions (as a semi-tax).

Salary tax

This is a monthly tax imposed on salaries, overtimes, bonuses, profit-sharings, and other benefits in cash or in kind accruing to employees. The important tax deductions for salary tax assessment include:

- representation allowance, given to managers, within E£2500 p.a.;
- production incentives within E£3000 p.a. given to employees if their employer's gross income (turnover) in the tax-year increased by at least 10 per cent from the previous year's gross income; and
- housing benefits (within reasonable limits) for foreign experts.

Tax reliefs or allowances include:

- the employee's share in social insurance subscriptions;
- 10 per cent of the remaining income (i.e., after the above-mentioned deductions and relief) as income earning allowance;
- cost of living allowance at E£2000 p.a.; and
- the family allowance at E£2,000 for the single person, E£2,500 for the married person without children, (or the not married person with one child or more) and E£3,000 for the married person with one child or more.

Foreign experts whose employment in Egypt does not exceed 183 days a year are subject to the tax on their total salary income from Egypt without any deductions or reliefs.

TAXATION AND INCENTIVES FOR FOREIGN INVESTORS

The Law for Desert Land encourages projects for reclamation and cultivation of barren land

Salaries and similar remunerations paid to executive directors of Egyptian companies within E£5,000 a year for each are subject to salary tax. Executive directors are also entitled to a tax-free representation allowance within E£3,000 a year. The remaining part of their remunerations will be subject to the tax on income from moveable capital at the rate of 32 per cent as described in the section on withholding tax.

The salary tax (annual) rate is progressive as follows:

- on the first E£50,000 p.a. the rate is 20 per cent;
- on amounts over and above E£50;000 p.a. the rate is 32 per cent.

The employer is required to compute the salary tax on a monthly basis, withheld at source, and then remit it to the tax authority within the first 15 days following the month of salary payment.

Withholding taxes on certain categories of income

Income taxes are withheld at source, without any deductions for expenses or costs, on three categories of easily earned incomes:

- income from moveable capital which is not closely related to the profession or main activities of the recipient of such income;
- royalties; and
- incidental commissions not directly related to the profession of the commission recipient.

The withholding taxes on these incomes apply to all kinds of persons receiving them whether they are individuals, partnerships, corporation, or governments, and whether they are residents or non-residents of Egypt. However, tax conventions between Egypt and other countries may grant exemptions, or exceptions or require lower tax rates.

Income from moveable capital

This category includes the following types of income:

- interest income from loans, debentures or bonds, and cash deposits;
- interest, dividends, profits, or gains from foreign securities or foreign investments in general; and
- remunerations paid to the chairmen and directors of Egyptian companies.

Income from moveable capital which is closely related to the profession or the main activities of the recipient of such income (such as interest on loans to banks extending such loans) shall not be subject to this withholding tax but will be included in the business profits of the recipient subject to the unified income tax or the corporate profit tax, as the case may be.

Dividends of Egyptian companies are not subject to this tax, nor to any other direct tax.

The important exemptions or reliefs from this withholding tax are interest on foreign loans extended to the government, governorates, public authorities, and public sector companies, such as interest on Treasury bills and bonds, interest on all kinds of cash deposits with local banks and post offices, and interest on debentures issued by companies. The latter being conditional upon at least 30 per cent of the debentures being offered for public subscription in the Egyptian Stock Exchange (ESE), and that the number of subscribers is not less than 150. Interest on debentures offered for public subscription by Egyptian joint-stock companies which do not fully meet these requirements but whose shares are listed at the ESE are tax exempt within the prevailing interest rate on time deposits with local banks. Interest on debentures issued by Egyptian public sector banks, and private sector banks in which the public sector holds at least 51 per cent of their share capital is fully exempt from the tax.

Royalties

This category includes all types of royalties or payments in consideration of know-how, copyrights, patents, and similar types of intellectual rights. The Egyptian tax law does not provide any exemptions or exceptions in this respect.

Incidental commissions

This category includes incidental commissions or brokerage not directly related to the profession of their recipients, and whether such commissions are paid locally or to persons residing outside Egypt. The Egyptian tax law does not provide any exemptions or exceptions for this category of income.

Withholding tax rates

The tax rate on income from moveable capital in all cases is 32 per cent.

For royalties and incidental commissions paid to companies and corporate bodies of all kinds the tax rate is also 32 per cent. For royalties and incidental commissions paid to individuals or simple partnerships the tax rate is progressive ranging between 20 per cent and 40 per cent as discussed hereunder the heading 'Unified personal income tax'.

Tax withholding and remittance

As a general rule, the person paying these categories of income would be required to withhold the tax at source from each payment, and to remit it to the tax authority. However, if the income recipient is an Egyptian company or a public authority, and the income payer is an individual, a simple partnership, or a non-resident, the recipient would be required in this case to deduct the tax, and to remit it to the tax authority.

Generally, the withheld taxes are required to be remitted to the tax authority within 15 days from the date of income payment-receipt. In exception to this, there are many cases specified in the tax law where remittance is allowed within the first 15 days of the month following the month during which income payment-receipt took place.

Unified personal income tax

As indicated above, the salaries, income from moveable capital, royalties, and incidental commissions are each taxed separately. Other types of income which may accrue to individuals whether working independently, or jointly in the form of simple partnerships are grouped together to form the tax base for the unified personal income tax. The types of personal incomes which represent the base for the unified tax are three-fold:

- profits from commercial and industrial activities;
- net income from free professions and non-commercial professions or activities; and
- net income from real estate.

Profits from commercial and industrial activities

Profits from commercial and industrial activities include, inter alia, the net profits realised by commercial or industrial enterprises, net profits of enterprises engaged in mining or petroleum activities, and net profits from renting of shops and furnished flats.

The accounting net profits of these activities have to be adjusted according to the provisions of the tax law to arrive at the taxable profits. These tax adjustments are quite similar to those explained under the heading 'Corporate profit tax'.

The tax law does not recognise the legal entity of simple partnerships and thus the share of each partner, active or sleeping, in the taxable profit of a simple partnership is included in his unified income tax base.

The tax exemptions include profits of honey-bee projects, (for unlimited time), profits of land reclamation and cultivation (for 10 years), profits of poultry and animal breeding (for 10 years), profits of fisheries and fish-catching projects (for 10 years), and profits of private insurance funds (for unlimited time).

Net income from non-commercial professions

The net income from non-commercial professions includes the net profits, as adjusted according to the tax law, of liberal professions (such as the professions of doctors and lawyers), and other non-commercial professions of self-employed individuals in which the work is the essential factor in generating the income. The important tax adjustments here include 15 per cent of net income as professional depreciation, and contributions to social insurance or pension systems.

Non-resident foreigners who may perform, on a temporary basis (ie, for a period not exceeding six months a year) the activities of non-commercial professions will be subject to the tax at 20 per cent on their gross incomes without any deductions or reliefs.

Income from real estate

The income from real estate includes the rental income (actual or hypothetical) accruing to the owners of agricultural land, and buildings. The rental value of agricultural land and buildings is assessed by the government every 10 years whether the real estate is actually rented by its owner or not. Of this rental value, 20 per cent is deducted for maintenance and expenses, and the remaining balance is included in the tax base of the unified income tax.

However, tax-payers have the option to ask the tax authority to assess their net income from real estate on an actual basis, in which case they have to maintain proper books of account which show their actual gross incomes from all real estate owned by them, and the actual costs and expenses incurred by them on their real estate.

Since the agriculture land and buildings are also subject to some direct income taxes, i.e., the real estate taxes as will be explained under the section on the real estate taxes, to avoid

TAXATION AND INCENTIVES FOR FOREIGN INVESTORS

Steps of Repentance, St Katherine's Monastery, Sinai

taxing the same income twice, tax-payers are allowed to deduct from their unified income tax due for payment, original real estate taxes already paid by them.

Assessment

The taxable incomes or profits from commercial and industrial activities, non-commercial professions, and real estate are totalled and the family allowance is deducted from this total as follows:

- for a single person the deduction is E£2,000 p.a.;
- for a married person without children, or the not married person with one child or more, the deduction is E£2,500 p.a.;
- for a married person with one child or more the deduction is E£3,000 p.a.

If the taxable income of an individual is composed of salaries as well as other types of income subject to the unified income tax the family allowance shall be deducted from the taxable amount of salaries, and if the allowance exceeds the taxable salaries amount the excess is deducted from the gross taxable income subject to the unified tax.

The annual taxable income from the three sources referred to above will be subject to the unified personal income tax at the following rates:

Slice	More than E£	Up to E£	Rate
1st –		2,500	20%
2nd	2,500	7,000	27%
3rd	7,000	16,000	35%
4th	16,000	open	40%

The taxpayer is required to file his tax return for the calendar year in question and remit the tax due before the first of April of the subsequent year.

In addition to the personal income taxes mentioned above a complementary tax called the 'development of state resources duty' is imposed on the following incomes:

- salaries of employees;
- remunerations of the chairman and directors of Egyptian companies;
- incomes from commercial and industrial activities; and
- incomes from non-commercial professions.

The state resources duty is imposed on the aggregate taxable income of the individual from the above-mentioned sources which is over and above E£18,000 a year at the rate of 2 per cent. The duty is payable with the unified income tax at the same due date, but for employees it is payable with the salary tax which is paid on a monthly basis.

Corporate profit tax
Scope
Corporate profit tax is imposed on the annual profits of joint-stock companies, limited partnerships by shares, limited liability companies established according to Egyptian law, public sector companies, and public authorities which may engage in taxable activities. The tax is also imposed on foreign banks, and foreign companies and enterprises operating in Egypt in respect

of the profits realised by them from their activities in Egypt. For simplicity we shall refer to these entities as the 'companies'.

Gross taxable profit

The Tax Law, Law No. 157 of 1981 requires certain adjustments to be made to the accounting profit (or accounting loss) to arrive at the gross taxable profit or tax loss that can be carried forward. The important points to be mentioned here are:

- The income from the 'company's' main activities as well as any other incomes, revenues, or gains realised by the 'company' shall be included in its gross taxable profit. In this respect, profits realised by the 'company' from exercising its activities outside Egypt are included in the gross taxable profit unless such activities are carried out by an independent enterprise.
- Gains from the disposal of capital assets are also includable, but if the proceeds from the disposal are fully utilised within two years to purchase new capital assets in replacement of the assets disposed of, the part of the corporate tax related to such capital gains shall be reimbursed or deducted from the corporate tax due for payment.

Costs and expenses

Generally, speaking, the costs and expenses incurred by the 'company' in carrying out its activities, or related to its objectives are tax deductible with some few restrictions, exceptions, and additions as highlighted here:

- the depreciation expense computed at the generally applicable rates in each industry is deductible;
- the notional rental value of the buildings owned by the 'company' and occupied by it to carry out its activities is tax deductible;
- an additional depreciation at the rate of 25 per cent of the cost of new machines and equipments purchased or manufactured by the 'company' to use them in its productive activities is tax deductible but only in the year during which the said assets are used for the first time in production. The normal depreciation plus the additional depreciation should not exceed the cost of the asset;
- provisions are generally not deductible. However, provisions to meet definite losses in the assets or definite liabilities whose amounts cannot be accurately determined are deductible within 5 per cent of the 'company's' net annual profit and within 10 per cent as to banks. The technical provisions of the insurance and reinsurance companies as required by the Egyptian Insurance Law are deductible in full;
- taxes paid by the 'company' are deductible with the exception of the corporate profit tax;
- donations to Egyptian charities are deductible within 7 per cent of the 'company's' net annual profit, and

- the amount of bonuses or remunerations to employees in excess of the equivalent of three months' salary is not deductible.

Income from moveable capital

The incomes accruing to the 'companies' from their moveable capitals which have been subjected to the tax on income from moveable capital (discussed previously) or have been exempt therefrom by law is tax deductible. Any financial costs as well as investment or administration expenses related to such incomes should also be excluded. However, this deduction of incomes from moveable capitals does not apply if such incomes are closely related to the profession or the main activity of the 'company' in which case the related incomes will be included normally in the gross taxable profit of the 'company'. The deduction does not also apply to dividends received on the 'company's' shareholding in another Egyptian company, and thus such dividends are included in the 'company's' gross taxable profit, but will enjoy certain allowances or reliefs as indicated below.

Similarly, 90 per cent of the (actual) income from buildings or agricultural land owned by the 'company' and on which the company has paid the real estate taxes or was exempt therefrom is tax deductible.

Carrying forward tax losses

If the adjustments required by the tax law as highlighted above result in a tax loss, this loss can be carried forward to five subsequent years, maximum. But tax losses cannot be carried backward.

Tax reliefs

The important tax reliefs or allowances deductible from the gross taxable profit to arrive at the net taxable profit are:

- an amount equal to the interest on the paid-up capital of a listed 'joint-stock company' at the prevailing interest rate on time deposits at banks in Egypt for one year;
- an amount equal to the dividends received by the 'company' from its shareholdings in another Egyptian joint-stock company on condition that the 'company' acquired the shares of the other company on its foundation;
- an amount equal to the income from shares and debentures owned by an investment joint-stock company which employs at least 90 per cent of its invested capital in securities on condition that this allowance does not exceed the amount of profit distributed by the investment company to its shareholders;
- an amount equal to 90 per cent of the dividends received by the 'company' from its shareholding in another Egyptian 'joint-stock company'. This allowance does not apply if the allowance under points two and three above is applied; and
- an amount equal to the income from funds of Egyptian insurance and reinsurance

TAXATION AND INCENTIVES FOR FOREIGN INVESTORS

'companies' held or deposited in foreign countries to meet their insurance liabilities in these countries.

Tax reliefs are also extended to profits arising from mergers between the 'companies', and to share-capital redemptions of 'companies' operating under concessions granted by the government.

Tax exemptions

The important tax exemptions provided by the Tax Law 157 of 1981 to profits on certain types of projects are:

- honey-bee companies for an unlimited period of time;
- land reclamation and cultivation companies for 10 years;
- poultry and animal breeding companies for five years;
- fishery and fishing companies for five years;
- industrial companies which employ at least 50 employees for five years; and
- mutual funds for unlimited period of time.

One of the treasures in the Egyptian Museum

Coptic Museum, Old Cairo. The area is being renovated with the use of private funding

Tax rate

The standard rate of the corporate profit tax is 40 per cent. Profits of industrial 'companies' from their industrial activities, and profits from exporting activities are subject to the tax at a reduced rate of 32 per cent. Profits of oil exploration and production companies which are not state-owned are subject to the tax at the rate of 40.55 per cent. The complementary tax called the 'development of state resources duty' is also levied on the taxable profits of the 'companies' which are over and above E£18,000 a year.

Tax return and tax payment

'Companies' are required to file their tax returns, together with their financial statements and the auditors reports, within 30 days of the date of the annual meeting in which the financial statements are approved, but not later than 30 days of the deadline for the convention of the annual meeting as stipulated in their articles of association. According to the Companies Law 159 of 1981 the deadline for the annual meeting is three months from the end of the company's financial year. Foreign branches are required to file their tax returns with the afore-mentioned documents within four months of the end of their financial years. The corporate profit tax and the state resources duty should be remitted with the tax return on due date.

Real estate taxes

These taxes are imposed on the rental income from buildings and agricultural land. This rental income is assessed or reassessed by the government every 10 years for all buildings (within city boundaries) and all agricultural land whether actually rented to others, or directly used or exploited by the owners.

Taxes on buildings

The original tax rate on buildings is 10 per cent for non-residential buildings, and ranges between 20 per cent and 40 per cent on residential buildings depending on the average rental value of the room in a flat. The original tax is assessed on the net rental value which is 80 per cent of (gross) rental value (that is, 20 per cent is deducted for maintenance and expenses). In addition to the original tax there is a complementary tax called guards tax (*khafar* tax) whose rate is 20 per cent of the original tax.

Both the original tax and the guards tax are borne by the owner. The owners of the buildings and the occupants thereof may also be subject to some local taxes or duties imposed by the governorates of Egypt (i.e., local self-governments such as counties in other countries). In Cairo Governorate, for example, the following duties are imposed:

- municipal duty at 2.67 per cent of the net rental value borne by the owner;
- occupancy duty at 4 per cent of the gross rental value borne by the occupant; and
- cleaning duty at 2 per cent of the gross rental value borne by the occupant.

Residential buildings which were established on 9 September 1977 or thereafter and which are classified as being of non-luxurious level became exempt from the original tax and the guards tax as from 1 January 1982.

Taxes on agricultural land

The rate of the original tax on agricultural land is 14 per cent and is assessed on the (net) rental value of the land, which is 80 per cent of the gross rental value. There is also a guards tax (*khafar* tax) whose rate is 20 per cent of the original tax. Both taxes are borne by the owner of the land. As in the tax on income from buildings, governorates may also impose some local taxes or duties on the rental value of agriculture land.

Customs taxes

Imported goods are subject to the custom taxes and duties as designated in the customs tariff. Customs tax rates on imports are in the range of 5-40 per cent except for means of transportation where the rate may go up to 135 per cent. There is also a service charge at 2 per cent if the import tax rate is 30 per cent or less, and at 3 per cent if the import tax rate is more than 30 per cent.

Machines and equipment imported by joint-stock companies, partnerships limited by shares, and limited liability companies for their own use are subject to the customs tax at a reduced rate of 5 per cent ad valorem. Other legal forms of enterprises (mainly simple partnerships and foreign branches) do not enjoy this reduced customs rate unless they come under one of the laws encouraging investment in Egypt. This point together with some exemptions from the customs taxes are indicated under 'Important tax exemptions and other investment incentives', sub-sections 'The Investment Law' and 'Tax incentives provided by other laws'.

Customs import tax on parts of completely knocked down products (such as motor cars) which are imported to be assembled in Egypt is assessed on the basis of the complete product and then reduced by percentages ranging between 10 per cent, if the local content of the final product is less than 30 per cent, and a maximum of 90 per cent, if the local content exceeds 60 per cent; if, however, the import tax as previously assessed is higher than the actual import taxes on the parts, the lesser amount shall be paid.

Customs taxes paid on imported parts used in manufacturing local products are reimbursed in full if such local products are exported.

Machines, equipment, and similar capital assets, with the exception of private passenger cars, which are imported on a temporary basis, are subject to the customs import tax at 20 per cent of the original customs tax rates according to tariffs for each year or fraction of year during which they remain in Egypt until exported.

Sales tax

Manufactured goods, operating or processing for the account of others, some intermediary services, and some tourism services are subject to the sales tax as imposed by Law No. 11 of 1991 which came into force from 3 May 1991. The sales tax is mainly imposed on manufactured goods (whether imported or locally produced) and is similar in many respects to value-added tax. The standard rate of the sales tax is 10 per cent but some goods are exempt from the tax and some other goods attract lower or higher tax rates.

The sales tax paid on goods which are exported, as they are or after some processing, shall be reimbursed in full.

As at mid-1999 the sales tax is applied to importers and manufacturers only. A second phase it will be applied to wholesalers and at third and final phase it will be applied to retailers.

Obviously the real burden of the sales tax will fall on the final consumer.

Stamp tax

The Stamp Tax Law 111 of 1981 classifies the stamp taxes into specific and proportional taxes. The specific stamp taxes are imposed on a variety of documents such as contracts and cash receipts at specific sums whose total burden is very reasonable.

The proportional stamp taxes are imposed on the values of certain financial transactions and instruments at prescribed rates; for example loans at 0.8 per cent, credits at 1 per cent, advertisements at 36 per cent, insurance premiums at 3 per cent to 20 per cent, and governmental payments for supplies, services, and contracting works at 2.4 per cent.

Social insurance contributions

Companies, or rather employers in general, are required to apply the Social Insurance Law No. 79 of 1975 to cover their employees against old age, disability, death, work accidents, unemployment and illness. Law No. 79 of 1975 covers Egyptian employees as well as foreign employees whose countries have treaties with Egypt for reciprocal social insurance treatment. Countries with reciprocal treaties are Greece, Cyprus, Morocco, Libya, Sudan, Jordan, Syria, Iraq, Lebanon, Somalia and Palestine.

Employers are required to withhold the employees' social insurance contributions from their salaries, and to remit them together with the employers' contributions to the Social

Insurance Organisation on a monthly basis. The salaries and related benefits or emoluments are divided, for social insurance purposes, into a basic salary, and variable elements. The maximum insured sum of the basic salary as at mid-1999 was E£525 a month, and the maximum insured sum of the variable elements was E£500 a month. Variable elements include the remainder of the basic salary if it is in excess of E£525 a month as well as overtimes, bonuses, representation allowances, and similar emoluments. The social insurance rates are:

Salary	Employer's contribution	Employee's contribution
On basic salary (up to E£525)	26%	14%
On variable elements (up to E£500)	24%	11%

The social insurance system for contractors' workers is different from the above system, and is regulated by Ministerial Decree No. 74 of 1988. Contractors' workers are the Egyptian temporary workers hired on contracts, and are directly involved in the execution of the contracting works, such as electricians, carpenters, masons, welders, plumbers or tillers. The contractor's social insurance contribution is assessed on a lump-sum basis according to the formula, whereby the contract amount is multiplied by the wages percentage and the social insurance rate at 18 per cent.

The wages percentage is determined by reference to Table 3 attached to Ministerial Decree No. 74 of 1988 which fixes a percentage for each type of contracting work. The social insurance rate at 18 per cent covers the workers against old age, disability, death and work accidents. If the main contractor subcontracts part(s) of his contract to a subcontractor(s) the social insurance contributions paid by his subcontractors(s) are deductible from the social insurance contribution due from him to avoid duplication. The contractor's social insurance contributions are payable gradually on each progress invoice when approved by his customer (or employer).

Contractors' workers are required to pay their social insurance contributions directly to the Social Insurance Organisation on a monthly basis.

Important tax exemptions and other investment incentives

In 1974, Egypt started to adopt the open-door policy, and to encourage foreign investors, as well as the Egyptian private sector to invest in Egypt. For this purpose Law No. 43 of 1974 for Foreign Investment and Free Zones was issued and proved to be very successful in attracting foreign investors. In 1989, this law was replaced by Law No. 230 of 1989 which was along the same lines of Law 43 with some limited changes to meet the changing circumstances. In May 1997 Law No. 8 of 1997 for Investment Guarantees and Incentives was issued to replace Law No. 230 of 1989, again to meet the changing circumstances and to give more incentives to investors where their endeavours are most needed by the Egyptian economy.

In the following section, the important provisions of Law No. 8 of 1997 are highlighted with emphasis on the tax and other incentives provided thereby. In a second section, the important tax incentives provided by other laws are summarised.

The Investment Law

On 11 May 1997 Law No. 8 of 1997 for Investment Guarantees and Incentives was issued to replace the Investment Law No. 230 of 1989. Companies and other types of enterprises that were established under the abolished law (Law No. 230 of 1989) will continue to enjoy the tax exemptions and guarantees provided thereunder until they legally expire.

The important activities or projects which can enjoy the tax exemptions and guarantees under Law No. 8 of 1997 include manufacturing, mining, land reclamation, hotels and tourism villages, tourism transport, air and marine transportation, petroleum services, residential housing, infrastructure projects, finance leasing, underwriting activity in the capital markets, venture capital activity, production of computer software and systems, fish, poultry and animal breeding, and so on.

Free zones also come under Law No. 8 of 1997. Projects in free zones can be established to carry out any of the activities mentioned above, in addition to any other activities approved by the Investment Authority. In this respect the Investment Authority approves the storing activity, transit trade, and repairing of goods entered from inside the country, or carrying out some industrial processes thereon, and returning them back to inside the country.

The project can adopt any legal form recognised by the Egyptian law but usually it takes the form of a joint-stock company.

The important tax exemptions, provided by Law No. 8 of 1997 to the projects established in accordance therewith are as follows:

Projects inside the country

1. Projects inside the country (therefore not in free zones) enjoy an exemption from the profit tax (corporate profit tax or personal income tax as the case may be) for five years from the first financial year following the year during which they become productive or operational (ie, capable of generating income from their main activity).

    However, projects established within the Old Valley in new urban communities, new industrial cities and remote zones enjoy exemption from the profit tax for 10 years. Projects established outside the Old Valley, such as in Toshka, enjoy tax exemption for 20 years.
2. Egyptian joint-stock companies under Law 8 whose shares are registered with the Egyptian Stock Exchange will enjoy an exemption from the corporate tax on their profits equal to the Central Bank of Egypt's lending or discount rate multiplied by the paid-up capital of the company.
3. The imported capital assets of the projects, whatever their legal form may be, are subject to

customs taxes at a reduced rate of 5 per cent ad valorem.
4. The foundation documents of the companies and enterprises (articles and memorandum of association or deeds), as well as loan and mortgage contracts related to their activities are exempt from the stamp taxes and notarisation fees, for a period of three years as from the date of registering the company or enterprise in the Commercial Register. Also the registration of pieces of land necessary for establishing the companies or enterprises thereon shall be exempt from the aforementioned taxes and fees without any limitation of time.
5. Interest from bonds issued by joint-stock companies under Law 8 is exempt from the tax on income from moveable capital provided that the bonds are offered for public subscription and that they are registered at the ESE.
6. Valuation gains related to in-kind sharecapital given on the foundation of a company under Law 8, or on the occasion of increasing its share capital shall be exempt from the profit tax.
7. Gains from mergers, divisions (splittings), or change of the legal form of companies or enterprises under Law 8 are exempt from all taxes and duties that may arise in this respect.

Projects established in the free zones

Projects established in the free zones and the profits distributed by them are exempt from all taxes and duties all through their lives. But these projects will be subject to an annual duty payable to the Investment Authority at 1 per cent of the value of goods received by the project for storage, or at 1 per cent of the value of goods manufactured or assembled by the project. Projects whose main activity does not deal with goods (i.e., service projects) will be subject to the annual duty at 1 per cent on their total annual revenues.

Materials and goods which are exported abroad by the free zone projects or imported to exercise their activity shall not be subject to the customs taxes, the general tax on sales, and other taxes and duties. Also articles, equipment, machines and means of transport which are necessary for exercising the activity licensed for the projects inside the free zones shall be exempt from the above-mentioned taxes and duty, with the exception of passenger cars.

Projects in the free zones are considered to be offshore projects and thus goods sold by free zone projects inside Egypt are subject to importation regulations and to customs taxes payable by the purchaser.

Guarantees and privileges

The important guarantees and privileges provided by Law No. 8 of 1997 are as follows:
1. Projects may not be nationalised or confiscated. The assets of the projects may not be seized, blocked, confiscated, or sequestrated except by judicial procedures.
2. Projects inside the country are exempt from some restrictive provisions in the Companies Law No. 159 of 1981. Free zone projects are also exempt from the Companies Law No. 159 of 1981, and Foreign Exchange Law. However, the employees of the company or enterprise are entitled to a profit-sharing not less than 10 per cent of the annual profits allocated for

distribution among the shareholders or partners (as the case may be) but the amount of profit-sharing should not exceed 100 per cent of the annual salaries of the employees.

3. Projects are exempt from legal restrictions on the ownership of real estate by foreigners, or projects with foreign participation.
4. Projects are exempt from applicable import and export regulations and these are replaced by much simpler regulations.
5. Projects are allowed to freely fix the prices of their products without any governmental intervention or control.
6. The Investment Authority will assist the investor in acquiring a piece of land for his project in one of the new urban communities or cities at quite low prices.
7. It is worth mentioning before ending this section that the current foreign exchange regulations are very simple and liberal, and thus they do not put any restrictions on the repatriation of the foreign invested capital, and the transfer of the foreign investor's share in the profits of the project.

Tax incentives provided by other laws

In addition to the tax exemptions and incentives referred to above, there are tax exemptions (mainly from the corporate profit tax) provided for by other laws of which we may highlight the following:

Law No. 143 of 1981 for Desert Land

This law encourages projects for reclamation and cultivation of barren and desert land owned by the state by granting such projects an exemption from the corporate profit tax for 10 years together with some other incentives similar to those given under the Investment Law.

The Reconstruction Law (Law No. 62 of 1974)

This law grants foreign construction companies, and foreign consultancy firms an exemption from the corporate profit tax as well as the other tax exemptions provided for under the Investment Law when such companies or firms are engaged in any reconstruction projects specified by the Ministry of Housing and Reconstruction within the national plan for economic and social development, for a period not exceeding five years for each project.

Law No. 29 of 1975 for Armament

This law exempts foreign companies and organisations which contract with the Ministry of Defence for the supply of armament, rendering of services, or construction works needed for this ministry from all taxes and duties including the corporate profit tax, and the customs taxes.

Egypt and the United States Agreement for Economic and Technical Assistance (1978)

According to this Agreement U.S. contractors who are assigned contracting works in Egypt which are financed by USAID shall be exempt from all taxes and duties including the corporate profit tax, and the customs taxes.

Tax treaties

The tax treaties between Egypt and 'other states' include certain exemptions or reductions in the tax rates not hitherto addressed. It suffices here to highlight the following standard provisions in the tax treaties:

- The tax rate on interest income, or dividends (currently Egyptian dividends are not subject to any tax) accruing to residents of the 'other states' from Egyptian sources should not exceed 15-20 per cent thereof. Similarly, interest income, or dividends accruing to residents of Egypt from sources in the 'other states' should not be taxed in the other states, at more than 15-20 per cent thereof;
- The tax on royalties accruing to residents of the 'other states' from Egyptian sources should not exceed 15-25 per cent of the gross amount of the royalty. The same thing applies to royalties accruing to Egyptian residents from residents of the 'other states';
- The incomes accruing to residents of the 'other states' from the performance of professional services in Egypt for a period or periods not exceeding 120 days a year may be exempt from the Egyptian personal income taxes. The same rule applies to Egyptian professionals who provide their services in the 'other states'.

Accounting and auditing

The accounting and auditing profession in Egypt is mainly governed by three pieces of legislation:

Law No. 133 of 1952

This Law regulates the general aspects of the profession and determines the qualifications required for accountants and auditors to practise the profession:

According to Law No. 133 of 1952, the accounting profession should be practised by individuals of Egyptian nationality and not corporations. However individuals may form simple partnerships to be able to properly serve big local companies as well as international companies operating in Egypt. The major international accounting firms (the big five) are represented in Egypt.

Registration as an authorised accountant requires the possession of a bachelor of commerce degree (majoring in accounting) and the completion of a period of three years of approved training but will not be allowed to audit Egyptian companies except after having completed another five years of practical experience in a recognised accounting firm.

The Decree Establishing the Egyptian Society for Accountants and Auditors (ESAA)

ESAA was established in 1946 by a royal decree, then was reorganised in 1977 as a non-profit organisation under Law No. 32 of 1964. ESAA's main object is to improve the professional standard of accountants and auditors. ESAA has been a member of IFAC since 1978.

Membership of ESAA requires training with a member of ESAA for at least three years and the successful completion of two professional examinations after which they are entitled to audit all types of business entities including Egyptian companies.

Minister of Economy decision No. 478 of 1997

Minister of Economy decision No. 478 of 1997 established a permanent committee to issue accounting standards, auditing guidelines, and professional ethics.

The permanent committee for accounting and auditing standards had, as at mid-1999, issued 20 Egyptian accounting standards (EAS) which are in line with the corresponding International Accounting Standards (IAS), issued by IFAC, with minor adaptations to conform to local requirements. Where no EAS exists, the International Accounting Standards should be followed.

Egyptian standards or guidelines on auditing are still being developed based on the International Standards on Auditing (ISA). The Egyptian Standards on Auditing would be very similar to ISA with minor modifications to comply with local requirements.

Filing requirements

With the exception of sole traders and simple partnerships, all Egyptian companies, and branches of foreign companies are required to file annually their financial statements and the audit report thereon with the relevant supervisory authority (i.e., the Companies Department, the Investment Authority, or the Capital Market Authority). The statutory audit reports should be based on financial statements prepared in conformity with the Egyptian accounting standards and audited in accordance with the international standards on auditing.

15 Legal environment

Helmy and Hamza
(Baker & McKenzie)

Establishing a presence

A foreign company may establish a direct presence in Egypt through a liaison or representative office, a branch office, or a locally incorporated entity.

Representative offices

Foreign companies are permitted to establish representative or liaison offices, as well as scientific or technical offices and other offices whose purpose is to carry out market surveys or to study the feasibility of production without carrying out any commercial operations or commercial agency activities.

A representative office may be registered under either Company Law No. 159 of 1981 or the Commercial Agencies Law No. 120 of 1982. Such offices should be entered in the register in the Companies Department. To register, the company must submit an application detailing the name, nationality, company objectives, capital, head office abroad, nature of office to be established in Egypt, its activities and address in Egypt and certain information relating to the manager.

The application must include the company's constitutive documents and a resolution of the board of directors of the company, which must be certified at an Egyptian embassy abroad. A certified Arabic translation of these documents is also required.

In certain cases such offices must be registered pursuant to the Commercial Agencies Law. Under this law, if a foreign company is required by a government authority to have a service facility for its products in Egypt, it must appoint a commercial agent and it may register its representative office under this law instead of the Companies Law. However, such registration will lapse immediately if the company ceases to have a commercial agent.

Representative offices must submit to the Companies Department annually the following information about their employees: names, positions, nationalities, salaries, and the total payroll earned by Egyptian employees. Details of the representative office's activities during the year in question must also be submitted.

These offices may not carry out any taxable activities, such as invoicing for services rendered or trading in the company's product(s). Their employees, however, will be subjected to salary tax regardless of nationality. In the case of Egyptian employees, social insurance

Foreign exchange generated from tourism or exports no longer needs to be repatriated into Egypt

contributions will be due and payable by both the employers and the employees. Foreign employees working for a representative office must obtain work and residence permits.

Scientific offices (for a pharmaceutical company)

To register, the company must address a letter to the Pharmaceutical Authority at the Ministry of Health requesting its approval for the establishment of a scientific office in the name of the company. The letter should include:

- the name of the individual who will carry out the procedures to establish the scientific office and the name of the office manager who must be either a physician or pharmacist; and
- the name of at least three pharmaceutical products registered in Egypt. (If the company has not registered any pharmaceutical products, it must address another letter to the Pharmaceutical Authority requesting the registration of at least three pharmaceutical products. The letter should include a description of the pharmaceutical products, the name

of the individual who will register them, and a list of all the pharmaceutical products of the company.)

The manager must submit plans of the proposed office premises to the Pharmaceutical Authority, which will then inspect the premises. The matter is then referred to the Ministry of Health, which will issue a ministerial decree authorising the establishment of the scientific office. (If the company wishing to establish the scientific office has licensed its products to a company in Egypt, part of the licence fee has to be paid in Egyptian pounds to cover the local expenses of the scientific office.) All employees of a scientific office, including the manager, must be Egyptian.

Branch offices

A foreign company may register a branch office in Egypt, provided that the foreign company has a contract (with either the private or public sector) to perform work in Egypt. Although a branch office can engage in commercial, financial, industrial and contractual activities, those activities (under the branch registration) will be limited to the work to be performed under its contract in Egypt.

To establish a branch office, the approvals of the Minister of Internal Trade, the minister supervising the field of activities of the branch, and the Investment Authority must be obtained. A branch office must also be registered in the Commercial Registry. The registration application must be accompanied by the following documents:

- the Articles of Incorporation of the company;
- an audited balance sheet for the most recent fiscal year;
- corporate resolution(s) authorising the establishment of the Egyptian branch, appointing its manager and allocating the necessary capital for its operations; and
- a copy of the contract it has signed in respect of its activities in Egypt.

The branch must also be registered with the Companies Department. The registration is valid for five years.

A branch of a foreign company must comply with Egyptian law including laws governing companies, taxation, labour, social insurance and foreign exchange. In particular, it must have an Egyptian auditor. Furthermore, the following must be submitted to the Companies Department annually:

- a copy of the balance sheet, the profit and loss account and the auditor's report;
- the names and nationalities of the managers;
- the details of all personnel and the salaries paid to the Egyptian employees; and
- the details of profits and the proportion of those profits distributed to employees.

LEGAL ENVIRONMENT

The branch may not employ foreigners in excess of 10 per cent of its workforce (excluding foreigners employed as managers) or pay them more than 20 per cent of the total payroll.

Employees will be subject to salary tax, and the branch must make the appropriate monthly withholdings in respect thereof. In the case of Egyptian employees, social insurance contributions will be due and payable by both the employers and the employees. Foreign employees working for the branch must have obtained, prior to starting work in Egypt, work and residence permits.

The branch is subject to corporate income tax at the rate of 40 per cent on net profits generated from its operations in Egypt. The branch must distribute at least 10 per cent of its net profits to its employees, up to a maximum of the total annual payroll.

Under Egyptian foreign exchange laws, to meet its local expenditures in Egyptian pounds, the branch must exchange foreign currency through the Egyptian banking system. The branch must keep financial books and records and submit audited tax returns annually.

Egyptian companies

There are various forms of business organisations used by the Egyptian private sector. However, the vehicles most commonly used by foreign investors are joint-stock companies and limited liability companies.

There are two regimes under which a foreign company may incorporate an Egyptian joint-stock or a limited liability company: the Investment Guarantees and Incentives Law, Law No. 8 of 1997 (known as the 'Investment Law') and Law No. 159 of 1981, as amended by Law No. 3 of 1998 (the 'Companies Law'). Foreign companies generally prefer to form entities under the Investment Law to be eligible for the benefits and privileges available under that Law. Generally, there are no minimum Egyptian capital participation requirements.

Joint-stock company

In general, the rules and regulations governing joint-stock companies are more comprehensive than those for limited liability companies, especially in the case of joint-stock companies offering shares to the public.

Law No. 3 issued in January 1998, amending the Companies Law, made it easier and faster to form joint-stock companies. Instead of having to submit an application with supporting documentation to the Companies Department for its approval, as was the case under the previous system, the founders now need only notify the Companies Department of the company's formation. The following documents must be attached to this notification:

- the constitutive documents of the company, such as the Articles of Association and Statutes. (Model Articles and Statutes have been issued by Ministerial Decrees for Law No. 159 Companies and Investment Law Companies);

LEGAL ENVIRONMENT

- a certificate from an authorised bank to the effect that the required capital has been deposited in a blocked account. This capital is then released upon the company's formation; and
- a receipt for payment in settlement of incorporation fees, which represent 0.1 per cent of the Company's issued capital (with a minimum of E£100 and a maximum of E£1,000).

An additional document indicating the Cabinet's approval is required in connection with companies engaging in the fields of satellites, newspapers, remote sensing systems and private associations.

Upon submission of these documents and notification to the Companies Department, a fast-track system, introduced by Law No. 3, ensures that a certificate is issued to confirm that all the documentation is complete and has been received. Once the company has this certificate it is automatically registered in the Commercial Register and acquires its legal status upon the lapse of 15 days from the registration date. The Companies Department has 10 days from the date it was originally notified of the company's formation to object on one of the following grounds:

- the Statutes or Articles deviate from the models with respect to mandatory requirements, or violate any law;
- the purposes of the company violate any law or public order; or
- one of the founders is not qualified under the law.

If the company does not rectify the grounds for the Companies Department's objection within 15 days of receipt of notification of objection, the company will be struck off the Commercial Register. The objection is deemed to have been waived if the company does not receive any comments on the rectification steps taken by the company from the Companies Department within 15 days of the receipt by the Companies Department of the company's response stating the rectification steps taken by it. Finally, to acquire full legal status, the company's Articles and Statutes must be published in accordance with the Executive Regulations in the relevant Government Bulletin.

The minimum share capital for a joint-stock company whose shares are not open to public subscription is E£250,000. If the shares are offered to the public it is E£500,000.

A further step towards facilitating investment in Egypt is the reduction of the paid-in capital required for the incorporation of joint-stock companies, from 25 to 10 per cent of the issued capital. Law No. 3 also stipulates that companies that are formed by public subscription do not have to offer a minimum of 49 per cent of the shares to the Egyptian public.

Moreover, Law No. 3 now allows a joint-stock company to raise its issued capital up to its authorised capital by way of an extraordinary general assembly resolution without the requirement of having the issued capital fully paid. The old rule of the Board of Directors' authority to increase the issued capital within the limits of the authorised capital is still valid, provided the issued capital is fully paid.

LEGAL ENVIRONMENT

The Investment Law guarantees against expropriation and nationalisation of companies established under it

Value of shares

The nominal value of shares must not be more than E£1,000 or less than E£5. Preferred shares may be issued. Previously, bearer shares were not permitted and all types of shares had to be registered (nominal). However, the Capital Markets Law (enacted on 22 June 1992) authorised the issuing of bearer shares, subject to some restrictions. Bearer shares carry no vote in the general meetings and may not exceed 25 per cent of the issued and outstanding shares of the company. Moreover, the full nominal value of bearer shares must be paid up in full at the time of incorporation. Share certificates are issued to each shareholder.

Number of shareholders

There must be a minimum of three founding shareholders (founding shareholders may be natural persons or legal entities). There is no maximum limit.

Purpose

Generally, there are no restrictions on a joint-stock company's intended commercial purposes provided they do not conflict with public policy or public morality. However, for joint-stock companies established under the Investment Law, the purposes must be within those listed in the Investment Law, or otherwise as provided for by the Council of Ministers to benefit from the incentives and guarantees granted under the Law.

LEGAL ENVIRONMENT

Name

The name of the company should indicate the activity or objects of the company. It must not include the name of any of the shareholders unless such name is a registered trade name.

Debentures

Negotiable debentures or bonds may be issued by a joint-stock company. They must be of equal value and have equal rights with respect to each security of the same series. Debentures convertible into shares may also be issued. Existing shareholders will then have rights of priority to subscribe to these debentures. Debentures may be issued to the public.

Transfer of shares

Founding shares and shares issued for contribution in kind may not be transferred (except to other founders) before the publication of the financial statements of the first two full fiscal years. Apart from that restriction, there are no restrictions on the transfer of shares unless specified in the statutes of the company.

Transfer of shares for companies established under the Investment Law are not subject to this restriction provided the approval of the Chairman of the Investment Authority, or his nominee, is obtained.

Management

A joint-stock company is managed by a board of directors whose members may not number less than three, and there must be an odd number at all times (except in companies established under the Investment Law where an even number is allowed). There are no nationality requirements for board members.

Profits

The company's after-tax earning in each fiscal year, as increased or reduced, as the case may be, by any profit or loss of the company carried forward from prior years, is available for distribution in accordance with the requirements of Egyptian law and the company's by-laws, as follows:

1. The company is legally required to establish and maintain a legal reserve (the 'Legal Reserve') equal to at least 50 per cent of paid-in capital. If at the end of a fiscal year the Legal Reserve is less than 50 per cent of paid-in capital, an amount equal to at least 5 per cent of after-tax earnings, if any, in respect of such fiscal year must be allocated to the Legal Reserve.
2. After funding the Legal Reserve, if required as described above, the balance of after-tax earnings after deduction of the Legal Reserve ('Distributable Profits'), may be distributed pursuant to a shareholders' resolution in a general shareholders' meeting.
3. The company is legally required to allocate to the employees an amount (the 'Employee Bonus') equal to a minimum of 10 per cent of the Distributable Profits and a maximum of

the aggregate annual basic salaries. If the 10 per cent of the Distributable Profits is higher than the aggregate annual basic salaries, the 10 per cent may be paid in cash to the employees and any remainder, if any, will be allocated to a special account for employees and to provide services for their benefit pursuant to the determination of the board of directors in accordance with Article 196 of the Executive Regulations of the Companies Law.

4 The Distributable Profits shall be distributed in order of priority as follows: An initial amount equal to a minimum of 5 per cent of the Distributable Profits to be distributed to the shareholders as dividends and to the employees as part of the Employee Bonus. An amount equal to no more than 10 per cent of the Distributable Profits may be paid to members of the board of directors as remuneration. The balance of the Distributable Profits may be: paid to the shareholders as additional dividends and to the employees as an additional payment on account of the Employee Bonus; carried forward to the following year as retained earnings; or allocated to fund a special reserve to be used as determined by a general shareholders' meeting, on the recommendation of the board of directors.

Payment of dividends is made to the share owner, based on a statement of account from a registered book-keeper, if the shares are deposited with the Central Depository, or by surrender of coupons attached to the share certificates if the company has physical shares, as the case may be. Dividends not claimed within five years of the date of payment become barred by the statute of limitations and are paid to the state treasury. Shareholders may decide at an ordinary general meeting to distribute all or part of the dividends included in the financial statements of the company accompanied by a report from the company's auditor.

Stock exchange registration
Stock exchange registration is obligatory within one year of formation in the case of a company offering its shares to the public, otherwise after the third year's published accounts.

Limited liability company

A limited liability company's constitutive documents are its Statutes. Model Statutes have been issued by Ministerial Decrees for Law No. 159 companies and for Investment Law companies.

Shareholdings
The minimum capital of a limited liability company is E£50,000. The capital must be fully paid up at the time of incorporation and placed in a blocked bank account. This capital is then released upon the company's formation. Quotas, or as is more commonly used in the market, shares, must be of equal value and cannot have a nominal value of less than E£100. No share certificates are issued for limited liability companies.

LEGAL ENVIRONMENT

The coptic 'Hanging Church' of al-Mu'allaqa, dating from the 11th century

Number of shareholders
A minimum of two founding shareholders is required and a maximum of 50 shareholders is permitted. (Shareholders may be natural persons or legal entities.) It is not permitted to offer shares in limited liability companies to the public.

Purpose
A limited liability company may not carry out the activities of insurance, banking, savings, deposit taking or the investment of funds for the account of third parties.

LEGAL ENVIRONMENT

Name

The name of the company may refer to its activities and may include the name of one or more of its shareholders.

Debentures

Debentures may not be issued by limited liability companies.

Transfer of shares

Shareholders wishing to transfer their shares to third parties must first offer them to existing shareholders, who have a period of one month within which to purchase the shares on a pro rata basis. (The statutes may require that no transfer of shares be effected except upon the approval of the other shareholders.)

Management

Limited liability companies are managed by one or more managers, of which at least one must be Egyptian. There must also be a supervisory council if there are more than 10 shareholders. There is no requirement that employees participate in management.

Profits

Profits are distributed to the employees of a limited liability company when the capital of the company reaches E£250,000. Then the rules are the same as for a joint-stock company.

Incentives for foreign investors

The Investment Law

To encourage investment in Egypt, the Investment Law provides certain incentives for foreign investors who carry out commercial activities in Egypt in accordance with its provisions. To qualify for these benefits and privileges and to receive the requisite Egyptian government approvals, certain specified procedures must be followed. These procedures are set out in detail in the Executive Regulations of the Investment Law. The Investment Authority is the governmental agency concerned with the review of all applications for companies to be formed under the Investment Law.

Qualification

To benefit from the privileges granted under the Investment Law, projects carried out by companies in Egypt must encompass any of the following activities: land reclamation and cultivation of barren land, animal, poultry and fish production, manufacturing and mining, tourist projects (including all means of tourist transportation, different kinds of hotels and hotel-related facilities), agricultural projects, aviation and transportation services, overseas maritime transportation, oil exploration services, housing and infrastructure projects (including installation, operation and management of cable and wireless communication systems), medical facilities that offer 10 per cent of its capacity free of charge, lease financing and underwriting securities, venture capital projects, information technology, projects funded by the Social Fund for Development and other activities as may be added by the Council of Ministers.

Egyptian, Arab and foreign investors are entitled to some guarantees and incentives with respect to activities falling under any fields of investment outlined under the Investment Law. There are no minimum Egyptian capital requirements.

Guarantees and incentives available under the Investment Law

Once a company's investment project has qualified and received the requisite Egyptian government approval, the following guarantees and incentives are available.

The Investment Law guarantees against expropriation and nationalisation of companies established under it. Moreover, companies and their assets cannot be attached, seized or expropriated by way of an administrative order. The law further provides that no administrative body shall either interfere in setting prices or profit margins; or revoke or suspend a license for the use of property except in those cases where licence terms are violated.

The basic tax holiday from corporate income tax enjoyed by companies established under the Investment Law is for a period of five years starting from the first fiscal year following the commencement of production or the company's activities. Projects established in new industrial zones, new urban communities and remote areas enjoy a tax holiday of 10 years, and projects established in areas outside the Old Valley enjoy a tax holiday of 20 years. The Council of Ministers is authorised by the Investment Law to issue Decrees specifying those areas.

Articles of Incorporation, mortgages and loan agreements are exempt from stamp duty, tax and notarisation fees for three years from the date of registration at the Commercial Register. Land purchased for the companies' and projects' use is exempt from real estate registration fees.

A flat rate of 5 per cent is assessed as customs and import duties on the value of materials that are imported for use in the operation and expansion of the project. All imports must be approved by the Investment Authority. Procedures for approval are set out in the Executive Regulations of the Law.

The Investment Law grants various exemptions from certain labour requirements under the Egyptian Companies Law and the Labour Law. For example, companies established under the Investment Law are exempt from the requirement that certain types of employees (such as drivers, office juniors and so on) be hired in the order of their registration at the labour employment office.

Free zones

Egyptian, Arab and foreign investors can also carry out projects in the Egyptian free zones, which are regulated by the Investment Law and considered as being located offshore. For example, most goods and materials imported to a free zone project are not subject to import duties or regulations.

There are two types of free zones – public and private. Public free zones are specific locations established by the Investment Authority in such areas as Alexandria, Suez, Port Said, Cairo, and so on. Private free zones are established exclusively for a specific project or company. Generally, the types of activities permitted in the free zones are mixing, blending, repackaging, manufacturing, assembling, processing and repair operations.

A company formed to operate in a free zone is exempt from all Egyptian income taxes for an unlimited period. Free zone projects are subject to a duty of 1 per cent of the value of goods entering or leaving the free zone, or to an annual duty of 1 per cent of the annual value-added in the project.

The New Urban Communities Law

Law No. 59 of 1979 (the 'New Urban Communities Law') was promulgated to encourage the development of specified regions in Egypt. For a foreign investor to qualify for the benefits and privileges under the law the project must be undertaken in certain designated new communities. Tax holidays, however, are granted by virtue of the Investment Law. A foreign investor may apply to establish an Egyptian joint-stock or limited liability company under the Investment Law and then request the New Communities Authority to license the project under the New Urban Communities Law. Profits from projects operating in one of the specified regions are exempt from corporate taxation for a minimum of 10 years from the first financial year following the commencement of activities.

Projects located in such regions are exempt from all tax on property for 10 years from the commencement of operations.

Tourism Law

Law No. 1 of 1973 (as amended by Law No. 102 of 1993) regulates hotels and tourist enterprises and encompasses all projects in this field. Tax holidays, however, are granted by virtue of the Investment Law.

Foreign Exchange Law

Law No. 38 of 1994 and its Executive Regulations issued under Ministerial Decree No. 331 of 1994, as amended, regulate foreign exchange operations in Egypt. The Decree lists entities authorised to deal in foreign currency. This includes almost all banks licensed to operate in Egypt and makes allowance for any new banks which might be authorised in the future. Banks under the Decree are permitted to buy foreign currency on their own account and on behalf of third parties. Banks are the only entities allowed to transfer currency outside Egypt. Branches of foreign banks are permitted to deal in local currency as well as foreign currency.

The law permits the establishment of authorised foreign currency exchange dealers. Dealers are authorised, under the law, to buy and sell foreign currency for their own accounts and on behalf of third parties. However, dealers are not authorised to transfer foreign currency outside

Egypt. Although the law does not prohibit the physical possession of foreign currency, it prohibits individuals or entities from dealing in foreign currency unless such dealing is accomplished through licensed banks or dealers.

Maintaining foreign currency
In accordance with the decree, both natural and legal persons are free to maintain foreign currency in any amounts. Foreign currency accounts may be held with any approved bank in Egypt. The funds kept in foreign currency accounts may be used in Egypt or remitted overseas. Companies that are formed pursuant to the Investment Law are allowed to maintain all of their foreign currency proceeds in foreign currency. Foreign currency generated from tourism or exports no longer needs to be repatriated into Egypt, and may be maintained abroad at the owner's discretion. Foreigners selling moveable capital are no longer required to deposit it in a blocked bank account.

This liberalisation is in stark contrast to pre-existing legislation, and is designed to encourage foreign investment.

Buying foreign currency
The decree authorises the purchase of unlimited amounts of foreign currency from any of the authorised banks or dealers. In accordance with the decree, banks and dealers are allowed to sell foreign currency either as cash or as transfers abroad to individuals or to private or public sector companies. Furthermore, banks and dealers are authorised under the decree to sell foreign currency for transferring stock dividends and interest from Egyptian bonds outside of Egypt.

The decree introduced the concept of forward exchange transactions whereby the purchase or sale of foreign currency at an exchange rate established at the time of agreement can be effected, with payment and delivery at a specified future date.

Free foreign exchange market
Ministerial Decree No. 331 of 1994 established a single market for foreign exchange transactions: the free foreign exchange market. The rates of exchange that apply to transactions effected within the scope of the market are determined by the Central Bank of Egypt (CBE), other approved banks, and dealers according to the free market mechanism.

Insurance Law
The insurance field has undergone a liberalisation process through the issuance of various legislation.

Under Law No. 10 of 1981, regarding the supervision and control of insurance in Egypt, all insurance had to be effected through wholly-owned Egyptian insurance companies. Law No. 91 of 1995 then authorised up to 49 per cent foreign participation in Egyptian insurance companies. Now, with the issuance of Law No. 156 in June 1998, 100 per cent foreign participation in Egyptian insurance companies is permissible.

Generally, under Law No. 156 any person acquiring 5 per cent or more of an insurance company must notify the Insurance Authority within two weeks of such acquisition. Holding or acquiring more than 10 per cent of an insurance company, unless by way of inheritance, requires approval of the Prime Minister.

Banking Law

Law No. 163 of 1957 (as amended by Law No. 37 of 1992, Law No. 101 of 1993 and Law No. 97 of 1996) regulates the activities of the banking system. Law No. 120 of 1975, as amended, regulates the activities of the Central Bank of Egypt.

Law No. 37 of 1992 and Law No. 101 of 1993

According to Law No. 101 of 1993, the Minister of Economy, in consultation with the CBE, in an attempt to ensure capital adequacy in all banks operating in Egypt, now imposes capital adequacy standards for each bank in relation to its assets and liabilities in accordance with the Basle Rules.

The CBE retains significant powers to undertake remedial measures when the provisions of this law are violated. For example, the CBE retains the right to send its own auditors to verify the accuracy of any suspect bank's records, and can order the suspect bank to increase its capital reserves if violation of the law is found.

Furthermore, according to Law No. 101 of 1993, the Minister of Economy in consultation with the Board of Directors of the CBE, may approve the dealings of a branch of a foreign bank in Egypt in local currency, without the need for the branch to take the form of an Egyptian joint stock company.

Law No. 37 of 1992 provides for the establishment of a fund by Egyptian banks to insure cash deposits with them.

Law No. 97 of 1996

Law No. 97 of 1996, amending Banking Law No. 163 of 1957, now allows foreigners to own more than 49 per cent equity shares in a bank, but no one person is permitted to hold more than 10 per cent of the shares without the prior approval of the CBE. Furthermore, Law No. 155 was issued in 1998 allowing the private sector to own shares in the capital of banks wholly owned by the government.

Bank Secrecy Law

Law No. 205 of 1990 (the 'Bank Secrecy Law') governs the obligation of Egyptian banks to keep information relating to their customers' bank accounts secret.

The Bank Secrecy Law provides that an Egyptian bank may not disclose any information relating to a customer's account, deposit, safe or related transaction in the absence of either the written permission of the customer or a decision rendered by a competent tribunal (whether judicial or arbitral).

Any party legally authorised to view information relating to a customer's account, deposit or safe is also prohibited from disclosing any information unless either of the above-mentioned criteria have been met.

The Bank Secrecy Law allows Egyptian banks to open secret numbered accounts or deposits in foreign currency. Disclosure of the name of the owner of such numbered accounts is prohibited unless either of the above-mentioned criteria have been met.

A court order that allows certain information relating to a customer's account to be disclosed may be obtained only if there is substantial evidence that a criminal act has been committed by the customer or to authorise a bank to release a bank statement for a given customer in order to execute a garnishment order.

Any infringement of the Bank Secrecy Law is punishable by imprisonment for not less than a year and a fine of not less than E£10,000 and not more than E£20,000.

Capital Markets Law

Law No. 95 of 1992 (the 'Capital Markets Law') regulates the capital markets in Egypt. The Executive Regulations of Law No. 95 were issued by Ministerial Decree No. 135 of 1993 and have been amended several times since then. Under Law No. 95, any company intending to issue a security must notify the Capital Market Authority (CMA), which then has three weeks in which to review the issue. Law No. 95 allows subsequent issues of shares to have different values.

For a public issue of securities the company must prepare a prospectus approved by the CMA and must provide the CMA with periodic reports and information relating to such public issue. Further, a company offering part of its shares in a public offering, or trading a minimum of 30 per cent of its shares on the stock exchange, must inform all shareholders owning at least one per cent of the company's capital of any other shareholder wishing to increase his holding above 10 per cent.

Law No. 95 allows the issuing company to set, at its annual shareholders' meeting, a return on the security that exceeds the limits established in other laws (the 7 per cent ceiling in the Civil Code).

Areas covered by the law

Law No. 95 covers, in general, joint-stock companies that offer their shares to the public as well as companies that deal in securities and in particular the following six fields of activities:
- the promotion and covering (underwriting) of investment in securities;
- participation in the formation of companies that issue securities, or in the increase of their capital (Egyptian equivalent to the Holding Company);

- venture capital;
- the clearance and settlement of securities dealings;
- the formation and management of securities portfolios and investment funds; and
- securities brokerage.

In addition, any other activities related to the field of securities may be added by a decision of the Minister of Economy after obtaining the approval of the CMA.

Registration (listing)

Joint-stock companies must register with the stock exchange in Cairo or Alexandria. The company's securities can be listed in either the official or the unofficial register.

The following securities may be listed in the official register:

- a public issue of a security that represents no less than 30 per cent of the company's nominal shares and that is subscribed to by no less than 150 persons; and
- a public issue of a security by the government or a public-sector company.

All other securities that do not meet the criteria for listing in the official register as well as foreign securities are to be listed in the unofficial register.

Investors that deal in a security listed in the official register are exempt from stamp duty at the time the security is issued as well as from the annual stamp duty.

A second unofficial register has been established for newly formed companies to trade and list their shares at more than par value.

Central depository

In 1996 the Mis Settlement & Central Depository (MSCD) was established. The purpose of the depository is to facilitate and encourage the trading of shares by implementing a system of electronic trading by which vendors of shares do not have to follow the traditional process of materially delivering the share certificates to the purchasers. Instead, the transaction is effected through MSCD where the companies' share certificates are deposited. Transfer of ownership is then effected by issuance of a receipt by MSCD indicating the name of the new owner.

It is not mandatory for companies to deposit their shares at MSCD, however many are depositing their shares to facilitate the trading process. MSCD has played a major role in encouraging paperless dealings in shares.

Investment funds and ESOPs

Law No. 95 provides that securities transactions may be undertaken only by financial services companies licensed by the CMA. Board members of such companies must have a minimum of five years' experience in the field of securities, or must have four years' experience and participated and passed the training course set up by the CMA in order to be granted a licence.

Furthermore, the Law stipulates that an investment fund must now take the legal form of a joint-stock company. The CMA has the authority to review and object to the members of an investment fund company's board of directors as well as the fund managers. An investment fund must be managed by a company that specialises in the management of such funds. The Law also provides that the ratio between the investment fund company's paid-in capital and the fund's financial resources must be maintained at a certain level. Only those banks that have been authorised by the Minister of Economy may deal in the subscription to investment fund shares.

Banks and insurance companies may establish investment funds, without having to create a separate joint-stock company, if they have received authorisation to do so from the CMA and the CBE (in the case of banks) and the General Organisation for Supervision on Insurance (in the case of insurance companies).

The Law further introduced the concept of Employee Share Option Plans (ESOPs) whereby employees in a joint-stock company may form an association that owns shares in the company's capital on behalf of the employees.

Sales of shares using a broker

The sale of shares listed on both the Cairo and Alexandria Stock Exchanges must be executed through a licensed broker. The commission for such service is set by ministerial decree at a maximum rate of 0.5 per cent of the transaction value if less than E£10,000 and a maximum rate of 0.2 per cent for transactions over E£10,000. In practice, however, the brokerage commission is subject to negotiations.

Brokers' obligations and restrictions

The amendment to the Executive Regulations of the Capital Markets Law, Law No. 95, by Decree No. 39 of 1998, sets out the obligations and restrictions of brokerage companies. In particular it adds new rules on insider trading.

Brokerage companies are bound by fiduciary duties of honesty and integrity. This includes brokerage companies having to inform the public of any conflict of interests that may exist. Also included in their fiduciary duties is the obligation not to disclose any information regarding their clients and their clients' transactions.

Article 244 of Decree No. 39 of 1998 sets out the law on insider trading whereby brokerage companies, their directors and employees are expressly prohibited from engaging in insider trading by using information that is not public. Brokerage companies may not effect transactions on behalf of their clients, without sufficient evidence justifying their advice and the resulting transactions. Brokerage companies are prohibited from participating in excessive trading, whereby transactions are entered into with the aim of increasing commission, expenses or any other fees. Generally brokerage companies may only deal on behalf of their clients in transactions for which they have been granted specific instructions. These instructions must be recorded by the brokers. The client must be informed of the completion of a transaction within 24 hours. Transactions on behalf of the brokerage companies' directors, employees or relatives of second degree are permitted provided that the explicit written consent of the Board of Directors of the brokerage companies is granted.

Privatisation and the Public Enterprise Law

The new Public Enterprise Law

Law No. 203 of 1991 (the 'Public Enterprise Law') and its Executive Regulations represents the first step towards the privatisation of public sector organisations in Egypt. Law No. 203 paved the way for the transformation of public sector organisations and the companies that they supervised into holding companies and subsidiary (or affiliated) companies.

Under the old public sector law (Law No. 97 of 1983) the sale of public sector companies was prohibited except to other public sector entities. Under the new law private companies and individuals may subscribe to, or purchase, the shares of the subsidiary companies. The proportion of private ownership in such companies is to be determined by the government on a case-by-case basis. If the government relinquishes its majority ownership in a particular company (51 per cent) then the company will no longer be subject to the provisions of Law No. 203 but will be subject to the Companies Law.

By virtue of Law No. 203 the shares of the subsidiary companies may now be traded on the stock exchange, a measure that substantially facilitates Egypt's privatisation programme. Previously, the shares of public sector companies could not be traded on the stock exchange.

The following forms of privatisation are available under the Egyptian government's privatisation programme:

i   the sale of all or part of the share capital (through private or public bidding);
ii the sale of part of the shares on the stock exchange;
iii the sale of all or part of the entity's assets (through private or public bidding); and
iv the full or partial utilisation of the existing facilities by way of subcontracting, leasing or management contracts.

In all cases, consideration shall be given by the evaluating authority to the modernisation of production facilities as well as the training of personnel and the transfer of technology.

Law No. 203 only represents the first stage in Egypt's privatisation programme. To update and streamline commercial activities in Egypt, the government is considering unifying Law No. 8 (Investment Law), Law No. 203 (Public Enterprise Law) and Law No. 159 (Companies Law) so that all rules governing companies can be found in a single text.

Privatisation trends

A number of reforms have taken place in Egypt in the privatisation area, boosting local and foreign private investment in the public sector. Two areas in particular have proven very successful using the BOOT (build-own-operate-transfer) concept: the telecommunications sector and the area of infrastructure projects.

The BOOT concept was first adopted in the power sector by virtue of Law No. 100 of 1996, amending Law No. 12 of 1976 regarding the establishment of the Egyptian Electricity Authority. Law No. 100 allows local and foreign private investors to build power generating plants and sell the electricity so generated to different electricity distribution companies. Law No. 100 stipulates that local and foreign investors are permitted to own and operate power plants, without restrictions, provided the concession period does not exceed 99 years. New enabling legislation extended this concept to building public highways, airports, water and sewage plants and other infrastructure projects.

The developments in the telecommunications sector began with the implementation of Law No. 19 in March of 1998, which segmented telecommunication services into basic and value-added services. ARENTO, the National Telecommunications Authority, which had been the operating and regulatory body of Egypt's telecommunications sector, was transformed into a joint-stock company. It remained the operator of the basic services, renaming itself 'The Egyptian Telecommunications Company' (Egypt Telecom). A new regulatory body was established by virtue of Presidential Decree No. 101, issued in April of 1998, as a separate body independent from the operating entity, Egypt Telecom.

Under Law No. 19, Egypt Telecom may trade its shares provided the majority of share capital remains with the government and a percentage of the shares be offered for sale to the employees.

The value-added services, such as the cellular and payphone services, have been offered to the public and are now wholly owned and managed by the private sector.

Labour Law

Law No. 137 of 1981, as amended (the 'Labour Law') together with Articles 674 to 698 of the Egyptian Civil Code (1948), contain the most significant rules governing the relationship between an employer and an employee in Egypt.

Work certificates and permits

All Egyptian workers (with some exceptions, such as those doing casual jobs taking six months or less to complete) must obtain a work certificate. An expatriate who wishes to work in Egypt must obtain a work permit from the Ministry of Manpower and Training. Work permits are usually granted for a period of 10 months and may be renewed.

Employment contracts
An employment contract must be in writing, drawn up in Arabic in triplicate with one copy each for the employer, the employee and the Social Insurance Office. The employment

contract must include certain information specified in the Labour Law. If an employee is hired on probation, the employment contract should indicate the probationary period, which cannot exceed three months. A contract may be drawn up for a definite or indefinite period of time. A fixed-term contract, if renewed, will thereafter be construed as indefinite. (This rule applies to Egyptian nationals only.)

An employee shall not work more than eight hours a day, or 48 hours a week. (A week is six days in Egypt, although most private sector employees work for only five days.) However, the number of working hours may be increased to nine hours a day in certain circumstances. Every employer must grant employees a weekly rest, which cannot be less than 24 hours. The employer is exempt from these provisions in certain situations; for example, where the added work is intended to prevent a serious accident or to cope with an unusually heavy workload. In such situations, the employee must be paid overtime.

An employee is entitled to annual paid leave of 21 days after a full year of service. This annual leave must be increased to one month after the employee has worked for 10 consecutive years in the service or is over 50 years old.

Every employee shall be entitled to full pay for holidays designated by the Minister of Manpower and Training (such holidays not to exceed 13 days per year). An employer may use the services of its employees during these holidays if work conditions so require, provided that the employer pays double-time.

The Labour Law also contains liberal provisions with respect to employee sick leave, with up to six months' sick leave per year with pay between 75 per cent and 100 per cent of the employee's normal wage.

Healthcare, pension payments

All companies in the Egyptian private sector must provide free healthcare for their Egyptian employees either through the Medical Insurance Plan of the Ministry of Social Insurance or privately. Every company in the Egyptian private sector must also contribute to the Pension Insurance Fund of the Ministry of Social Insurance.

Dismissal and termination

An employee cannot be dismissed unless a grave fault has been committed. Article 61 of the Labour Law sets out a list of such faults. As a general rule, an employer cannot lawfully dismiss an employee in Egypt unless the matter has first been brought before the local conciliation committee at the Ministry of Manpower and Training and a hearing has been held. The conciliation committee seeks to help the parties settle their dispute. The committee's recommendation, however, is not binding on the parties and the employee retains the right to challenge the dismissal in an Egyptian court.

The Egyptian labour courts have discretion in assessing an employment dismissal compensation award on the basis of their review of the facts of each particular case. An employee is usually entitled to 30 days' notice of dismissal or one month's salary in lieu of the 30 days' notice. In addition, previous court decisions have awarded an unjustified dismissal payment, which could be between one to three months' salary for each year of employment.

The Labour Law sets out a number of grounds for termination without notice including expiration of the contractually fixed period, retirement or resignation of the employee, or the death of the employee or the employee's total incapacity to work.

Commercial aspects of business activities

A foreign company may appoint a commercial agent from the private or public sector to represent its interests in Egypt. The appointment of a commercial agent is obligatory for making tenders or for purchase offers to committees of public sector organisations and government agencies in Egypt. Commercial agents are, as a matter of policy, not permitted with respect to offers made to the Ministry of Defence. A commercial agent is defined under Law No. 120 of 1982 (the 'Commercial Agency Law') and Ministry for Economy's Decision No. 342 of 1982 as a natural person or legal entity carrying out the business of submitting tenders or concluding purchase, sale or lease contracts on behalf of and for the account of producers, manufacturers or distributors. Such a person or entity must be recorded on the register for commercial agents maintained at the Ministry of Economy and Foreign Trade. To be registered the following conditions must be satisfied:

- if the commercial agent is a natural person, the individual must be of Egyptian nationality and cannot be a government official or employee of any public sector organisation; or
- if the commercial agent is a legal entity, it must have its head office in Egypt, be wholly owned by persons of Egyptian nationality, and if one of the shareholders of such legal entity is another legal entity it must be majority owned by Egyptians, and the deed of incorporation of the company must specify commercial agency work as one of the company's purposes.

The agency contract must be submitted with the application for registration. The contract should provide for the following: the geographical area and the commodity covered by the contract, the nature of the agent's work, the mutual obligations of the parties, the percentage of the commission, and the conditions and currency of payment. Any amendments to the contract must be notified to the Egyptian consulate in the country of the principal. The commissions and fees payable pursuant to such contracts for commercial agents must be stated in the bids or tenders in question and be paid through a bank registered with the CBE. It is not required that the agent be exclusive. However, if the agent is a public sector company no other private sector agent may be appointed for the same line of products.

Neither the Commercial Agencies Law nor any other special legislation in Egypt limits the rights of a foreign company to terminate (or not to renew) a commercial agency, or obliges the foreign company to provide a statutory minimum notice of termination or non-renewal, or pay termination or non-renewal compensation to its commercial agent. However, Egyptian law requires that termination be upon adequate notice. Notice provisions are generally agreed upon and defined by the parties in the commercial agency agreement. Egyptian law also contains the abuse of rights doctrine, under which a court can grant a commercial agent damages for its principal's abusive exercise of a right to terminate an agreement.

The Anti-dumping Law

As a member of the World Trade Organisation and in compliance with the covenants included in the final treaty comprising the results of the Uruguay round for multilateral commercial negotiations and the lists of Egypt's promises in the field of trade commodities, which was signed in Morocco in 1994, a new law was introduced in May of 1998 regarding the protection of the national economy. This law, aimed at dealing with the consequences of damaging practices carried out in international commerce, has already lead to a series of decisions by the Ministry of Trade and Supply in which anti-dumping penalties were imposed and collected.

Law No. 161 of 1998 grants the Ministry of Trade and Supply powers to protect the national economy from the damaging consequences of subsidies, dumping or unjustified increases in importation. Its responsibilities include providing required studies, information and all other necessary data needed to evidence incidents of subsidies, dumping or unjustified increases in importation. The Ministry of Trade and Supply is also charged with providing technical aid to local producers facing complaints from member countries of the World Trade Organisation regarding incidents referred to above. Furthermore, the Ministry of Trade and Supply may issue decisions that include compensatory measures to confront such named incidents. A list of experts specialising in areas needed for such incident reports is issued by the Ministry of Justice with the approval of the Ministry of Trade and Supply. The list can be found at a special register established with the Ministry of Justice. In addition the Ministry of Justice with the approval of the Ministry of Trade and Supply may identify those who have law enforcement authority to evidence violations of Law No. 161. Finally, individuals and public authorities responsible for investigating a complaint must maintain the confidentiality of the information and data given as evidence by the parties. Violation of this confidentiality may be fined up to E£50,000 and no less than E£10,000.

Patents, trademarks and copyright

Patents and industrial designs

Law No. 132 of 1949, as amended, on Patents and Industrial Designs, closely modelled on British patent law, allows inventors to obtain patent protection for 15 years from the date of application and may, in some instances, be renewed for one additional five-year period (10 years for pharmaceutical process patents). The patent-holder has the exclusive right to exploit the invention, including the right to pledge, assign or license the patent. The patent-holder must exploit the patent (or be subject to compulsory licensing for failure to do so) and pay specified annual fees to the Patent Office. After 15 years and any applicable renewal the patent-holder's exclusivity right ends and the invention enters the public domain. Only the manufacturing process, and not the pharmaceutical products are patentable in Egypt.

Industrial designs

A separate office and register is maintained in connection with industrial designs. The protection accorded by the law is for a period of five years from the date of registration, renewable for two similar periods.

International agreements

Egypt is a signatory to the Paris Convention. If a patent application is made in a member country of the Paris Convention or in any other country offering reciprocal treatment, the applicant may apply for a patent in Egypt within one year of the related application abroad. Egypt is also a member state of the Patent Cooperation Treaty.

Trademarks

Law No. 57 of 1939 as amended (the 'Trademark Law') allows trademark holders protection for 10 years from the date of application, renewable indefinitely for similar periods. Any renewal must be specifically applied for and the procedure involved is the same as that for the first registration of the trademark. (Trademarks may also be protected if they relate to services.)

A trademark is deemed to be owned by the person who effects the registration. Ownership cannot be challenged if the registered owner has used the mark for a continuous period of five years from the date of registration.

Trade statements

The Trademark Law also provides protection to the public against false or misleading trade statements, including any description or statement relating to:

- the number, measurement, weight, components and contents of goods;
- the date of manufacture and expiry date on food products;
- the area or country where the goods were manufactured or produced; and
- the name and other details of a manufacturer or producer.

International agreements

Egypt is a signatory state to the Madrid Convention of 1954.

Copyright

The Copyright Law, Law No. 354 of 1954, generally defines copyright protection to include, among other things: architectural designs, speeches, theatrical pieces, musical works, photographic and cinematographic works, maps, and works for broadcast on television or radio. Law No. 38 of 1992 amended the Copyright Law to broaden the scope of its protection to include video tapes and computer software. Law No. 38 also increased the penalties, which apply in cases of copyright infringement.

Protection under the Copyright Law ends 50 years after the death of the author. In the case of a legal entity, the protection period begins on the date of first publication. In certain circumstances in the field of photographic and cinematographic works the protection ends after a period of 15 years from the date of first publication.

Egypt is a member state of the Berne Convention of 1886 on copyright, although Egypt does not consider itself bound by the provisions of Article 33 of the Berne Convention concerning the jurisdiction of the Court of International Justice. Further, Egypt is also a member state of the 1971 Convention for the Protection of Producers of Phonograms Against Unauthorised Duplication of their Phonograms.

Licensing

In general, the contract terms entered into between the parties will govern the terms of any technology licensing agreements. Technology licensing agreements for Investment Law projects are subject to review by the Investment Authority.

A withholding tax of 40 per cent is levied on royalty payments unless an appropriate treaty to avoid double taxation exists between Egypt and the home country of the foreign company reducing the tax to a lower percentage.

Sale of goods

Vienna Convention

The United Nations Convention on Contracts for the International Sale of Goods (also known as the Vienna Convention) has come into force in a number of countries, including Egypt and the United States. This convention, based on elements from both common law and civil law, would generally apply to contracts between nationals or residents of member states.

Some rules in the convention concerning contracts and contract interpretation differ from local rules. Therefore importers and exporters should carefully review the sales contract in light of the convention, to ensure that the convention's rules do not conflict with the parties' intentions. Parties to a contract may agree not to apply the provisions of the convention.

Import regulations

Import regulations provide that goods may be freely imported and exported, provided they are not on the prohibited list and the relevant duty is paid. Law No. 121 of 1982 requires that an importer who wishes to import goods for the purposes of trade must be registered in the Register of Importers and be an Egyptian national. Law No. 121 requires a number of other conditions for such registration, including conditions relating to minimum capital and past commercial experience. However export activities can be conducted by companies with foreign participation.

Public Tender Law

Public tender regulations have also changed recently with the introduction of a new Public Tender Law, Law No. 89 of 1998, which eliminates Law No. 147 of 1962 in relation to the implementation of economic development plan projects and Law No. 9 of 1983, the old Tender Law. The new Public Tender Law governs all supply, service and construction contracts entered into with an Egyptian government entity. Generally, government contracting must be by way of public tenders or by public negotiations between the government entity and the contractor. Certain exceptions are listed whereby contracting may be either by:

- limited tender, where the nature of the contract requires certain types of suppliers, contractors, consultants, technicians or other experts, whether situated in Egypt or abroad;
- local tender, whereby all contracts up to the value of E£200,000 are confined to local suppliers;
- limited negotiations, where items manufactured are only available from certain contractors or certain production locations, where technical works require certain specialists, or where national security dictates confidentiality; or
- direct contracting in extraordinary cases.

There is no standard government contract and, generally, each government ministry or agency uses its own form of contract (which must, however, conform to the provisions of the new Public Tender Law). Public tenders must be advertised in a daily newspaper locally or abroad, depending on the nature of the contract, and must ensure equal opportunity and free competition.

Although a government contract must be awarded to the contractor who submits the most qualified and lowest bid, an Egyptian domestic contractor is accorded priority if its bid does not exceed the lowest foreign bid by more than 15 per cent.

Each tender must be accompanied by the payment of a provisional deposit of up to 2 per cent, which is returned to unsuccessful tenderers, and a final deposit of up to 5 per cent must be paid within 10 days of a tender being accepted. The contract may be cancelled if payment of the final deposit is not made, and any losses suffered as a direct result may be recovered.

A maximum fine of up to 10 per cent of the value of construction contracts and up to 3 per cent of the value of supply contracts and up to 4 per cent for technical assistance contracts may be levied on contractors for late performance or late delivery.

The new Public Tender Law permits government entities to terminate contracts where the bidder has acted fraudulently, declared bankruptcy or induced government officials to act contrary to the provisions of the new Public Tender Law. Furthermore, tenders may be rejected upon receipt due to:

- public interest and welfare;
- only one tender being submitted; or
- the lowest tendered price exceeding the estimated value of the contract.

The contract may be terminated at any time if the contracting party defaults on its terms and conditions. Any losses incurred may be recovered.

Generally, in cases of late performance or non-performance the concept of *force majeure* is recognised in accordance with principles of the Egyptian Civil Code. Certain events (for example, the unavailability of materials, strikes and shipping delays) must be expressly mentioned in the contract if they are to be considered force majeure.

Oil and gas concessions

These concessions are granted on the basis of production-sharing arrangements between the Government of Egypt and EGPC, the state-owned organisation for oil, and a foreign oil company, usually known as the contractor. The concession agreement is issued by a special law for each concession. Under this arrangement the contractor undertakes to bear all exploration risks.

Exploration

The contractor is given an initial exploration phase. The maximum period granted ranges from three to four years. This phase may be extended at the contractor's option, two renewals of shorter duration (usually two years each) being granted. The agreement will automatically terminate at the end of the agreed extensions, if applied for, provided there has been no commercial discovery of oil as defined in the concession agreement.

The agreement may, nevertheless, be extended beyond the automatic termination date at the contractor's option for a period not exceeding six months to enable it to complete the drilling or testing of a well that had been started during that phase.

Minimum work and financial obligations

A minimum of one exploration well has to be drilled in each phase. Wells drilled in excess of the minimum work obligation in one phase can be offset against the minimum work for the next phase. Usually the concession agreement specifies the number of wells to be drilled in each phase.

The contractor must provide all necessary financing during the exploration stage in freely convertible currency. It may buy Egyptian pounds at the official rate of exchange. The contractor will be required to spend certain amounts during each phase of the exploration period. If the contractor fails to spend that minimum amount, then it has to pay to EGPC upon the end of the concession the amount of the shortfall.

Usually, a bank guarantee in favour of EGPC is posted to ensure payment of any shortfall amounts. The guarantee is reduced by the amounts expended by the contractor. The amounts spent by the contractor are recoverable in the event of a commercial discovery from what is known as the cost recovery crude oil. If no discovery is made, then the contractor cannot claim any amounts spent from EGPC. Minimum financial obligations differ from one concession to another and from one phase to another.

Area relinquishments

The concession agreement will provide for both voluntary and mandatory relinquishment of parts of the area covered in the concession agreement in which there has been no commercial discovery of oil. At the end of the initial phase of the exploration period, the contractor is required to relinquish a part of the area, which has not been converted into a development lease. The figure will be based on the proposal made by the contractor in its bid submission. If the exploration period has been extended, a further relinquishment takes place at the end of the second phase, and the balance of the area is relinquished at the end of the third phase.

At any time the contractor may voluntarily relinquish all or any part of the area, provided that it has complied with its expenditure obligations during the exploration period.

Commercial operations

Once oil or gas is discovered in commercially exploitable quantities, the contractor is awarded a development lease of between 20 and 30 years (usually 20 with a five-year extension) from the date of the commercial discovery. The approval of the Minister of Petroleum is sufficient and no additional legal instrument is required.

An operating company must be established and owned equally by EGPC and the contractor. The operating company must be liquidated upon the termination or expiry of the concession agreement. In all cases the term cannot exceed 35 years from the date of commercial discovery of any oil or gas well.

The charter of the operating company will be contained in an appendix to the concession agreement. The agreement provides that the operating company shall come into existence in the form of the charter automatically and without the need for any further legal procedures, 30 days after the date of the commercial discovery.

The operating company is completely exempt from the provisions of the Company Law and therefore it is governed primarily by the provisions of the charter, the by-laws adopted by shareholders, and the provisions of the concession agreement. Despite the shareholding of EGPC, the operating company belongs to the private sector. The contractor is responsible for financing the activities of the operating company. The operating company is responsible for providing the contractor with a written estimate of its cash requirements each month in US dollars.

Recovery of costs and production sharing

The contractor will recover all costs of exploration out of a percentage of oil, known as Cost Recovery Crude Oil, the percentage of which will form part of the bid of the contractor. The contractor will take and dispose of all Cost Recovery Crude Oil. If the value of this oil exceeds actual recoverable expenditure, the contractor will be deemed to have purchased such excess oil and shall pay its value to EGPC. The value of the oil will reflect the prevailing market price for crude oil.

The market price for each calendar semester is taken to be the weighted average price for comparable quantities on comparable credit terms in freely convertible currency from FOB point of export sold to third parties on an arm's-length basis by EGPC or the contractor, whichever is the higher. Cost Recovery Crude Oil is permissible up to 40 per cent of the crude oil produced.

The principles relating to cost recovery of oil apply to gas with some differences. All costs and expenses relating to exploration and the development of gas are recoverable out of 50 per cent of all gas, gas condensate, gas products and/or gas derivatives produced and saved from all development leases that are not used in petroleum operations. This can be increased to 60 per cent for one or more years if the cost warrants it, provided that the total cost recovery gas during the first 12 years does not exceed 50 per cent of the total production over the same period.

The price of gas will be determined according to the formula contained in the concession agreement.

The remaining percentage of crude oil will be divided between EGPC and the contractor, according to the terms of the concession agreement, which is usually between 80 per cent to 88 per cent for EGPC and 12 per cent to 20 per cent for the contractor. The division for gas ranges between 70 per cent to 75 per cent for EGPC and 25 per cent to 30 per cent for the contractor.

Royalties
Some 10 per cent of total quantity of petroleum produced is paid in kind or cash by EGPC (not the contractor) from its share of oil to the Egyptian government.

Customs duties and taxation
The contractor is subject to corporate income tax, which for petroleum production companies is 40.55 per cent. The contractor should keep the required books and file the required tax returns. However, typically, the concession agreement provides that EGPC's share of the oil includes a quantity of crude equal to the contractor's tax liability and that EGPC will pay the contractor's taxes out of the proceeds of this quantity. All taxes paid by EGPC on behalf of the contractor shall be considered income to the contractor. The contractor's personnel are subject to personal income tax on salaries.

Customs duties
Wide-ranging customs exemptions are granted to the parties to a concession agreement and to foreign employees working for the contractor or the operating company. The equipment (except passenger cars) of the contractor and all his subcontractors' required for their operations are exempted from customs duties. However, this equipment must be re-exported after the completion or termination of the concession or customs duties must then be paid.

Title to assets
All assets acquired and owned by the contractor in connection with the operations performed under a concession agreement by the contractor or the operating company will become the

property of EGPC, as the full costs are recovered by the contractor under the provisions dealing with cost recovery, or upon termination of the agreement, whichever is earlier.

Environment

EGPC has recently altered its concession agreements by incorporating certain provisions for the protection of the environment.

Ownership of real estate

The ownership of land by foreigners is governed by three laws, Law No. 15 of 1963, Law No. 143 of 1981 and Law No. 230 of 1996.

Law No. 15 of 1963

Law No. 15 provides that no foreigners, whether natural or legal persons, may acquire agricultural land.

Law No. 230 of 1996

On 14 July, Law No. 230 of 1996 was issued superseding Law No. 56 of 1988. The new law allows non-Egyptians to own real estate whether built or vacant with the following conditions:

- ownership be limited to only two real estate properties throughout Egypt for accommodation purposes of the person and his family (family meaning spouses and minors), in addition to the right to own real estate needed for activities licensed by the Egyptian government;
- the area of each real estate not be in excess of 4,000 square metres; and
- the real estate is not a historical site.

Exemption from the first and second conditions is subject to the approval of the Prime Minister. Ownership in tourist areas and new communities is subject to conditions established by the Cabinet of Ministers.

Further, non-Egyptians owning vacant real estate in Egypt must build within a period of five years from the date their ownership is effective (the date on which the realty is recorded at the competent Notary Public Office). Non-Egyptians may only sell their real estate five years after registration of ownership, unless the consent of the Prime Minister is obtained.

Law No. 143 of 1981

Law No. 143 governs the acquisition and ownership of desert land. Certain limits are placed on the number of *feddans* (one *feddan* is equal to approximately one hectare) that may be owned by individuals, families, cooperatives, partnerships and corporations. Partnerships are permitted to own 10,000 *feddans*. Joint-stock companies are permitted to own 50,000 *feddans*.

Partnerships and joint-stock companies may own desert land within these limits even if foreign partners or shareholders are involved, provided that at least 51 per cent of the capital is owned by Egyptians. However, upon liquidation of the company, the land must revert to Egyptians.

Article 1 of Law No. 143 defines desert land as the land 2 kilometres outside the border of the city.

Further, the lease of such land for more than a period of 50 years shall also be considered to be ownership under Law 143. Although companies formed under the Investment Law do not require Egyptian participation, companies that undertake projects over desert land must be owned in their majority by Egyptians (the President of the Republic may decide to treat Arab nationals as Egyptian nationals for purposes of this law.)

Environmental Law

There has been a heightened level of concern by the Egyptian public and government over environmental issues over the past few years. This trend is due to an awareness of the value of natural resources and a desire to provide for the general welfare of the Egyptian people. This increase in public interest has manifested itself in the form of the creation of new legislation (Law No. 4 of 1994) and increasing environmental commitments.

International conventions

Egypt has joined and ratified 16 international conventions and treaties on the environment. Some of the more prominent ones include the Basle Convention on the disposal of hazardous materials, the Convention of London of 1954, as amended, concerning maritime pollution by oil and the Protocol of 1978, attached to the Convention of London of 1973, for the prevention of pollution by ships. Egypt has signed but not ratified a number of other conventions on the environment.

The Law on the Environment

Law No. 4 of 1994 concerning the environment radically transformed the field of Egyptian environmental law through both the consolidation of enforcement authorities within the newly established Agency for Environmental Affairs (AEA) and the introduction of comprehensive regulations superseding earlier environmental legislation.

The AEA has been charged with the enforcement of this law and provided with an independent budget to ensure its autonomy. In the past, Egyptian environmental enforcement was hampered by rivalry among the numerous bodies charged with environmental regulation. The new law supersedes all conflicting prior legislation (except Law No. 48 of 1982 concerning the protection of the River Nile and the water courses), and creates important new bodies of law in previously omitted areas (for example hazardous waste disposal). Air, water and land pollution are among the topics addressed in the law.

Protection of land

Investors engaging in all new developments are now required to obtain Environmental Impact Statements (EIS) to obtain a licence to build and the law places a duty upon the developer to monitor his compliance with the environmental laws. Pre-existing facilities must also obtain an EIS for all new development.

Hazardous waste and materials

The law provides detailed restrictions concerning the use, transportation, handling and disposal of hazardous wastes and materials. Qualifying materials and wastes are defined in the law.

Air pollution

Egypt's air pollution control efforts include emission control standards, zoning restrictions, controls on the use of pesticides, noise limits and standards for the maintenance of acceptable levels of radiation. Furthermore, limits are prescribed for the amount of heat, humidity and the quality of ventilation in the workplace.

Salt water environment

The law regulates ship-based pollution of the marine environment, including discharges of oil and hazardous materials and the disposal of sewage waste and rubbish. The force of these provisions extends to both Egypt's territorial waters and its exclusive economic zones. Land-based sources of marine pollution are also dealt with through zoning restrictions and the granting of sweeping enforcement powers to deal with polluters.

Other elements

The law contains incentives for entities that operate in Egypt in an environmentally friendly manner, thus encouraging investors to observe the law. The law provides a three-year grace period from the date of publishing the Executive Regulations of the Law for all entities operating in Egypt to implement the provisions of the law and abide by them. Such grace period ended on 28 February 1998, but it may be extended for an additional two years upon the approval of the Council of Ministers, provided that the applicant shows evidence that it is taking serious steps in implementing the Law. It also prescribes fines and prison sentences (in extreme cases) for violations of its provisions.

LEGAL ENVIRONMENT

Disputes

Egypt has a civil law system. Under Article 166 of the Egyptian Constitution: 'Judges shall be independent subject to no other authority but the law. No authority may intervene in court cases or in the affairs of justice'. There are two levels of civil courts of primary jurisdiction, the Summary Courts (which include Urgent Matters Courts) and the Courts of First Instance. (These courts also hear criminal, labour and commercial matters.) Courts of First Instance hear appeals from the Summary Courts and appeals from the Courts of First Instance are made to the main Courts of Appeal, located in the principal cities of Egypt. The Supreme Court of Appeal (Court of Cassation) reviews the decisions of the Courts of Appeal. The Court of Cassation reviews the legal issues that are the subject of appeal but does not review the questions of fact.

There is also a separate judicial system for administrative disputes involving government ministries and agencies. These administrative courts fall within the jurisdiction of the Council of State (Conseil d' Etat), which is empowered to hear actions brought by persons challenging the validity of presidential decrees and ministerial decisions as well as disputes involving contracts with the government. The Council of State also has a Legislative Department that reviews draft legislation and government contracts and renders legal opinions for the government.

Under Article 175 of the Egyptian constitution, the Supreme Constitutional Court is 'vested solely with judicial control over the constitutionality of laws and regulations'. The Constitutional Court also reviews administrative decisions and conflicts of law between the civil and administrative courts.

Arbitration

Most international contracts provide for some form of international arbitration for the settlement of contractual disputes. The Court of Cassation has confirmed on a number of occasions the validity of such arbitration clauses. An Egyptian court will respect an arbitration clause and stay proceedings brought before it. Arbitration may be conducted under any set of rules. One of the most popular set of rules is the International Chamber of Commerce (ICC) rules. An arbitration under the rules of the ICC may be held in Egypt or abroad.

A local body of arbitration is the Cairo Regional Center for International Commercial Arbitration, which applies the rules of the United Nations Commissions on International Trade Law (UNCITRAL). However, there are no requirements in Egyptian law that an arbitration be conducted under the auspices of the Cairo Regional Center.

Law No. 27 of 1994 concerning arbitration in civil and commercial matters brings Egypt further into line with the UNCITRAL model law on international commercial arbitration (after which it appears to have been largely modelled).

Law No. 27 of 1994 is a comprehensive statement of the law and therefore facilitates the conduct and enforcement of international arbitral proceedings in Egypt. The new law now requires only that the following conditions be met for the enforcement of an arbitral award in Egypt:

- it does not contravene any judgement issued by Egyptian courts on the subject matter of the dispute;
- it does not contravene public order or policy in Egypt; and
- the defendant received due notice of the award.

The law also clarifies certain aspects of Egyptian arbitration law by legislating in areas that were previously neglected. Under the new law, the Egyptian government is specifically deemed accountable for arbitration agreements it enters into and may no longer take the position that it is not subject to commercial arbitration clauses. In addition, the procedures surrounding the appointment of experts are outlined in the text of the new arbitration law. Prior to the law on arbitration this appointment of experts had been left entirely to the discretion of the arbitrator.

The new law provides that annulment proceedings against all arbitration awards must be initiated within 90 days from notification of the award's issuance. However, this requirement does not preclude the enforcement of the award except under extreme circumstances (for example when there is clear evidence of fraud).

Applications for the enforcement of arbitral awards must be accompanied by the original award or a signed copy; a copy of the arbitral agreement; an Arabic translation of the award, authenticated by the competent authority if the award was not issued in Arabic; and a copy of the minutes evidencing the deposit of the award with the competent court in Egypt (usually the Cairo Court of Appeal). This law provides a firm base for arbitration and enforcement of awards in Egypt.

Enforcement of foreign arbitral awards
An award issued pursuant to an arbitration that has taken place outside Egypt may be enforced in Egypt if it is covered by one of the international conventions to which Egypt has adhered or if it satisfies the conditions set out in Law No. 27 of 1994.

Egypt is a signatory state to:

- the New York Convention of 1958 on the Recognition and Enforcement of Foreign Arbitral awards;
- the Washington Convention of 1965 on the Settlement of Investment Disputes between States and the Nationals of other States; and
- the Convention of 1974 on the Settlement of Investment Disputes between the Arab States and the Nationals of other States.

Egypt has also signed a series of treaties with a number of countries for the encouragement and reciprocal protection of investment.

These countries include Belgium, France, Germany, Greece, Iran, Italy, Japan, Lebanon,

Luxembourg, Morocco, Netherlands, Romania, Sudan, Switzerland, the United Kingdom, the United States, and Yugoslavia. Each of these treaties contains arbitration provisions in the event of a dispute. In the case of disputes between one of these countries and a national or company of another such country concerning an investment of the latter in the territory of the former, the dispute shall be settled in accordance with the provisions of the Washington Convention.

Generally, the treaties provide that arbitration awards issued in one country may be enforced in the other if the award is supported by written evidence of the parties' agreement to arbitrate, the dispute in question is capable of arbitration in the country where the award is to be executed, and the award does not conflict with public policy. Where no international convention applies, then the provisions of Law No. 27 of 1994 must be satisfied for a foreign arbitral award to be enforced.

Enforcement of foreign court judgements
To enforce a foreign judgement in Egypt the party enforcing the judgement must obtain an *exequator*. To apply for an exequator the normal procedures for initiating a lawsuit must be followed. In order for an Egyptian court to issue an exequator, it must be satisfied that the following conditions have been met:

- reciprocity: the country in which the judgement was rendered enforces judgements from the Egyptian courts;
- competence of the court rendering the judgement: the foreign court has jurisdiction over the dispute and Egyptian courts do not have exclusive jurisdiction over the dispute;
- due process: all parties to the dispute are duly notified and represented (i.e., not in contravention of the rules of natural justice);
- final judgement: the judgement is final (*res judicata*); and
- conflict of judgements: the judgement does not conflict with any existing judgement by any Egyptian court and the enforcement of such judgement will not contravene public policy, order or morality in Egypt.

Egypt is a signatory state to the Arab League Convention that allows enforcement of awards issued in a signatory state in another signatory state.

Conclusion

This review of the legal and regulatory environment in Egypt for starting a business and conducting business in Egypt is intended to give an idea to a prospective investor about the laws and regulations that such investor and his or her counsel will consider when starting a business or conducting a business in Egypt. However, because it is only an outline, it is not and cannot be a substitute for sound legal advice from qualified Egyptian counsel.

LEGAL ENVIRONMENT

Changes in the laws in the last few years have encouraged foreign investment in Egypt through the implementation of open market principles. As a result, it is now easier to start and operate a business in Egypt than in the past. Consistent with the economic and monetary reforms currently being introduced in Egypt, the government has initiated a legislative reform programme in which legislation in the following areas is expected to be drafted or amended: transfer of technology, labour law, corporate law, landlord and tenant law, commercial and bankruptcy law and competition law.

16 Egypt leading the way

Fulfilling the promise of the mid-1990s

Almost alone in the Middle East and North Africa, Egypt has experienced something of a revolution during the past few years. And it has been a revolution that has taken place on more fronts than would first appear. The changes have impacted upon economic, political, cultural and social affairs. At the heart of this revolution has been the realisation that unless reform was drastically accelerated, the economy was headed for catastrophe. Closely connected to this has been the realisation that unless it attracted more enlightened and highly-educated personnel to the bureaucracy, it would not have the talent to design and implement this vital economic reform. It became obvious that past obsessions with security, control and centralisation, had to be loosened if the foreign and domestic private sectors were to be given a real role in the economic reform process, and that this required a significant change in cultural thinking within key national institutions. Finally, the social implications of change, particularly in the areas of privatisation and land reform, had to be addressed to avoid social upheaval during the transition period.

In a country of 65 million people, which has disparities of wealth, and pronounced social and cultural differences between the rural and urban populations, nationwide reform is a daunting task. The government has concentrated its efforts in particular areas which are regarded as holding the key to securing a trickle-down benefit for the country as a whole. And it is the economic fundamentals which have allowed this strategy of gradual reform to be instigated. Debt forgiveness by Arab states to the tune of US$7 billion after Egypt's support of the US-led war against Iraq in 1991 set the groundwork. This was followed by an agreement with the Paris Club of government donors for the rescheduling of foreign debt, which eased the debt service ratio to 11 per cent. The 1991 Gulf crisis also led to around US$6 billion being repatriated by Egyptians leaving the Gulf states. These windfalls provided the foundations upon which the government was able to take dramatic decisions to launch economic reform.

A number of events have thrown any assessment of the achievements of the past eight years into stark relief. On 17 November 1997, 58 foreign tourists and six Egyptians were killed by Islamist militants at a temple in the southern city of Luxor. Aside from the horror of the event and the political concerns it created, the incident cost Egypt 1 per cent of its projected real GDP growth. While the number of tourists visiting Egypt has now reached 85 per cent of the level before the Luxor killings, many have been lured by discount holidays. Those who are visiting the country are generally staying for shorter periods, but it is clear that a recovery is now under way. The oil price slump will add substantially to the current account deficit, while

In a country of 65 million people, which has disparities of wealth and social and cultural dfferences, nationwide reform is a daunting task

a variety of economic analysts estimate that income from the Suez Canal and the US$3–4 billion earned in remittances from Egyptians working abroad are now at their peak.

In the face of these severe tests, Egypt has shown its resilience, while its reformers have taken the necessary steps to ensure that they are not diverted from the reform programme upon which the country has embarked. This immediate resilience is perhaps one measure of the extent to which the fruits of the stabilisation programme are being harvested and the process of building solid foundations for the future can also be seen as having emerged from this period. The sustainability of reform is therefore the key test by which success can be judged. With this in mind, all the main economic indicators show clearly that the foundations remain solid. Real GDP may not have reached the desired 7 per cent level, but the trend is clearly in that direction. Inflation remains on a downward trend, having fallen by more than 1 per cent a year since 1990. The level of new direct investment, both domestic and foreign, has been marked, clearly in response to both the liberalisation of industrial sectors, and the more favourable investment climate engendered by the guarantees and incentives the government is now offering. Throughout these changes, the financial system has gone from strength to strength. The burgeoning number of players in the capital markets stands as testimony to the growing strength and importance of the financial system, not only as a facilitator of the process of reform, but as a new, profitable and growing business in itself.

Judging these achievements in Egypt's own terms is more appropriate than assessing progress on the basis of comparison with other emerging markets. Egypt has essentially emerged from its own past. This is the major promise to have been fulfilled. The state is withdrawing from economic activity and leaving the private sector to take over. To fully bolster that private sector role, the government is seeking ways of broadening credit facilities for the medium and small businesses which are the real economic underbelly of the country. It is their future growth which will determine whether the mass of the population is able to make the transition to the market economy. To achieve this promise, the pace of reform will require acceleration to encourage the strengthening and diversification of the financial sector and to allow it to meet the capital needs of business in a manner which Egypt has yet to see.

Egypt in the region: economic leadership to complement political clout

Egypt's political influence in the Arab world is unrivalled, and is a vital element in the pivotal three-way relationship with Syria and Saudi Arabia, the lynchpins of official Arab opinion. President Mubarak has retained a dialogue with Israel, and has meanwhile kept open the door with such diverse regional states as Libya, Turkey, Iran and Sudan, while also remaining the regional sponsor of the Middle East Peace Process by offering vital guidance to the Palestinian leadership.

Middle East intraregional trade averaged a mere 9 per cent in 1985–95, compared with 60 per cent for trade with the EU. In 1998–99, Egyptian exports to Arab countries fell by 21 per cent, from 13.9 per cent of total exports to 10.9 per cent. Between 1991 and 1996, less than 2 per cent of Jordanian and Palestinian Authority imports came from Egypt. Egypt must create 450,000 new jobs annually, to match the growth of its workforce. It must increase exports by 11 per cent to achieve an 8 per cent growth in GDP – the level necessary to meet the job-creation target. Few Egyptian officials believe this is possible based on what is on offer from the European market, to which 40 per cent of Egypt's exports now go. It must find new markets in the region. The most obvious one is Israel, whose officials estimate that the potential value of annual Egyptian-Israeli trade could be US$200 million.

In 1995 Israel accounted for 0.64 per cent of Egypt's exports, compared with 10.08 per cent in 1992. Israeli studies suggest that as many as 500,000 Israeli tourists could visit Egypt every year, bringing up to US$750 million to the Egyptian economy. Since the creation of diplomatic ties between the two countries, following the 1979 Camp David agreement, Egypt and Israel have seen the value of their non-oil trade rise to US$85 million-worth in 1997. Israel is now Egypt's second biggest trading partner in the Middle East and North Africa (MENA) region, after Saudi Arabia. In addition, Egypt sells Israel 2 million tons of crude oil annually, and has in theory agreed to the construction of a gas pipeline to Israel.

Finding new and deeper markets for its goods is the major challenge facing Egypt's reformers. To this end, a three-phase programme aimed at improving financial facilities for exporters is now being put in place. During the first phase, Egypt's export priorities, capabilities and targets for the next decade will be identified. This will be followed by an examination of the role, functionality and effectiveness of the financial facilities available to exporters which are currently in place. Coupled with new bureaucratic reforms, tariff reduction is also set to continue, while customs procedures are currently being examined with a view to streamlining.

Liberalisation of trade has been accompanied by agreements to raise trade levels on a bilateral basis, notably with Morocco and Turkey, as well as through Egypt's recent accession to membership of COMESA, the Southern and East African trading bloc. Trade relations with Russia and the Commonwealth of Independent States have also been strengthened with the signing of a protocol to insure export revenues.

The intensification of trade-related activity in advance of Egypt's full membership of the World Trade Organisation and the completion and phased compliance with a partnership agreement with the EU, have created the potential for a marked acceleration in the level of exports. This potential will have to be fulfilled from beyond the MENA region. While Egypt's economic liberalisation programme has become the envy of the region – for its design, application and pace – the region has yet to satisfy what Egypt requires from it. The financial services industry which has emerged, is now ready to extend its business abroad, a process already evidenced in Jordan. The major leap now required depends upon the political resolution of the Arab-Israeli question. With Egypt's growing needs, the pressure for that resolution has rarely been greater. All sides in the dispute must eventually realise they have no choice but to resolve their differences fairly, if the Arab states are to create the regional market vital to sustaining their domestic needs, and Israel is to incorporate itself into the region which is the obvious source of its oil, gas and water needs, as well as the natural market for its goods.

Conclusion

As investors and fund managers scour the world for new tigers to feed, does Egypt figure as a credible alternative? It is close to Europe, it has a large population, it has the facilities for trade, and a trading environment which is becoming more user friendly. But has it done as much to

EGYPT LEADING THE WAY

Egypt's political influence in the Arab world is unrivalled and it has played a vital role in the Peace Process

Ramses Temple, Luxor

exploit its advantageous position in the current global climate as it could or should have done? A successful reform process has been carried through without creating instability. Egypt's economy has started to change because of the ability of President Mubarak and his reformist team to embrace the vision and instigate that change. The details of reform – the detailed plans, the detailed understanding, the detailed strategies – remain in the hands and minds of these significant people, and the need to continue to broaden the reformist constituency is obvious.

Egypt has undoubtedly embarked on a fully-fledged path to reform. It has emerged convincingly from a deeply troubled past, of economic mistakes and mismanagement. The foundations of a market economy are being put in place, and will create an attractive climate for investment. The steady success of the reforms and the absence of alternatives has chipped away at any scepticism. The reformers have steam-rollered their way into sectors ranging from power generation to cotton marketing, from airport privatisation to private sector roads. All these achievements have been instigated on the back of a solid economic fundamentals. Meanwhile, the financial sector has remained firm, and is fast playing a key role in facilitating this change. Eventually it will take the initiative from the government, as the role hitherto played by privatisation is replaced by a private sector-led boom, in which the government will play the part of the regulator, leaving the economy to determine Egypt's direction at the dawn of the 21st century.

The co-publishers

Company background

Commercial International Bank (Egypt) S.A.E. (CIB) was incorporated in 1975 under the name Chase National Bank (Egypt) S.A.E. as a joint venture between National Bank of Egypt (NBE), which initially held 51 per cent of its share capital, and Chase Manhattan Overseas Business Corporation (OBC) which held the remaining 49 per cent. The bank was the first to be established by Egypt's 'open door' policy under Law No. 43 of 1974 (amended by Law No. 230 of 1989). Its establishment marked the resurrection of non-state-owned banking in Egypt after two decades of socialist economic policies. The original purpose of the bank was to provide trade and project financing and other services to the increasing number of private sector companies, including multinational and joint venture companies, established in Egypt.

Chase Manhattan OBC acted as the managing shareholder under a 10-year management and technical services agreement pursuant to which Chase Manhattan OBC provided several operating officers on secondment – including the managing director and the senior credit officer – as well as management systems and computer software. In 1987, Chase Manhattan Bank N.A. decided to reduce its involvement in developing countries and to withdraw from Africa and the Middle East. Chase Manhattan OBC therefore closed down its operations in Egypt and sold its shareholding in the bank to NBE, as a result of which NBE's holding of the bank's shares increased to 99.9 per cent. The bank's name was then changed to Commercial International Bank (Egypt) S.A.E. (CIB), its current name.

Following Chase Manhattan OBC's withdrawal, CIB maintained its business strategy of servicing the commercial banking requirements of upper-tier large and medium-sized private Egyptian companies and multinationals operating in Egypt. It focused on the industrial and service sectors. NBE allowed CIB's management a high degree of autonomy, monitoring its investment at the strategic level through the Board of Directors. Executive management was effectively delegated to CIB's senior personnel. NBE also made public at this stage its intention to dilute its equity interest and provide CIB with a broad-based shareholding structure.

The period from mid-1987 to early 1990 was a period of consolidation during which CIB initially defended and then expanded its market share as it established itself as a leading Egyptian bank without foreign share capital or management involvement. Following the execution of the Economic Reform Programme sponsored by the International Monetary Fund in mid-1991, the Egyptian banking sector was significantly deregulated and liberalised. This resulted in rapidly declining margins on traditional banking products and in turn created pressure for banks in Egypt to raise additional capital in order to compensate for the tightening margins. This development, together with the government's new policy of encouraging the Egyptian capital markets, led CIB to adopt a step-by-step strategy to broaden and increase its share capital base.

This process began with a series of offerings of tranches of NBE's shareholding in CIB to employees of both banks between February and December 1992. As a result of these offerings, NBE's holding of CIB's share capital was reduced to 69.9 per cent by December 1992. The sale of 30 per cent of NBE's stake to the employees was a radical incentive programme by Egyptian standards and the largest single sale to staff by any Egyptian company. Apart from broadening CIB's shareholder base, the purpose of the employee offering was also to develop, motivate and retain CIB's personnel. Subsequently, CIB adopted a policy of progressive capitalisation of retained earnings and reserves to increase its paid-in capital. This was complemented by low dividend payments in each of 1990, 1991 and 1992, during which period an aggregate of only 13 per cent of net profits was paid out to shareholders.

The next stage of the capital restructuring process was a public offering of new shares in CIB – completed in November 1993. In the largest public offering to date of shares by an Egyptian company, CIB increased its issued share capital by 43 per cent. After an intensive marketing effort, the shares were placed with institutional investors – including an investment by the IFC – with large Egyptian and foreign corporate and individual investors and with CIB's retail depositors and the Egyptian public. This transaction is generally considered to have been the key catalyst for the emergence of the domestic capital markets. CIB is currently the largest company in terms of market capitalisation (approximately 6.5 per cent of the total market) and by number of shareholders. It is also the most actively traded share, accounting for 10 per cent of total turnover to date.

In 1996, CIB became the first Egyptian company to issue global depository receipts. Following orders from 170 international institutions, the GDR issue was heavily oversubscribed and, at US$119 million (20 per cent of CIB's paid-in capital), it is the largest GDR from the Middle East to date. This further diluted NBE's share to 19.5 per cent.

In 1997, CIB tapped the international syndicated loan market in a highly successful transaction which was raised from the originally envisaged US$100 million to US$200 million. Over 30 major international banks participated. Chase, UBS, ING Barings and Commerzbank were the arrangers. Beyond the obvious funding and profitability implications for CIB, the real significance of this landmark transaction was that it re-opened the Euro-syndicated loan markets for Egyptian borrowers.

Commercial Banking

At year-end in December 1998, CIB had a market share of 16 per cent of total loans to private companies in Egypt. The bank's customer base comprises primarily private-sector corporates, embassies and export-oriented companies. CIB's network of 30 main branches and 30 sub-branches is efficiently positioned in areas of considerable corporate activity, and of upper and middle income population density throughout Egypt.

CIB concentrates in particular on industrial sectors such as pharmaceutical, chemical, textile and food companies; in the service sector the bank concentrates on oil service companies and tourism. CIB has successfully built up important long-term relationships with the majority of US and European companies in Egypt.

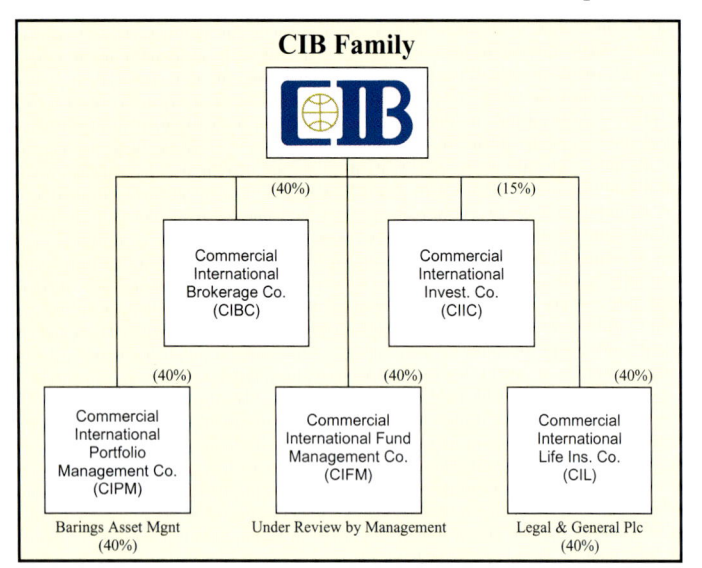

CIB provides short- and medium-term loans to commercial enterprises in Egypt and arranges, syndicates and participates in longer-term project finance loans. Additionally, the bank provides a range of overdraft and revolving credit facilities.

CIB Family

- CIB
  - Commercial International Brokerage Co. (CIBC) (40%)
    - Commercial International Portfolio Management Co. (CIPM) (40%) — Barings Asset Mgnt (40%)
  - Commercial International Invest. Co. (CIIC) (15%)
    - Commercial International Fund Management Co. (CIFM) (40%) — Under Review by Management
    - Commercial International Life Ins. Co. (CIL) (40%) — Legal & General Plc (40%)

Other products and services

Since 1992, CIB has expanded its role as financial intermediary and agent for mobilisation of donor funds by foreign governments and supranational organisations. CIB has been the leading bank in Egypt in utilising USAID commodity import programme funds since November 1986. The bank has also been named as sole agent for the European Union Ecu43 million Food Sector Development Programme and its Ecu55 million Multi Sector Support Programme. CIB is also the sole agent for the E£50milion Buffalo Fattening Programme of the US government and is the largest user of the 'GSM 102' export credit guarantee programme for US commodity imports since April 1992.

Ownership Structure

See chart opposite for CIB's ownership structure after the 1996 GDR issue.

Financial performance and rating

At year-end 1998, CIB had net profits of E£310 million (US$91 million) showing that the bank has maintained its position as the most profitable bank in Egypt for the sixth consecutive year. Thompson BankWatch confirms that profitability has been increasing at a constant rate over the past few years with cost-efficiency ratios being maintained at a low level. Return on equity stands at 24 per cent. Thompson also recognises the bank's prudent risk management and cautious loan loss provisioning.

CIB's total assets reached E£13,277 million (US$3,905 million) in December 1998, making it the country's fifth largest bank, preceded only by four state-owned banks.

CIB is also the third largest Egyptian bank in terms of shareholders' equity (E£1,282 million or US$377 million) and the best capitalised, with a Tier-1 BIS ratio of 10.2 per cent. CIB's accounts are prepared in accordance with international accounting standards by the local affiliate of Deloitte & Touche.

CIB carries a triple-B and A-3 rating by Standard and Poor's. Capital Intelligence rated the bank A and A-2. Thompson BankWatch gave CIB a senior debt rating of BB+ with a positive outlook. For the past six consecutive years, the bank has been awarded the Best Bank in Egypt award by *Euromoney* and was chosen as Best Domestic Bank in Egypt in June 1998, and Egypt's Premier Bank in May 1999 by *Global Finance*.

Future strategies

Since its beginnings as a 49 per cent-held subsidiary of Chase Manhattan, CIB has become the country's premier bank, never compromising quality at any stage of its development. CIB has been a pioneering institution not only in the context of Egypt's financial sector but also in the country's overall business evolution, particularly with the outside world. This is demonstrated by its unique track record in the GDR, syndicated loan, domestic IPO and ESOP areas. CIB has also been a case study of know-how transfer in financial services in the region. This is clearly evidenced by the bank's versatility and successful development following the departure of its foreign shareholder.

This pioneering mentality is reflected in CIB's well-planned and focused corporate strategy. CIB aims to become the leading financial services conglomerate in Egypt by means of:

1. consolidating its position as the top provider of wholesale banking services to the higher-quality Egyptian private sector, multinational and export-oriented companies. In parallel with its corporate expansion, CIB is diversifying and expanding its funding base through organic branch growth (target 35-40 branches by 2000) and by tapping domestic and international debt markets at competitive terms;

2. diversifying into low-risk, fee-based activities such as corporate finance advisory work, stockbroking and asset management both directly and through its group of affiliated companies;

3. expanding the scope of its activities on a selective basis to benefit from the rationalisation of the Egyptian financial sector by entering the insurance and leasing sectors.

With its solid capital structure, increasing earnings, focused business strategy and management approach, CIB is uniquely positioned to develop its lines of business and become Egypt's first integrated financial services company.

Egypt's first Eurobond

In July 1999 CIB was preparing to issue its first Eurobond: a true landmark event for the company and for Egypt. It is all the more impressive given that it should pre-empt the planned sovereign issue from the ARE: that issue had been planned to establish a benchmark for corporate issuers. The bank has secured a BBB- rating from Standard & Poor's and in the first quarter of 1999 profits nearly doubled to US$25.6 million. At the same time provisions had fallen by 47 per cent and the bank's assets were up by 6 per cent to over US$4 billion.

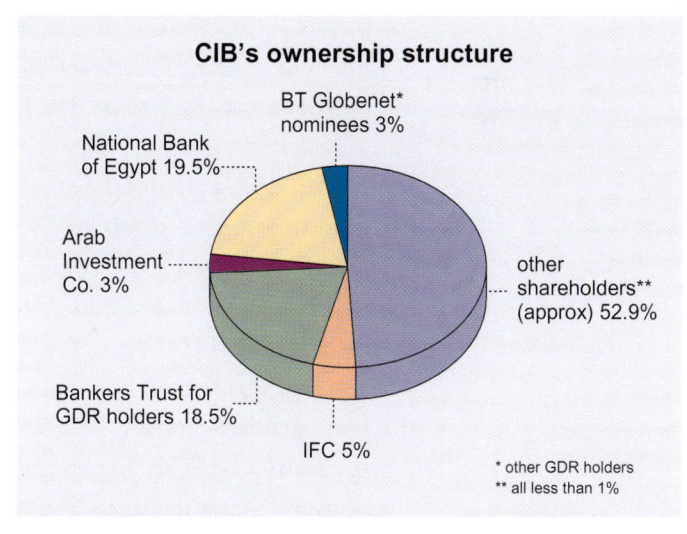

CIB's ownership structure

- BT Globenet* nominees 3%
- National Bank of Egypt 19.5%
- Arab Investment Co. 3%
- Bankers Trust for GDR holders 18.5%
- IFC 5%
- other shareholders** (approx) 52.9%

* other GDR holders
** all less than 1%

Background

Founded in 1958, Ezz Group initially engaged in the local distribution of steel products. In the mid-1970s the business expanded into the importation of steel products and rebars, ceramic tiles and sanitary wares, and the group became the largest private sector importer of such products for nearly 20 years. In the late 1980s, the group diversified its activities to include industrial investments. This move capitalised on Egypt's rapidly growing construction industry and improved economic environment as well as the strong market knowledge and positioning gained by the group through extensive market experiences.

Today, Ezz Group is considered one of the leading industrial groups in Egypt focusing on heavy industries, namely steel, ceramics and porcelain tiles in addition to development of industrial zones development. The group is Egypt's second largest producer of reinforced steel rebars and a leading manufacturer of high-quality ceramic and porcelain tiles. It controls industrial investments exceeding E£2 billion (US$590 million). Further expansion into the flat steel production with a total investment value of E£2.5 billion (US$740 million) is currently under way, scheduled to be operational by the end of the year 2000. The group is the major private sector sponsor of planning and development of the new industrial zone north-west of the Gulf of Suez. This is the first national development project aimed at establishing a world-class industrial park to be developed, promoted and managed by the private sector.

Capitalising on 40 years of market experience, Ezz Group successfully achieved an average growth rate of about 60 per cent per annum for its industrial business during the last 10 years, capturing market shares of 25 per cent and 30 per cent of the steel rebars and upscale tiles markets in Egypt, respectively.

Human resources are key to the group's success. Extensive training programmes, which include an MBA programme sponsorship with above-market benefit schemes for employees, aim to upgrade staff skills and knowledge as well as building group loyalty. Ezz Group believes that qualified human resources are an indispensable asset to successful growth and the maintenance of a leading position in an increasingly competitive environment. The group's staff of over 2,400 is managed by a highly qualified management team.

Engineer Ahmed Ezz is the group's CEO and major shareholder. For the last 18 years, Mr Ezz provided the driving force behind the group's growth, specifically in the industrial fields.

Product quality and efficient management systems are primary organisational targets. Ezz Group is committed to quality, enhanced by maximising the efficiency of management systems.

Efforts to optimise business processes include periodic in-house management reviews as well as utilising the expertise of international management consultancy firms such as Booz Allen & Hamilton, Arthur Andersen and Oliver Wight. Both methods help ensure the implementation of best business practices. The group supports its objectives by utilising state-of-the-art technologies to ensure the highest-quality product at the most competitive cost. Strict quality control measures are applied throughout all process stages in the group's plants. The group's quality management systems are certified by Germanischer Lloyd of Germany as complying with ISO 9002 and/or ISO 9001 for quality standards and ISO 14001 for environmental standards.

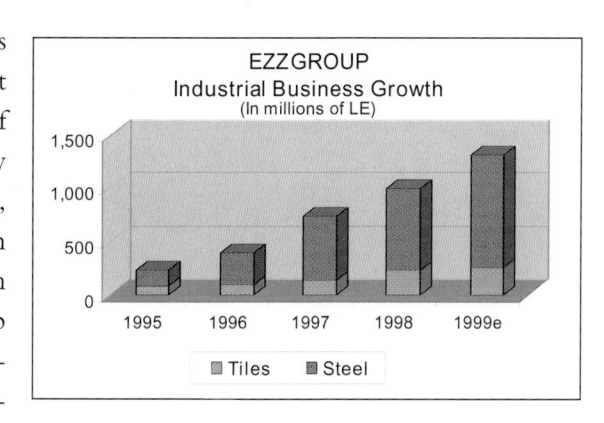

Ezz Group's strategy focuses on building competitive strengths to consolidate and strengthen its market position in Egypt and to support its objective of becoming a regional market leader. Economic reform policies and ambitious development plans adopted by the Egyptian government reinforce the group's strategy. High GDP growth continues to create strong growth opportunities. The group intends to capitalise on these opportunities by expansion and investment in its core businesses.

The steel business

Ezz Group's steel long products business consists of two operating companies, Al-Ezz Steel Rebars (ESR) and Al-Ezz Steel Mills (ESM). Both are Egyptian joint-stock companies manufacturing reinforced steel rebars with a combined production capacity of 1.1 million tonnes. The operations were recently consolidated whereby ESR currently owns about 90 per cent of ESM. In a global equity offering, which was successfully closed in June 1999, 30 per cent of ESR's shares were offered and are currently being traded on the London and Cairo Stock Exchanges. Mr Ahmed Ezz owns and controls the remaining 70 per cent.

Production facilities include a melting shop and three rolling mills. The plants are located in the new satellite cities – Sadat City, about 100km north of the capital, and 10th of Ramadan City, about 35km north-east of Cairo. The total combined area of the plants is approximately 453,000m^2. Danieli of Italy designed, supplied and installed the plants.

International industry experts describe Ezz steel plants as world class. Indeed, we have been named as the most efficient Egyptian steel producer in terms of optimised consumption and production output. The first rolling mill, commissioned in June 1989, operates at 139 per cent of its design capacity. The second rolling mill, commissioned in September 1996, reached design capacity after eight months and currently operates at 120 per cent of design capacity. The learning curve was even more impressive for the third rolling mill, commissioned in

September 1998, which reached design capacity level after only three months and currently operates at 110 per cent of design capacity. The challenging melting shop operation that began in August 1998 attained design capacity after only eight months.

Ezz Group – efficiency and growth in the steel business

	1996	1997	1998	1999e
Design capacity ('000s tonnes)	210	510	610	910
Production output ('000s tonnes)	275	525	738	1,050
Operating rate (%)	131	103	121	115
Growth in production (%)	56	91	41	42

Source: Ezz Group.

Coping with the growing demand of steel rebars in Egypt, further planned capacities are under consideration for all existing lines to increase total rebar production to about 1.4 million tonnes per annum by 2001.

Over the past 10 years the Egyptian market for steel rebars has grown at a much faster rate than the growth of GDP. Despite the fact that local production has doubled since 1995, the Egyptian market witnessed a shortfall of about 23 per cent, which was covered through importation in 1998. Further growth is forecast, given the current development stage of Egypt, which will require higher consumption levels of steel rebars. The anticipated growth rate is forecast as a minimum of 7 per cent annually.

Further expanding into the flat steel industry, Ezz Group, together with Danieli, established Al-Ezz Heavy Industries Company (EHI) which will build, own and operate a steel manufacturing, casting and hot strip rolling complex in Egypt's new development area northwest of the Gulf of Suez. The design capacity is 1.175 million tonnes of hot rolled coils per annum. Danieli of Italy will design, supply, install and commission the plant under a turn-key contract. The total investment is about US$740 million, comprising US$270 million equity and about US$470 million in long-term bank financing. The financing was arranged through a project finance, limited recourse scheme provided 52 per cent by a syndication of international financial institutions and 48 per cent by Egyptian institutions. The project obtained a guarantee from the Italian export credit agency SACE to partially support financing provided by the offshore banks syndication. This is the first time that such a guarantee was obtained by an Egyptian private sector project covering this amount of financing for a tenor exceeding 13 years. The project is also supported by long-term off-take agreements covering about 60 per cent of the production with prime European steel trading companies and a reputable pipe manufacturer. The plant is currently under construction and scheduled for operation by the end of the year 2000.

The tiles business

Ezz Group's tile manufacturing business is composed of two operating companies: Al-Ezz Porcelain Company (EPC) and Al-Ezz Ceramics Company (ECC). ECC produces wall, floor and decorative ceramic tiles. EPC manufactures ceramic tiles in addition to porcelain tiles, the first to be introduced to the Egyptian marketplace. The ceramic and porcelain tiles retail under the brand name of Al-Jawhara in the local market and GEMMA in export markets. As part of a consolidation strategy, EPC acquired 98 per cent of ECC's shares. EPC shares are listed on the Egyptian Stock Exchange; 70 per cent are owned and controlled by Mr Ahmed Ezz and 30 per cent are traded on the exchange.

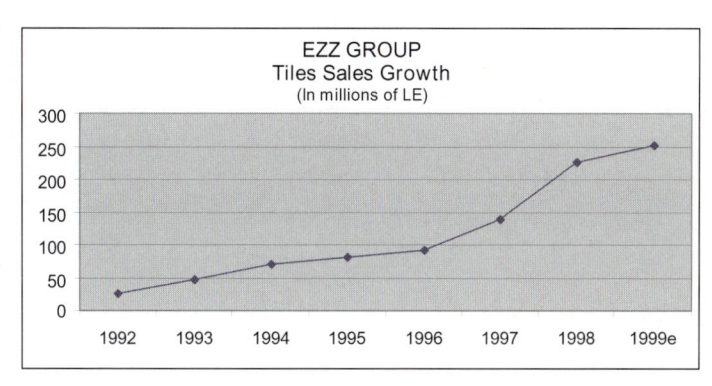

Production facilities include two adjacent plants with a total area of 150,000m^2, in Sadat City. Operations began in February 1991 with an initial capacity of 1.2 million square metres of tiles per annum. Due to growing demand for GEMMA products, capacities gradually increased to reach the current level of 12.6 million square metres of product (10.6 million square metres of ceramic tiles and 2 million square metres of porcelain tiles). SACMI of Italy, the world largest machinery supplier for the tiles industry, supplied the plants.

Since its inception, GEMMA witnessed a growing market share, which reached 30 per cent in 1999. GEMMA's average growth rate is 42 per cent per annum throughout the last eight years. Currently, Al-Jawhara has a very strong market position. It is recognised as the leading producer of high-quality tiles in the Egyptian marketplace. Al-Jawhara offers a wide range of size formats (15 formats) and more than 250 designs created and developed by the company's in-house designers and product development team. The company was ISO 9001 certified by Germanischer Lloyd of Germany in 1995.

Fleming CIIC

Fleming CIIC is a new joint venture between Flemings, the international investment banking and asset management group, and CIIC, Cairo's leading investment house.

Fleming Mansour | **Research** EGYPT
LEISURE AND HOTELS

Orascom Hotel Holdings, Orascom Projects and Touristic Development
Let's talk about tourism

Robert Fleming & Co Limited
25 Copthall Avenue London EC2R 7DR
Telephone +44 171 638 5858
Facsimile +44 171 628 0683

Sherine Moussa +20 2 393 7580
fmr@egyptonline.com

Fleming CIIC, which is headquartered in Cairo, consolidates both partners' existing positions in the primary and secondary markets in Egypt and will build a significant presence in the fund management business. The joint venture will also offer its services to domestic and international clients in North Africa and the Near East.

The new group has over 80 professional specialists and is active in the following areas:

- Capital Markets
- Corporate Finance
- Securities Sales and Research
- Asset Management
- Project Finance

The Flemings Group

Flemings is a global investment banking and asset management group employing over 7,500 staff and operating in over 40 countries.

The global asset management business manages E£66.7 billion (US$107.4 billion) on behalf of private investors, pension funds, companies, institutions, governments and central banks around the world. It is a leading manager of mutual funds and institutional money in the UK, Continental Europe, Asia and the US. The investment management process is based on a disciplined approach to stock selection, a significant in-house research capability and a strong local presence in all of the world's main financial markets. In Europe, it has over E£28 billion (US$45.1 billion) of funds under management, including E£3.1 billion (US$5 billion) in the award-winning Flagship pan-European mutual fund range. In Asia, it manages funds of over E£15 billion (US$24.2 billion) with asset management operations in Hong Kong, Tokyo, Taiwan and Singapore. In the US, it directly manages close to E£3 billion (US$4.8 billion) alongside its joint venture, Rowe Price-Fleming International, which manages over E£20 billion (US$32.2 billion) for US investors.

The global investment banking business provides securities, corporate advisory, capital markets and banking services to an international client base that includes major companies, governments, institutional investors and central banks. It has an extensive equity research and distribution network, with over 300 analysts covering more than 2,800 stocks, and is widely recognised as one of the world's leading securities houses in both Asia and the emerging markets. Its global corporate finance business has a presence on every continent and in every significant financial centre. Specialising in international M&A, European mid-cap companies and emerging markets, Corporate Finance has strength in depth in its chosen sectors and a track record of handling complex and demanding transactions. Capital Markets assists companies around the world to raise equity and equity-linked capital from institutional and retail investors in both developed and emerging markets. Its banking business provides money market and foreign exchange services, retail banking and private banking. It is also a major provider of debt and debt advice to enhance the performance of investment funds, to support property development and investment clients, and to fund MBOs/MBIs and private equity acquisitions. It also provides a stock lending capability and custody services.

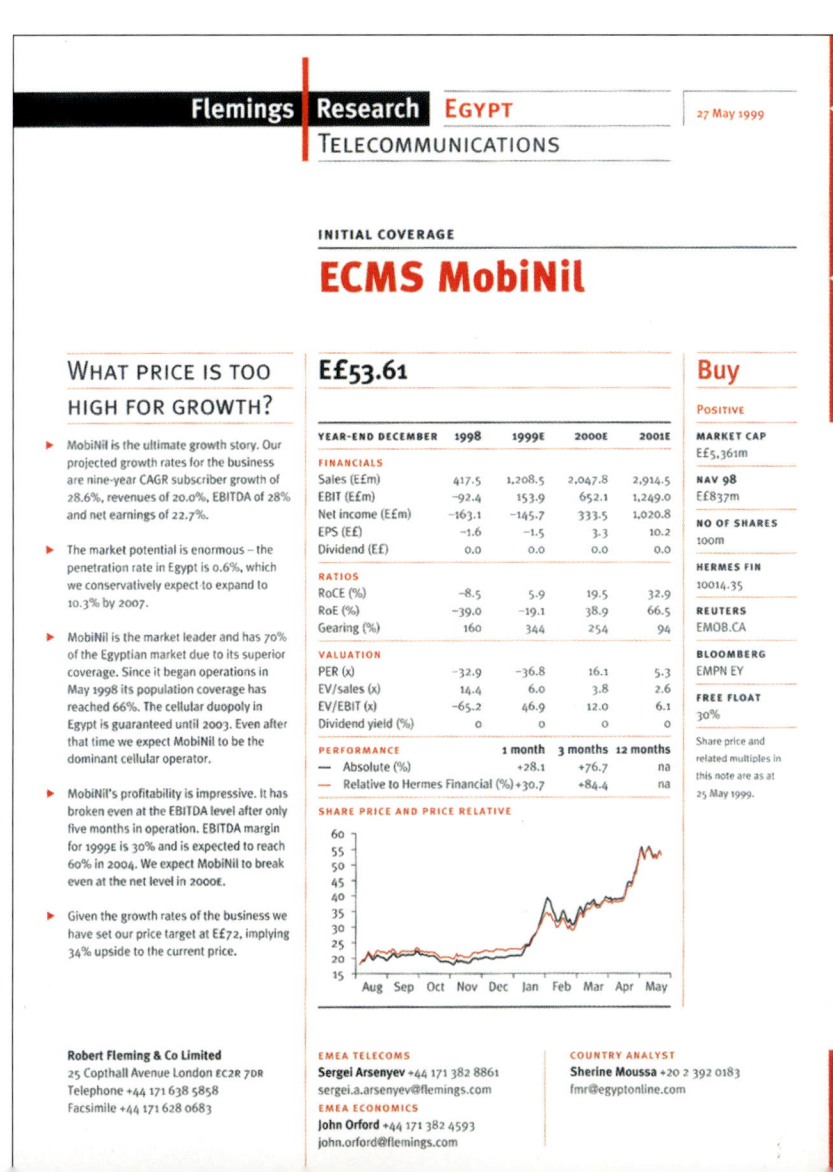

Fleming Mansour | **Research** | **EGYPT**
CONSTRUCTION

September 1998

Arabian International Construction

Robert Fleming Securities Limited
25 Copthall Avenue London EC2R 7DR
Telephone +44 171 638 5858
Facsimile +44 171 628 0683

Mohamed Abdel-Hadi +44 171 282 4523
mohamed.abdel-hadi@flemings.com

Recent Awards in the Region

Flemings is ranked No.1 Securities House (Sales and Research) for the Middle East, North Africa and the Mediterranean region by:

- Financial Times Extel Survey
- Greenwich Associates

CIIC

CIIC was established in 1994, as a closed shareholding company, to provide and expand the investment banking services previously extended by the Commercial International Bank's Merchant Banking Division to become one of the leading financial institutions in Egypt. The company's two institutional shareholders are the National Bank of Egypt and the Commercial International Bank.

The company has established itself as a pioneer player in investment banking, including corporate finance advisory work, privatisation issues, equity and debt issues, underwriting services and mergers and acquisitions.

Landmark transactions by the Corporate Finance Division include: the Egyptian first initial public offering, the first private placement in the privatisation process, the first GDR out of Egypt, the first private sector IPO on the Egypt Stock Exchange. Total issue business of CIIC to date exceeds E£5.5 billion.

In addition, Intercapital Securities, a brokerage firm established in 1995, which was 50% owned by CIIC, is included in the joint venture. Intercapital currently holds an 11% market share of secondary market turnover and has a particularly strong domestic position, as well as a significant regional and international placing power.

CIIC has recently incorporated a fund management company. Over its first few months of operations, the company has managed to secure mandates for the launch of 3 funds sponsored by Al Watany Bank of Egypt. CIIC is also co-managing the largest offshore fund dedicated to Egypt.

Selected transactions for clients in Egypt include:

- Alexandria Real Estate
- Arabian International Construction
- CIB
- Cairo for Housing and Development
- Coca Cola
- El Watany Bank
- EGEMAC
- Egypt Duty Free Shops
- Egyptian Electrical Cables
- International Electronics
- MISR Aluminium
- OGFI
- PACHIN
- Savola Sime

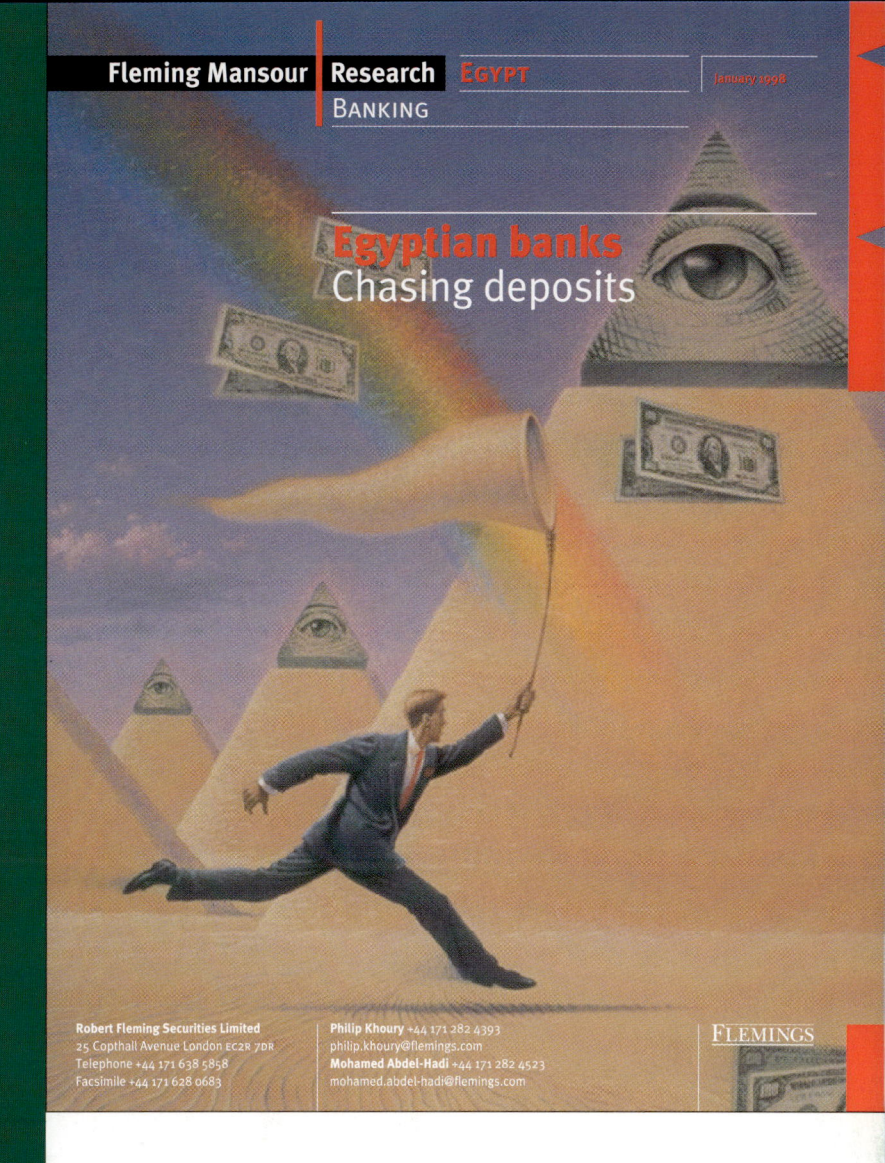

Fleming Mansour | Research EGYPT
BANKING

January 1998

Egyptian banks
Chasing deposits

Robert Fleming Securities Limited
25 Copthall Avenue London EC2R 7DR
Telephone +44 171 638 5858
Facsimile +44 171 628 0683

Philip Khoury +44 171 282 4393
philip.khoury@flemings.com
Mohamed Abdel-Hadi +44 171 282 4523
mohamed.abdel-hadi@flemings.com

FLEMINGS

Fleming CIIC Contact Details:
Fleming CIIC
9 Mohamed Fahmy Street
Garden City
Cairo
Egypt

Tel: +202 594 3875
Fax: +202 594 3869

Yasser El Mallawany
Chairman

Rupert Wise
Managing Director,
Flemings Middle East

Tel: +44 171 282 4212
Fax: +44 171 256 8592

GlaxoWellcome
Glaxo Wellcome Egypt S.A.E

Brief history

In less than a decade of doing business in Egypt, Glaxo Wellcome Egypt (GWE) has emerged as the country's leading pharmaceutical company with an annual turnover exceeding E£300 million and a market share of almost 9 per cent. The Egyptian pharmaceutical industry is currently valued at E£3.5 billion (US$1.03 billion) and is growing at a rate of 5 per cent per annum.

It was as a shareholder in Advanced Biochemical Industries (ABI), a local pharmaceutical company founded in the 1980s, that GWE first entered the Egyptian pharmaceutical market. At the time ABI had a market-place ranking of 22 with 30 licences, 10 local products and a 1 per cent market share.

By the time Glaxo acquired control of ABI in May 1990, the company ranked 12th in the industry, with its market share almost tripling. By applying novel sales and marketing strategies, quality assurance and critical financial restructuring, sales at the new Glaxo-ABI Company evidenced a dramatic increase. Furthermore, the August 1995 merger of Glaxo with Wellcome plc predictably set off new expansions in Glaxo Wellcome's Egyptian operation.

Today, British-based Glaxo Wellcome plc owns almost 90 per cent of GWE. The remaining shareholders comprise a number of institutional investors including Misr International Bank, Banque Paribas and Mohandes Insurance Company, in addition to individual investors.

Dr Negad M. Shaarawi, Chairman and Managing Director

The acquisition

In GWE's brief history, January 1999 represents a definitive breakthrough when the company, represented by its current chairman and managing director Dr. Negad M. Shaarawi, finalised the purchase of 97 per cent of Amoun Pharmaceutical Industries Company (APIC) for the sum of E£387.2 million (US$112 million). With this acquisition GWE not only acquired APIC's domestic and export rights to 30 products, its machinery and production facilities, GWE also expanded its premises from 33,000m^2 to 48,000m^2. APIC's geographic contiguity to GWE facilitated the smooth and complete integration of the two companies.

As a result of the takeover, GWE's workforce increased to over 1,500 employees. These are distributed between the head office, six distribution branches and six sales and marketing offices covering the different regions of Egypt.

During the signing ceremony, Egypt's Minister of Economy remarked how GWE's takeover was a vote of confidence for the Egyptian economy. Dr. Youssef Boutros Ghali went on to emphasise the private sector's achievements free from any government interference.

At the same ceremony Dr. Ibrahim Fawzi, Chairman of the General Authority for

Investment, stressed the strength of FDIs, intimating that GWE's noteworthy investment proved that Egypt's market-oriented reforms were attracting investors both at home and abroad.

Also present at the signing ceremony were Sir David Blatherwick, the British Ambassador; Mr. Abdel Hamid Ibrahim, head of the Egyptian Capital Market Authority; and Mr. Fouad Benghalem, Glaxo Wellcome (GW) area director for the Middle East and North Africa.

Maintaining international standards

GWEs unwavering efforts to attain excellence were rewarded in 1994 when GWE became one of 512 companies worldwide to receive the MRPII (Manufacturing Resource Planning) Class 'A' certificate.

ISO 9002 and 9001 soon followed in 1995 and 1997 respectively. These were granted by the prestigious British Standards Institution (BSI), ISO 9001 once the approved design-control and development laboratories were introduced at GWE. BSI awarded the company ISO 14001 in August 1997, underlining GWE's commitment to preserving and controlling its impact on the environment.

In February 1999 BSI reassessed GWE against the BS 8800 criteria for Occupational Health and Safety Management. Not only was the company in full compliance but BSI acknowledged the complete integration of all of the above systems (ISO 9001, ISO 14001 and BS 8800) into a smoothly running operation. GWE was granted the Integrated Management Systems Assessment Service Certificate, the eigth such certificate to be issued in all industries and the first in the pharmaceutical industry worldwide.

Technology and IT

GWE has consistently played an important role in transfer technology both in the production-related and information systems technology fields. It has become routine that fresh innovations are swiftly incorporated into the GWE system and introduced to the staff. Moreover, information technology is continuously updated and a two-way channel of information flow is open and accessible to employees.

Internet and Intranet are part and parcel of everyday work for both technical and administration staff members.

Y2K compliance

One of the areas under scrutiny at GWE is the Year 2000 computer problem. To this end GWE set up its own task force in 1997 as a part of the overall GW effort to ensure that its global operations will be year 2000 compliant before the target date of September 1999.

The Y2K project team communicates with GWE employees at regular intervals thus increasing awareness of the problem. The project team is also working with vendors, clients, and suppliers helping them to solve their own Y2K problem so as to minimise any outside interference with the running of GWE's operations.

Staff training

Training, being an essential part of the GWE culture, has invariably benefited Egyptian workers. Training is carried out in-house as well as with the assistance of special training centres in Egypt or in collaboration with academic institutions offering specialised courses.

Centres of excellence

At the invitation of GW's head office in the UK, GWE participated in the establishment of the group's Manufacturing and Supply Quality Management Systems. The resultant scheme will be applied in all GW operations around the world.

Economic issues: foreign direct investment

Without doubt the Egyptian government's policies encouraging FDI helped the pharmaceutical market gain momentum, which is why in 1990 GW invested E£70 million in Egypt acquiring the majority of shares of a local pharmaceutical manufacturing company. Nine years later, President Hosni Mubarak's continued support for FDI together with the country's sustained political stability and economic progress proved GW right, encouraging it to increase its investment in Egypt by as much as E£387.2 million in 1999.

Geographic location

Besides being Africa and the Middle East's gateway to Europe, Egypt's unique location in the centre of the Arab world makes it a focal point between North and South.

Both the combination of its historic ability to adjust to and absorb change and its political and economic weight in the North Africa-Middle East region favoured Egypt as one of 10 targeted emerging markets worldwide with great potential for future trade and investment.

Largest market in the Middle East

With a population of 62.6 million, a good infrastructure, a functional telecommunications network and a solid industrial base, Egypt is the largest market in the Middle East. Moreover, its labour force of approximately 17 million, which is growing by nearly 3 per cent annually, dominates the market. It is not surprising therefore that Egypt's share in the region's pharmaceutical market is a robust 20 per cent.

GWE partnership with Ministry of Health and Population

1996: Asthma management
In association with the Egyptian Society of Chest Disease, GWE provided a three-part comprehensive programme on asthma management.
1997: Hypertension
In association with the Egyptian Hypertension Society, with the aim of supporting a continuous

medical education programme for hypertension diagnosis and management. It was designed for the physicians working at the Ministry of Health and Population hospitals and polyclinics across Egypt.
1998: National asthma guideline
In collaboration with the Egyptian Society for Chest Diseases GWE supported the formulation and implementation of the first national guideline for asthma management.

GWE a corporate citizen

GWE took part in a nationwide effort launched by Egypt's first lady, Mrs. Suzanne Mubarak, to help children in need of regular blood transfusions.

GWE also participated in a national campaign launched by the Future Foundation. As outlined by former US president George Bush who was principal guest speaker at the foundation's November 1998 fundraiser, one of Future's aims is to provide low-income Egyptian youth with reasonably priced housing.

GWE was one of the first pharmaceutical companies to donate medical products to victims of the October 1992 earthquake and to the subsequent flash floods in Upper Egypt.

GWE regularly sponsors students' activities at local universities. For two consecutive years it was an official sponsor for the International Students' Leadership Council at the American University in Cairo. In 1999 it sponsored the Cairo International Model United Nations.

Moreover, a large number of college students studying medicine, pharmacy, veterinary medicine and science are welcomed every summer on GWE's premises for a 2-3 week training course. Notwithstanding GWE's ongoing efforts to familiarise students with the pharmaceutical industry as a whole, it vigorously underscores those quality systems and environmental issues related to industrial sites.

Student visits are conducted all year-round acquainting tomorrow's decision-makers, researchers and scientists with the latest technologies in the manufacturing processes, information systems and management.

Also within the framework of co-operation between industry and academia, GWE recently organised a number of managerial workshops for the medical staff at Alexandria University's Faculty of Medicine.

GWE's major products
Group products
Zantac, Septrin, Zyloric, Eltroxin, Fortum, Zinnat, Ventolin, Semprex, Zofran, Ceporex, Imigran, Serevent, Lacipil, Becotide, Beconase, Dermovate, Cutivate, Eumovate, Flixonase, Flixotide, Betnovate, Marevan, Actifed.
Local products
Supravit, Haemoton, Flurest, Abimol, Abivit, Adenophose, Abilaxin, Ultrafen, Primaleve, Starleve, Fortevit.

Manufacturing functions
Tablets; hard and soft gelatin capsules; syrup and suspensions; ointments and creams; suppositories; primary manufacturing; inhalers; clean liquids; injectables; oral cepholosporins (tablets, dry syrup); sterile cephs.

HELMY & HAMZA
BAKER & MCKENZIE

An international law firm

Baker & McKenzie is the largest law firm in the world. With 61 offices in 34 countries and over 2,400 attorneys worldwide, it pioneered the idea of a multinational legal practice within a single firm. When other firms followed its example, it maintained its lead by taking advantage of some 50 years of experience in combining an extensive international network with strong local, regional and international expertise at offices in major commercial centres around the world. It offers clients a solid local practice, with access to worldwide experience and expertise.

This unique global partnership was founded in Chicago on 1 July 1949. It began its initial expansion by opening its first office outside the United States in Caracas, Venezuela. By the end of the decade, influenced by the great outflow of US investment around the globe, and with particular emphasis on tax and the transfer of technology across international boundaries, Baker & McKenzie offices started operating in Amsterdam, Brussels, New York, São Paulo, Washington, DC, and Zurich.

The 1960s witnessed continued expansion of the firm internationally with the opening of offices in Tokyo and Sydney. Offices in Frankfurt, Geneva, London, Manila, Mexico City, Milan, Paris, Rio de Janeiro, Rome and Toronto soon followed.

In the 1970s the San Francisco and Bogotá offices were opened. Reflecting the growth of the economies in the Asia/Pacific region, offices in Bangkok, Hong Kong and Taipei were also opened in this decade.

Baker & McKenzie first entered the Middle East in the mid-1970s with the establishment of an office in Riyadh. In the 1980s, offices were established in Moscow, Beijing, Buenos Aires, Dallas, Melbourne, Miami, Shanghai, Guangzhou and Singapore, as well as in Juarez and Tijuana in order to serve the Maquiladora industry on the US/Mexican border. In 1986, Baker & McKenzie established its office in Cairo, Egypt.

Baker & McKenzie has been at the cutting edge of developing innovative solutions to legal problems for five decades. It has developed centres of expertise in particular fields and has formed a Middle East Experts Group at the head office in Chicago, which can be instantly contacted and accessed by the regional offices. An exchange of attorneys between offices fosters a close working relationship as well as developing bilingual capability.

Cairo office of Baker & McKenzie (Helmy & Hamza)

The Baker & McKenzie office in Cairo (Helmy & Hamza) is the only law firm in Egypt that combines a detailed knowledge of local law and the ability to offer the experience and discipline of an international law firm with access to a vast global network of resources and expertise in international corporate and litigation practice in a rapid and cost-effective manner.

It can advise clients on any aspects of complex multijurisdictional transactions. It provides legal services to both domestic and international companies in a diverse range of specialisation including corporate, banking and finance, commercial, taxation, privatisation, transfer of technology, capital markets, joint ventures, restructuring, mergers and acquisitions, debt-equity swaps, oil and gas. The firm also conducts a strong commercial litigation and international arbitration practice.

Dr. Taher Helmy, admitted in the US, Egypt and Saudi Arabia, practiced in the US for nine years before co-founding the Riyadh and Cairo offices of Baker & McKenzie. Samir Hamza, a senior Egyptian lawyer with practice experience in the US, Kuwait, Saudi Arabia and Egypt, is the other co-founder of the Riyadh and the Cairo offices of the firm.

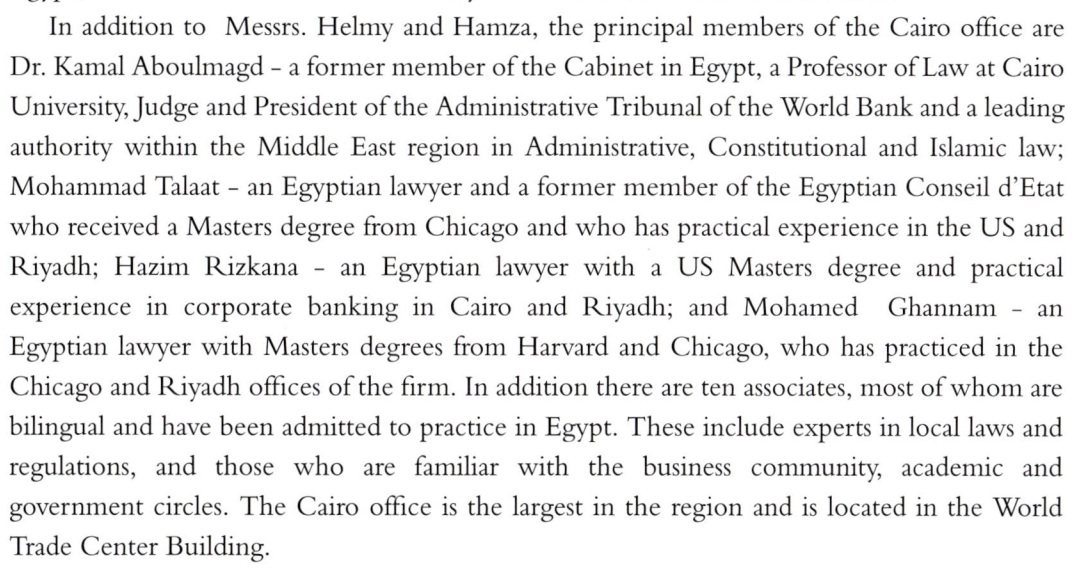

Taher Helmy and Samir Hamza, Senior Partners and founders of the Cairo office.

In addition to Messrs. Helmy and Hamza, the principal members of the Cairo office are Dr. Kamal Aboulmagd - a former member of the Cabinet in Egypt, a Professor of Law at Cairo University, Judge and President of the Administrative Tribunal of the World Bank and a leading authority within the Middle East region in Administrative, Constitutional and Islamic law; Mohammad Talaat - an Egyptian lawyer and a former member of the Egyptian Conseil d'Etat who received a Masters degree from Chicago and who has practical experience in the US and Riyadh; Hazim Rizkana - an Egyptian lawyer with a US Masters degree and practical experience in corporate banking in Cairo and Riyadh; and Mohamed Ghannam - an Egyptian lawyer with Masters degrees from Harvard and Chicago, who has practiced in the Chicago and Riyadh offices of the firm. In addition there are ten associates, most of whom are bilingual and have been admitted to practice in Egypt. These include experts in local laws and regulations, and those who are familiar with the business community, academic and government circles. The Cairo office is the largest in the region and is located in the World Trade Center Building.

The Cairo office advised the Egyptian government on a number of legislation reforms. The firm's role in the privatisation process in Egypt ranges from helping to draft the Public Enterprise Law, Law No. 203 of 1991 (the Privatisation Law), to executing three of the four major anchor investor transactions including the first privatisation transaction in Egypt.

The scope of activities carried out in the corporate practice are widespread, from advising and assisting first in the bidding for Egypt's first private power plant project on a BOOT (build, own, operate and transfer) basis, to acting as lenders' counsel to the banks on the same project. Baker & McKenzie is now considered a leader in securities transactions, acting as local and international counsel in key debt and equity offerings, as well as a leader in project finance.

The government called upon the firm's expertise in the recent amendments to the Copyright Law, as well as drafting the Environmental Law. The firm is also successful in international arbitration and major local commercial litigation.

Baker & McKenzie's clients include large multinational corporations and the leading local businesses. Baker & McKenzie's worldwide network of offices enables the Cairo office to refer Egyptian clients to its own offices abroad when they intend doing business outside the Middle

East. Clients rely on the Cairo office of Helmy & Hamza for the best legal advice, and a stable presence in the region. As part of the Baker & McKenzie international network, the Cairo office is deeply committed to furthering its clients' business interests both within the Middle East region and globally.

The following is an index of legal services offered:

Banking and finance

- Banking and financing transactions;
- Project finance;
- Financial regulatory work and structuring.

Corporate law and investment

- Incorporation of Egyptian companies, mergers, acquisitions, sales, dissolutions/liquidations;
- Setting up branches, technical, liaison and representative offices;
- Privatisation: asset and share purchase agreements; due diligence and legal audits;
- Establishing joint ventures, financial services companies and mutual funds;
- Securities transactions; local and international debt and equity offerings;
- Commercial and distributorship agreements;
- Handling foreign investment within and outside the free zones.

Construction and infrastructure

- Advice on construction and civil engineering contracts such as fresh water, sewage, waste water treatment, public utilities and administrative contracts for:
- Infrastructure and power plant projects (including BOOT transactions);
- Building and construction projects.

Environment

The Cairo office is at the forefront of this growing field, with expertise in hazardous waste; oil spillage; air pollution and water pollution.

Intellectual property

The firm is mainly involved in:
- Enforcement of IPR, specifically cases dealing with combating piracy;
- Transfer of technology, including licensing agreements.

Islamic law

'Mudaraba' and 'Murabaha' contracts under the 'Shari'ah' or Islamic law as well as other issues under Islamic law.

Labour

- Drafting all types of labour contracts;

- Preparation of work and disciplinary measure regulations;
- Social Security requirements.

Litigation and arbitration

The firm handles international and local arbitration, inter-jurisdictional litigation and local litigation in the following areas:
As all attorneys are licensed in Egypt, local litigation covers the following:
- Civil and commercial;
- Criminal aspects of commercial cases;
- Labour, administrative and tax cases.

Manufacturing

Advice is available on manufacturing requirements under Egyptian law, including labelling requirements and registration procedures for pharmaceutical, food, and cosmetic products.

Natural resources

International oil and utilities companies are major clients in the following fields:
- Exploration, production and oil concessions;
- Upstream industry, transportation of crude oil and development leases.

Taxation

- Corporate and personal income tax, sales tax, and stamp duty;
- Tax incentives for foreign investment within and outside free zones.

Telecommunications

The firm offers advice on a wide range of matters, including:
- Broadcasting regulations and downlink satellite agreements;
- Pay-TV programming and distribution agreements;

Tourism

The firm has advised on hotel and resort projects, construction and operation of cruise ships (including the preparation of ancillary contracts such as hotel management, technical services, licences, employment and operations contracts).

Trade and commerce

- Import/export and supply contracts and customs requirements;
- Agencies and distributors;
- Internal trading requirements, including profit margins and mark-up limitations;

Helmy & Hamza (Baker & McKenzie), World Trade Center, 1191 Cornich El Nil Eighteenth Floor, Cairo, Egypt. Tel: 20 2 579 1801/2/3/4/5/6 Fax: 20 2 579 1808

KPMG Hazem Hassan
Public Accountants & Consultants

KPMG International

Our mission

KPMG is the global advisory firm whose aim is to turn knowledge into value for the benefit of its clients, its people and its communities. New challenges demand new solutions. Global competition and information technology are creating a new dimension of client needs which require a new type of business adviser – an integrated team of specialists who combine industry expertise with functional knowledge.

KPMG is committed to building on this new type of a global professional services firm: integrated market teams combining the right people with the right skills and in the right place – where their clients need them.

By further developing its growing consultative skills while maintaining its high professional standards, KPMG is well-positioned globally to participate in the accelerating pace of activity as developed countries continue to transform their information-based economies and developing countries enter a new era of consumerism and growth.

As we approach the new century, we are extremely confident in our ability to meet these challenges and opportunities to grow our business, our people and our presence.

Services

As the business world changes in response to new political and economic realities, so, too, does KPMG. Building on our traditional base of audit and compliance work, we have expanded our role into that of a comprehensive consultancy firm, providing services to support our clients' needs to become more competitive.

Our consulting, tax and audit professionals work closely together, sharing their collective knowledge and expertise to provide integrated business solutions for clients.

KPMG audits more of the top 20 transnational corporations than any other firm. Major international companies come to us for management consultancy, advice and guidance in areas such as business process re-engineering and international tax structuring, for example.

Naturally, building new areas of expertise and creating new services go hand in hand. By listening to our clients and focusing on their business issues, we are constantly developing new services on an international and a domestic basis.

Key areas of functional expertise

Accountancy and auditing

Optimising the benefits of audit to our clients is a major priority. KPMG provides advice in the areas of financial and business management. We render opinions in accordance with statutory requirements and in compliance with relevant regulations and agreements. KPMG is also relied on for valuations, buy-out arrangements, prospective financial information, internal audit reviews, and many other services. For many clients KPMG serves as independent counsel and intermediary in making business contacts.

Tax

By using the resources of our international network, KPMG is better able to offer tax consultancy and compliance services to companies, other organisations and private individuals. Our aim is to ensure that each client pays no more tax than the law requires, which means we remain familiar with national and international tax laws, anticipate changes in those laws and provide clear-cut advice and quality services tailored to meet each client's specific needs.

Among our services are corporate and individual tax planning and compliance, and diagnostic reviews, which include designing and implementing tax planning strategies.

Management consultancy

Our objective in this area is to work together with our clients to achieve sustained improvements in their results through cost reduction or revenue generation and in the quality of their work and products. To achieve these results, our world-class resources provide advanced industry-focused end-to-end solutions in the areas of performance improvement, enabling technologies and strategic financial management, through a global network.

Specific services include IT strategy, world-class IT, electronic commerce, data warehousing, enterprise-wide package implementation, year 2000 compliance consultancy, supply chain management, business performance improvement, and world-class finance management.

We ally ourselves with major software vendors such as Oracle and Peoplesoft and have established global practices with SAP and Baan to help clients improve their business performance and boost return on investment.

Corporate finance

Whether the client is buying or selling, KPMG has the experience to handle every detail involved in structuring a transaction deal. Our mergers and acquisitions specialists effectively serve as deal managers, helping clients to formulate an offer and handle negotiations. We offer objective advice on raising funds to the client's best advantage, and can help with post-acquisition integration.

Industries

Although there are trends and developments shared by every industry, each segment presents its own set of challenges. As an advisory firm, KPMG has dedicated itself to becoming unrivalled industry experts in most major fields. We have specialists in a very broad range of disciplines and industries. With an in-depth understanding of the market and the industry, KPMG specialists foresee specific developments and offer advice on how best to proceed.

Being able to offer general professional services is no longer enough. Both the market and our clients demand industry expertise.

With this in mind, KPMG is structured by international industry groups. Each provides targeted knowledge gained in the client's own industry. KPMG's major industry groups are:

- banking and finance;
- building and construction;
- energy and natural resources;
- government;
- health care and life sciences;
- industrial products;
- information, communications and entertainment;
- insurance;
- retail and consumer products; and
- transportation.

KPMG is qualified to serve clients in each of these sectors and many others. We provide services to 26.4 per cent of the world's top 1,000 commercial and industrial companies. With so many premier clients, it is hard to find an industry sector that we do not actively serve. Our infrastructure makes it possible to create international or local multidisciplinary client teams which are united in their commitment to find inventive, client-focused solutions.

KPMG Hazem Hassan

KPMG Hazem Hassan is the leading independent accounting and consulting firm in Egypt. While retaining its national status, it is also a member of KPMG International. As Egypt's economy has developed and grown over the past decade, KPMG Hazem Hassan has advanced its capabilities and resources to meet the needs of the clients it serves. As a result the firm now has more than 1,000 professionals with national and international experience in the functional areas of consulting, tax, and accounting and auditing. KPMG Hazem Hassan's clients demand industry expertise.

KMPG Hazem Hassan's specialised industry groups are structured and staffed in the same way as those at KPMG International and include:

Mr Hazem Hassan, Chairman.

KPMG HAZEM HASSAN

- banking and finance;
- building and construction;
- energy and natural resources;
- health care;
- manufacturing;
- information, communication and entertainment;
- insurance;
- retail and consumer product; and
- transportation.

KPMG Hazem Hassan is therefore positioned to deliver its comprehensive array of services to its clients with multidisciplinary teams across all business sectors.

KPMG Hazem Hassan has offices in Cairo and Alexandria:

KPMG Hazem Hassan
72 Mohi El Din Abul Ezz Street, Mohandseen, Cairo, Egypt
Tel: +202 33 69094 +202 33 69098 Fax: +202 34 97224 +202 34 87819

KPMG Hazem Hassan
1 Gamal El Din Yassin Street, Flat 6, Raml Station, Alexandria, Egypt
Tel/Fax: (203) 4801863